In this book, Wonsuk Ma provides a valu[illegible] [illegible]y past, present, and future. By combining pe[illegible] [illegible]nd spiritual insights, he shares deep wisdom born of leadership on three continents. Ma's reflections inform and inspire. I recommend this book very highly.

Dana L. Robert, Ph.D.
William Fairfield Warren Distinguished Professor
Boston University, Boston, MA

Mission in the Spirit: Formation, Theology and Praxis is a refreshing and inspiring look at the growth of the Church in the Global South through the eyes of one who participated in the movement from the very beginning. Dr. Ma is a practical Pentecostal scholar who has trained national leaders who are on the "cutting edge" of the growth of the Church. He has tested his Pentecostal Missions Theology among some Unreached People Groups (UPGs) and has witnessed the work of the Holy Spirit in the Global South.

While Harvey Cox and Philip Jenkins have cited the statistics of the growth in the Global South Church, Wonsuk Ma is one who inspired leaders in the Global South to believe in a biblical Pentecostal theology and put it into practice in the marketplaces of the countries. He has had the distinct privilege of helping to shape the theology of these leaders of the Global South Church. He has a great part in shaping the national leaders of this remarkable growth.

This is a must read for anyone who wants to understand the work of the Spirit in the Church of the Global South. The future of Pentecostal scholarship will use this volume as a guide to the formation of practical Pentecostal outcomes.

Bob Houlihan, Ph.D.
Former Dean of Southeastern University, Lakeland, FL and
Missionary in Asia Pacific

If I would pick out three necessary elements in mission, I'd say first, the guidance of the Holy Spirit, second, deep knowledge or reflection on the Word, and finally personal maturity, spiritual formation in other words. If I choose someone who has these three elements integrated, I will name Dr. Ma without hesitation. This book speaks of mission and the Holy Spirit, yet it is a record of the three things mentioned above being integrated.

Sung Chan Kwon, Ph.D.
Director, GMF, Seoul

Reading the introduction, I wondered why Dr Wonsuk Ma decided to use himself as a case study for this book. However, after reading through the script, I realized that he is an epitome of mission, a reservoir of global Christianity that many people can drink from. The complexity of his theological education, his ministry among Asian Pentecostals, his ministry in Oxford Centre for Mission Studies that ushered him to ecumenism, and his work with Oral Roberts University that links him with Pentecostals and Charismatics qualify him to write a book that demonstrates that we serve "One Christ, [with] Many Witnesses".

Opoku Onyinah, Ph.D.
Immediate Past Chairman, The Church of Pentecost, Ghana

What does mission formation look like that is initiated, developed, and empowered by the Holy Spirit? Missiologist Wonsuk Ma, with invaluable help from Julie Ma, gets at the heart of this question. And it's a crucial question for a couple of reasons. First, mission is often treated as an appendage to Christian formation. This book makes the case for mission to be at the core of it. And second, authentic Christian formation is finally not in programs and curricula, but in the hands of the Holy Spirit. This book at once applauds the contributions of Pentecostalism to mission and encourages all to be faithful to the full range of God's mission in the world in the power of the Holy Spirit!

Al Tizon, Ph.D.
Affiliate Associate Professor of Missional and Global Leadership
North Park Theological Seminary, Chicago, IL

REGNUM STUDIES IN MISSION

Mission in the Spirit
Formation, Theology, and Praxis

Series Preface

Regnum Studies in Mission are born from the lived experience of Christians and Christian communities in mission, especially but not solely in the fast growing churches among the people of the developing world. These churches have more to tell than stories of growth. They are making significant impacts on their cultures in the cause of Christ They are producing 'cultural products' which express the reality of Christian faith, hope and love in their societies.

Regnum Studies in Mission are the fruit often of rigorous research to the highest international standards and always of authentic Christian engagement in the transformation of people and societies. These are for the world. The formation of Christian theology, missiology and practice in the twenty-first century will depend to a great extent on the active participation of growing churches contributing biblical and culturally appropriate expressions of Christian practice to inform World Christianity.

Mission in the Spirit
Formation, Theology, and Praxis

Wonsuk Ma

First published 2023 by Regnum Books International

Regnum is an imprint of the Oxford Centre for Mission Studies
St. Philip and St. James Church
Woodstock Road
Oxford OX2 6HR, UK
www.regnumbooks.net

British Library Cataloguing in Publication Data
A catalogue record for this book is available from the British Library

ISBN: 979-8-8898-3321-5
eBook ISBN: 979-8-8898-3322-2

Cover design by Prof. Jiwon Kim with the image of Tito Inio © Wonsuk Ma 2002

Typeset by Words by Design

Distributed by Fortress Press in the US, Canada, India, and Brazil

Dedication

To the memory of Rev. Dr Sungkyu Choi,
Inchon Full Gospel Church, Inchon, Korea,
for his investment in my study and partnership in mission.

Contents

Foreword

I met Wonsuk Ma while he was serving as the Executive Director and Mission Tutor at the Oxford Centre for Mission Studies (OCMS). The breadth and depth of his experience in mission and theological education were indisputable. From Asian Pentecostalism to global Pentecostalism, his Pentecostal theology was, and remains, informed by his meticulous academic research and analysis, authenticated by their grassroots mission experience among the tribal groups in the northern Philippines and enriched by their global interdenominational engagements.

My earliest encounter with Pentecostal-Charismatic beliefs and practices took place in the 1980s. Around this time, I had just completed my theological studies and began my journey in pastoral ministry at my home church in Singapore. But while this new movement gained momentum in the Global South, it was initially met with scepticism; unsurprising, as even the raising of hands during worship was frowned upon.

Over time, however, my church grew to be very mission-minded. All members were taught to obey the Great Commission in Matthew 28:16-20, and this scripture passage, together with the verse in Acts 1:8, was upheld with great importance. "But you will receive power when the Holy Spirit comes on you; and you will be my witnesses in Jerusalem, and in all Judea and Samaria, and to the ends of the earth." This enabled the church to embrace a kingdom perspective, allowing room for the Spirit of God to work outside our comfort zone like a "wind that blows where it pleases" (to reference Jesus' words to Nicodemus in John 3:8).

This book, *Mission in the Spirit: Formation, Theology and Praxis* by Wonsuk Ma would have been an immense help to churches like mine and young leaders like myself had it been available. It contains timeless and crucial information concerning all global Pentecostal *families* – denominational Pentecostal, Charismatic in different churches, and the independent or indigenous Pentecostal churches (or "neo-Charismatics"). It reveals the importance of the Holy Spirit in the process of mission formation, which affects theological shaping and mission engagements. It addresses controversial topics such as power encounter, prosperity gospel, the tension between evangelism (caring for life after death) and social action (caring for life before death), and the reality of human suffering in the midst of faith healing. Most of all, its balanced and non-judgmental approach would appeal especially to sceptics and honest inquirers.

We see the author's laudable passion for the future of mission in the new era of global Christianity. His primary concern is addressing the commonly raised issue of spiritual renewal and unity of the global church. He believes the Holy Spirit will bring "diverse Christian churches into one place in worship and spiritual experience." For him, spirituality is to be demonstrated in our daily living at home, at work, and community. Relatedly, blessings received from above are not meant just for ourselves but to be shared for the collective benefit. Readers will appreciate the author's vigilance concerning extreme teachings and practices. For example, on whether the level of attention given to evil spirits is theologically healthy, they consider it "a matter of theological balance." All must be evaluated according to scripture, with contextual and pastoral sensitivity.

Throughout my personal interactions with him, I was struck by his servant leadership. In *Mission in the Spirit: Formation, Theology and Praxis*, his humility is self-evident through his self-critiquing posture, maintaining a sincere awareness of the flaws in the Pentecostal-Charismatic movement even as he details its numerous triumphs. As he concludes in his final chapter:

> We Pentecostals must humble ourselves. Despite the giftedness and opportunities of the Spirit God gave us, we must critically reflect on our shortcomings and repent before the Lord and other churches… I, along with my fellow Pentecostals worldwide, plead to other Christian families to pray with us and help us be faithful in our stewardship of the gifts… to seek together a theological humility and a learning spirit from our shared past. …We can begin with a theological affirmation of oneness in Christ. Then, through life, worship, service, and studying together, we recognize and experience unity.

Christianity in the Global South owes much of its exponential growth to the Pentecostal churches and their variants. For those who are willing to learn and wish to examine this phenomenon and the work of the Holy Spirit with an open heart and mind, start with this book.

Loun Ling Lee
Editor, Lausanne Global Analysis

Acknowledgements

As Africans teach us that it takes the whole village to raise a child, so is a book. There are two groups I want to express my particular appreciation. The first is the "villagers" at Oral Roberts University. My two dean's fellows deserve a special commendation. Mr Lemuel Godinez converted the old pdf files into editable ones and checked the texts with care and professionalism. When we were going through the proof, Ms Caroline Polly Ueriraisa Tjihenuna provided an exceptional help by testing all the URLs and many footnotes. They also brought their unique perspectives, Latin American by Lemuel and African by Polly. Professor Jiwon Kim shined with his artistic talent by crafting the cover using my old photo. He went through at least five renditions before we reached the final choice. Our long-time friend, Judy Gilliland, carefully read through the entire book to improve the texts.

The second group of "villagers" are the journal publishers which granted their permission for my previously published studies in their periodicals and book. They were revised and updated for this book.

Asia Pacific Theological Seminary for its permission for:

- "Pentecostal Eschatology: What Happened When the Wave Hit the West End of the Ocean," *Asian Journal of Pentecostal Studies* 12:1 (2009), pp. 95-112.

OMF Literature for its permission for:

- "'In Jesus' Name…': Power Encounter from an Asian Pentecostal Perspective," in Violeta V. Bautista, John F. Baxter, Wonsuk Ma, et al., *Principalities and Powers: Biblical Reflections in the Asian Context* (Manila: OMF Lit., 2007), pp. 21-40.

Overseas Ministry Study Center for its permission for:

- "My Pilgrimage of Mission," *International Bulletin of Mission Research* 40:4 (Oct, 2016), pp. 340-48
- "The Holy Spirit in Pentecostal Mission: The Shaping of Mission Awareness and Practice," *International Bulletin of Mission Research* 41:3 (July 2017), pp. 227-38.
- (With Julie C. Ma) "Empowered by the Holy Spirit to Serve the Least: Hawaii (Korean) Cedar Church in the Lost Paradise," *International Bulletin of Mission Research* 46:3 (2022), pp. 384-395.

Oxford Centre for Mission Studies for its permission for:

- "'When the Poor Are Fired Up': The Role of Pneumatology in Pentecostal-Charismatic Mission," *Transformation* 24:1 (Jan 2007), pp. 28-34;
- "'Life" in Theological Education and Missional Formation: A Reflection for a New Christian Era," *Transformation* 33:1 (2016), pp. 1-15;
- "The Theological Motivation for Pentecostal Mission," in Emma Wild-Wood and Peniel Rajkumar, eds., *Foundations for Mission*, Regnum Edinburgh Centenary Series 13 (Oxford: Regnum Books, 2012), pp. 220-35.
- "Blessing in Pentecostal Theology and Mission," in Wonsuk Ma, Veli-Matti Kärkkäinen and J. Kwabena Asamoah-Gyadu, eds., *Pentecostal Mission and Global Christianity* (Oxford: Regnum Books, 2014), 272-91.

World Council of Churches for its permission for:

- "Today's Global Context of Evangelism and Its Challenges and Opportunities," *International Review of Mission* 103:1 (April 2014), pp. 93-102.
- "Pentecostal Gift to Christian Unity: Its Possibility in the New Global Context," *International Review of Mission* 107:1 (June 2018), pp. 33-48.
- "Theological and Missional Formation in the Perspective of 'New Christianity'," *Ecumenical Review* 66:1 (March, 2014), pp. 53-64.

World Evangelical Alliance for its permission for:

- "David Yonggi Cho's theology of Blessing: Basis, Legitimacy and Limitations," *Evangelical Review of Theology* 35:2 (April 2011), pp. 140-159.

The third are my close mission thinkers and practitioners who kindly provide the foreword and commendations. I delightfully followed a suggestion of a prominent mission leader to include younger mission leaders. Their voices signal the freshly unfolding plan of the missional God in each generation. Three established but very young in their missionary spirit also graciously wrote their commendations. I am deeply grateful.

The fourth is the Regnum team, led by Paul Bendor-Samuel. He not only suggested the younger leaders for the commendations but also expertly and patiently guided the publishing process. Tony Gray's editorial professionalism shines bright.

The last is my family. My wife, Julie, co-authored one chapter; thus, participating in this book project. Her missiological expertise and passion has contributed much to my thinking. The encouragement received from my missionary son, Woolim, and his family has been a constant reminder that mission is God's priority. Our second son in Seoul, Boram, reminds us of our pilgrimage in life as a Philippine-born missionary kid is learning to adopt his passport country as his new home.

This book is affectionately dedicated to the memory of Dr & Mrs Sungkyu Choi, the founding pastor of Inchon Full Gospel Church in South Korea. Their mission generosity helped me to complete my doctoral study, and the ensuing mission partnership in the Philippines played an important role in the formation of my mission understanding.

1. Introduction

Mission Formation

Mission formation received extra attention in the study process of Edinburgh 2010. To the eight study themes (thus, commissions) for the 1910 Conference, the Towards 2010 Conference added the ninth theme: Mission Spirituality and Authentic Discipleship. Its study commission translated the theme in the form of a question: what motivates and sustains mission? Along with another study commission on theological education, how a believer or a community develops the awareness of and call to mission is a matter of mission formation.

This subject motivated me on several fronts. My own missionary life became the subject of an enquiry. After decades of mission engagements, research, and training, I began to ask where and how I developed my own journey of mission. Thus, mission formation has become a natural subject for investigation. Also, to the Korean church, like many in the Global South, mission was something completely new or strange. Then as I zoomed out to see the broader picture of mission, several crucial questions surfaced: "How can the non-Western 'new' churches become vibrant missionary communities?" and "What has prevented them from fulfilling the biblical mandate?" I suspected that the crux of the questions was not the teaching of Jesus but how the understanding and practice of mission had been developed in the church. As a Pentecostal believer, I was also drawn to the role of the Holy Spirit in the formation process of mission, its theology, and practice. Considering its impressive expansion in a century or so and the global landscape of fierce competition among religions for "souls", how to sustain its growth impetus is now critical.

In the formative process of mission, an individual or community has a deposit of the received tradition. This includes how one understands mission, and how it fulfils God's missionary mandate. It also inherits layers of assumptions, often not articulated or even consciously known, but which decisively influence one's understanding and practice of mission. And they were built through a lengthy process, inevitably influenced by their historical context. As some pointed questions will demonstrate in this book, I wondered why we Koreans did not think we were equally qualified to undertake God's mission as the Western churches. It had not much to do with the different Bible we had; it was the unique way that the understanding of mission was shaped through the layers of theological and contextual assumptions.

After the publication of our book, *Mission in the Spirit: Towards Pentecostal/Charismatic Missiology*, I realized that mission formation was not adequately discussed, especially from the perspective of the "new" Global South. As I reviewed my published pieces on mission, I realized how profound the subject of mission formation was. I identified as someone who was not formally trained as a missionary and was part of the first wave of Korean missionaries who began to reach various parts of the world from the late 1970s.

My starting point is clear: mission awareness does not happen automatically. There is a critical place for pedagogy in the church. "Mission" to me belonged to another planet, and I began to suspect that this unbiblical anomaly is NOT inherent in the Bible, but that the concept of mission was shaped to keep many of us out. From my hindsight, my fellow Christians were deep into mission, but it was called "evangelism", often distinguished from "mission". Unfortunately, the Korean economy steadily rose while Christianity grew. Thus, the country "earned" the privilege of mission. But this mindset is completely foreign to the teaching of Christ, I realized later. I believe this is a good place to begin this journey of enquiry.

This Book

This book, therefore, is a theological enquiry. Initially, I set out neatly compartmentalized parts: formation, theology, and praxis. However, the writing revealed that the three were closely interwoven with one another, and it was simply impossible to divide them into three parts. I still attempted to set out the book with mission formation, presenting myself as a case to study. In a sense, this is a sort of action research: I become the subject of an academic enquiry. Thus, I began with two autobiographical narratives, which reflect the Pentecostal tradition of "sharing testimonies".[1] This self-oriented perspective raises the question of credibility: I was certainly biased for and/or against myself. As my Christian formation, for example, occurred in a small but closely knitted Pentecostal church, I had to experience another "conversion" when I was in a different (but still Pentecostal) context in a large city. How, therefore, this "case" study is useful to others in different contexts remains an open question. At the same time, I suspect that my formation journey would represent a mission "conversion" that many in the Global South will go through. My own context would also resonate with many in the South: living with other faiths, experiencing poverty and social injustice, and negotiating my Christian faith vis-à-vis my friends' religions. By and large, these contextual elements are found in the South, while fewer or none of them in the Global North.

---

[1] This method was adopted by the Global Christian Forum as their mode of ecumenical engagement. See Global Christian Forum, "Our Unfolding Journey with Jesus Christ: Reflections on the Global Christian Forum Experience" (2013), https://globalchristianforum.org/wp-content/uploads/2018/07/GFC-Our-Unfolding-Journey-ENG.pdf. (accessed 5 January, 2023).

Due to my intention, I often start with a descriptive discussion and then move to a theological analysis, often digging deep to reach out to unarticulated or subconscious spiritual and theological assumptions. I try to articulate the theological impetus that motivates a particular mission behaviour. Usually, I offer (self-) criticism with suggestions for correction, revision, or reinforcement of the existing theological orientation.

As this book complements our earlier one, I decided to continue the main title. However, this has a clear starting point: mission formation, and its impact on one's mission theology and practice. Therefore, my intention is not to cover every major area of mission studies; for example, creation care.

After the Introduction, the first narrative chapter (Chapter 2) presents my own missionary journey from hindsight. I offer a developmental path of my mission awareness. Chapter 3 highlights three unlikely figures who helped my mission journey, illustrating the informal process of my mission formation. Chapter 4 moves straight to today's mission anomalies, which took Christian mission far from the intention of Christ. Perhaps in the most provocative part of the book, I offer new opportunities that will require radical new thinking in mission. Chapter 5 takes our attention to the role of the Holy Spirit in the process of mission formation, revealing how it affects theological shaping and mission engagements. Chapter 6 continues the focus on Pentecostal mission formation, with examples of mission "behaviours". Presented initially to an ecumenical audience, the chapter demonstrates the empowering and transformative potential of Pentecostal mission. Chapter 7 moves from mission formation to theological and mission education. While arguing that mission should be the final goal of theological education, the chapter also proposes that "life" is at the heart of Christian mission. Flourishing life is the creation intent of God, and mission, as the consummation of God's creation intent, takes the fullness of life as the final goal (*telos*) of mission. This telos would eliminate the binary between evangelism (or "life after death") and social service (or "life before death"). Chapter 8 brings another theological influence to mission formation: eschatology. It sets the direction of the church and its mission as illustrated in early North American Pentecostal mission. I trace the transmission of the Pentecostal faith to Korea with a diluted or revised eschatological framework which has significantly impacted the life and mission of the Korean Pentecostal church. Chapters 9 and 10 pick up the two "life" dimensions of mission: evangelism (Chapter 9) and this life's concern (Chapter 10). Reiterating that saving souls is the foundation of Pentecostal mission, it also has a decisive role in the future affair of global Christianity. Chapter 10 focuses its attention on "blessing", the centre of David Yonggi Cho's keyword on the Pentecostal life and mission. I tried to guard this popular concern from spilling over into the controversial prosperity gospel on the one hand and to balance between the emphasis on this- and other-worldly life on the other. Chapter 11 takes up another theological topic: demonology. As Pentecostals actively engage in ministries of healing and exorcism, they have awakened this challenging theology, long buried by most Christian traditions under the rug. Coinciding with the growth of the global "southern" churches, Pentecostals have formed a practical demonology. Dialoguing with the resurgence of the Third Wave of demonology, I present a delicate theological path for Pentecostals. Chapter 13 interweaves a case study of an immigrant Pentecostal church and its social service with Pentecostal theology of leadership and transformation. The final chapter (14) presents a unique Pentecostal contribution to church unity and corporation. Pentecostal ethos and life have much to strengthen the efforts to bring churches together, while complementing the existing structural ecumenism.

Terms and Concepts

I use several keywords and concepts frequently in this study, with varying interpretations.

Pentecostal, Pentecostalism

Defining and describing these terms have been an ongoing discussion, proving the task increasingly difficult. There appear to be two considerations in this task. The first is the grid between the narrow and the more accommodating extremes in the experience of the Holy Spirit.[2] Pentecostals tend to claim a "radical experience" with the Holy Spirit. The problem is that both "radical" and "experience" are subjective. Other Christian traditions also claim experientiality of the Christian faith, and some are "radical". Still, there is an apparent extent of spiritual experiences that distinguishes Pentecostals from others. Thus, as argued by Jacobson, it may be more a matter of degree (that is, "how much") than boundary-setting.[3] Thankfully, however, not everything is subjective. For example, Pentecostals believe in supernatural healing in Jesus' ministry *and* anticipate it today. This leads to the second element in characterizing the Pentecostal identity. They are often called (Pentecostal) "distinctives", commonly shared by classical Pentecostals. And the most significant of them is "baptism in the Holy Spirit" (or expressed in various terms such as "fullness of the Spirit"). This spiritual experience is unique to the Pentecostals, and other Christian traditions cannot claim it in the same way as the Pentecostals. When "speaking in tongues" is added as the "initial and physical evidence" to it, this doctrine's uniqueness is further strengthened. It is true that not every "Pentecostal" adheres to this belief in the same way, especially among the Neo-Charismatics. Nonetheless, the Spirit's overwhelming presence in the believer's

---

[2] Wonsuk Ma, "Lord and Giver of Life: The Holy Spirit Among the Spirits in Asia," in Timoteo D. Gener and Stephen T. Pardue (eds), *Christian Theology in Asia: Evangelical Perspectives*, (Carlisle, UK: Langham Global Library, 2019), pp. 123–25.
[3] Douglas Jacobsen, "Pentecostalism Today: A Review of Brill's *Encyclopedia of Global Pentecostalism*," *Pneuma* 44.2 (July 2022), p. 259.

life characterizes Pentecostalism in its incredible diversity. Thus, these two elements should be considered in defining or characterizing Pentecostalism.

As I revisit an earlier definition or characterization, there is not much change. I tend to use the terms as a broad categorical expression for a particular group of Christianity. Various umbrella terms are proposed but with no agreement, such as Charismatic Christianity, Renewal Movement, and Spirit-Empowered Christianity. In each local context, there may be other terms used. For example, in Korea, the "Holy Spirit movement" refers to this broader category.[4]

> [It] refers to a wide range of Christians who are open to, believe in, and expect the work – particularly a supernatural kind – of the Holy Spirit, often characterized by an emphasis on the experiential and emotive dimension of religious life … The outward expression of such a value includes vibrant and participatory worship, commitment to prayer for God's direct intervention to human needs, zealousness for evangelism, and the like.

Traditionally, Pentecostal spirituality has a significant appeal to people of lower socio-economic strata:

> This form of Christianity tends to attract the marginalized and the poor in society. As the religion of the poor, Pentecostalism has brought an empowering effect to masses who are socially and even eccelestically marginalized.

Mission(s)

The meaning of "mission" has been more complex, moving further away from any consensus. My "lay" status as a mission thinker-practitioner does not help either. As seen in the Pilgrimage chapter, I began with the narrowly understood notion, referring to the act of witnessing, often through verbal proclamation. The usage also assumes one moving geographically from one place to another. However, as I have been exposed to diverse mission movements: from non-Western Pentecostal to holistic mission and ecumenical mission, any attempt to build a clear understanding of mission to satisfy every stakeholder has also been frustrated by my broader exposure. At least the Edinburgh Centenary brought all these camps together. Thus, adopting the two-page nine-point "Edinburgh 2010 Common Call" was a milestone for the world church and me.[5]

My time in Europe also helped me to see the different understandings of mission between North America (especially Evangelicals) and Europe. I have adopted a broad understanding of mission, encompassing life after and before death, and evangelism and caring for life. This two-pillar structure of mission,

---

[4] Julie C. Ma and Wonsuk Ma, *Mission in the Spirit: Towards a Pentecostal/Charismatic Missiology* (Oxford: Regnum Books, 2010), p. 4.

[5] Edinburgh 2010 Common Call (2010), http://edinburgh2010.org/fileadmin/Edinburgh_2010_Common_Call_with_explanation.pdf (accessed 10 March 2023).

as defined in the Lausanne Covenant, allows me to embrace the challenging realities of many social settings in the Global South. Indeed, a hungry stomach has no ear to hear the gospel. The debate on the priority may not be an issue when these are the two sides of one coin, each serving and strengthening the other.

My Old Testament foundation also informs my broader understanding. I began with God's master plan for creation and the unique place of humans, in whom God placed something essential to his own existence. This unidentified part is called, in various ways, "image", "breath", and "Spirit". When the first humans sinned, the immediate consequence was, in my view, the damage of this God-element in humans. Although the extent of the damage is a theological debate, this "corrupted" gift of God also corrupted the nature of humans and their relationship with the Creator, fellow humans, and the rest of creation. And the whole record of the Bible or human history itself is God's careful plan and execution to restore his creation.[6] And this is rightly called *missio Dei*. The recovery of God-essence, or his Spirit, in us is the beginning of his plan being fulfilled. Thus, the vision of God's fulfilled mission is the restoration of his creation order from humans to the land, from justice to security:

> … till the Spirit is poured on us from on high, and the desert becomes a fertile field, and the fertile field seems like a forest. The Lord's justice will dwell in the desert, his righteousness live in the fertile field. The fruit of that righteousness will be peace; its effect will be quietness and confidence forever. My people will live in peaceful dwelling places, in secure homes, in undisturbed places of rest (Isa. 32:15-18).[7]

This broader understanding also permits me to go beyond the academic separation between "mission" and "missions", and "evangelism" and "mission". If moving from God's realm to the world, as sent by Christ, is the step of mission, the totality of a believer's life in and to the world is missional. If every word, act, and the totality of Christ's life were not just "for" mission but mission itself, then so is the believer's presence in the world, which is the beginning of Christian mission. This messianic commission (in John 17) laid the foundation for mission, and the post-resurrection giving of the Spirit (John 20:21) completed the commissioning process. This Johannine version does not replace the Great Commission but complements it.

This inclusive understanding would be challenged by Stephen Neill's oft-quoted expression, "If everything is mission, nothing is mission." However, he defined mission as "the Church's particular responsibility for 'the heathen'". His argument is clear: not everything the church does contribute to the proclamation

---

[6] For example, Wonsuk Ma, "The Spirit of God in Creation: Lessons for Christian Mission," *Transformation* 24.3/4 (2007), pp. 222–30.

[7] Scriptures are from the New International Version (NIV), unless stated otherwise.

of the good news to the lost.[8] The resolution of this quandary is found not in the creation of another term to refer to his vision of mission, but in aligning everything the church does to the mission of God. This holistic notion of mission also highlights the role of life in this world. It is the only opportunity to hear and respond to the good news of Christ and the rare opportunity to disciple God's people to be "sent" to the world with the same good news. This may be compared with the incarnation of the Son to come to the world.

Global or World Christianity

Studies of Christianity in the world have been exploding, making this a new discipline. More universities and seminaries are creating professorial posts on World or Global Christianity. The birth and development of this discipline coincided with the steady and accelerated north-to-south shift of Christianity, particularly from the second half of the twentieth century. As well attested in several reference works, Todd Johnson has statistically and graphically presented these changes, which include the early 1980s as the tipping point of Christianity toward the southern continents.[9]

For the study of Christianity worldwide, Lalsangkima Pachuau provides a useful historical overview of its development. Andrew F. Walls looms tall in Pachuau's presentation as the pioneer of studying the global expansion of Christianity.[10] Initially leading the Centre for the Study of Christianity in the Non-Western World at Edinburgh University (now renamed the Centre for the Study of World Christianity), he made the "discoveries" of Christian growth in Africa, Asia, and Latin America. In Pachuau's view, his distinct contributions impacted the birth and development of studies of Christianity worldwide. Some of Walls's students, such as Lamin Saneh and Kwame Bediako, followed in his footsteps and strengthened the emerging discipline.[11] Also, more journalistic presentations of the changing religious landscapes in the world advanced the interest in the world's Christian phenomenon. Samuel Huntington's *The Clash of Civilizations and the Remaking of World Order* (1997) set a broader context, while Philip Jenkins's *The Next Christendom* (2011) highlighted the rise of Christianity in the southern continents of the world.

---

[8] Stephen Neill, *Creative Tension* (London: Edinburgh House Press, 1959), p. 81.

[9] Two major publications are good examples: Todd M. Johnson and Kenneth R. Ross (eds), *Atlas of Global Christianity* (Edinburgh: Edinburgh University Press, 2009); Todd M. Johnson and Gina A. Zurlo (eds), *World Christian Encyclopedia*, 3rd ed. (Edinburgh: Edinburgh University Press, 2019). He and his team have also published an annual update of world or global Christianity in the *International Bulletin of Mission Research*.

[10] Lalsangkima Pachuau, *World Christianity: A Historical and Theological Introduction* (Nashville, TN: Abingdon, 2018), pp. 7–8.

[11] Liverpool Hope University now hosts the Andrew F. Walls Centre for the Study of African and Asian Christianity.

The present discussion is about "world Christianity" and "global Christianity." As a burgeoning new area of Christian study, terms and concepts are being proposed and discussed with the hope of a reasonable consensus. "World Christianity" is now considered generally favoured by academics over "global Christianity". It is not clear if the former was used, for example, by Walls, with a clear differentiation from the latter. As "global" is often linked with globalization through the hegemony of the West, the voices from the southern continents (or non-West) are more conscious of the potential implications of the term "global". Sometimes with a "post-colonial" slant, the "world" group tends to bring out the presence and vitality of Christianity and its theological and missiological contributions. And this is a valuable development to balance out the heavily North- (or West-) based orientation and perspective from the previous era. With various local pieces from the traditionally marginalized but now fast-growing areas, a more accurate larger picture of Christianity emerges. For those who are using "global" in their studies, there appears to be less discernible ideological motivation. My search on Amazon.com with the terms "world Christianity" and "global Christianity" results in the impression that the two terms are used almost interchangeably. Sometimes, the same author uses both "world" and "global" in the titles of publications. Suppose I am compelled to distinguish between the two expressions. In that case, I may argue that "world Christianity" gives priority to the churches in the South (or the "majority world"), and "global Christianity" stresses the overall picture of the Christian faith both in the South and the North. In this sense, I am using "global Christianity" in this book.

2. My Pilgrimage in Mission, So Far

Looking back on decades of my missionary life, I still find mission a complex subject to grasp. The purpose of this reflection is to trace the development of my mission awareness as my wife, Julie, and I have lived our lives as "missionaries". This is not a biography as such; if readers are interested, they may find elsewhere a brief recollection of our life on mission.[1]

Context and Christian Formation

I was born in 1949, between the liberation of Korea from the harsh Japanese colonial rule (1910–45) and the devastating Korean War (1950–52). This generation went through the war, poverty, the post-war dictatorship, the Vietnamese war, military rule, the struggles for democracy, and more. Despite human rights violations, keeping food on the table was every family's priority; the nation, in general, was thus tolerant of military rule. The church also joined this national campaign for a prosperous life, and coincidentally this period saw a significant growth in Christianity. The rise of David Yonggi Cho's mega ministry with the message of a good God was not an accident. Already motivated toward hard work, the poor masses heard the message of God's miracles, healing, and blessing as welcome good news. Prayer mountains were full of people, including non-believers, who desperately sought God's helping hand and miracles.

My own spiritual encounters with God were fundamentally Pentecostal in nature. My mother was from a Presbyterian family tradition but was the only Christian in her new family when she married my father. Her non-religious family suddenly became religious zealots by adamantly opposing her Christian faith. However, she persisted, and all five of us kids happily followed her to the church, enjoying Sunday school classes. In my early teen years, when she took a polio-stricken sister of mine to a healing revival in a nearby city, my Christian faith was challenged for the first time. Although my sister was never healed, her lifelong service to the Lord has been an enduring "healing" testimony. The second challenge was my daily spiritual life under a Pentecostal widow pastor,

---

[1] For example, Wonsuk Ma and Julie C. Ma, "The Making of Korean Pentecostal Missionaries: Our Personal Journey," in Arto Hämäläinen and Grant McClung (eds), *Together in One Mission: Pentecostal Cooperation in World Evangelization* (Cleveland, TN: Pathway, 2012), pp. 159–76.

whose "weeping" church was looked down upon even by other Christians in our town. The church attracted people who were desperately searching for ways of survival, which was possible only through God's help.

My decision to go to a Bible college was the result of painfully giving up on the entrance to a university because of poverty. During the disappointing years after high school, I received a call to ministry through the powerful (but erroneous) preaching of a revivalist on the imminent return of the Lord. Before the end of my freshman year, I began my mandatory military service. When I returned to Bible college from my three-year military service (two of which were in Vietnam) by the middle of the 1970s, the national mood had started changing. Many people finally began to feel a possibility that the nation could grow out of its chronic post-war poverty and dictatorship. The hosting of the Olympic Games in 1988 brought the liberalization of international travel with growing economic and national confidence.

My first theological training began at Full Gospel Bible College, which stood where the famous Full Gospel Church of David Yonggi Cho began in 1955. By the 1970s, the whole atmosphere of the College could be called "Cho-fever". Most students emulated his spiritual life, which included prayer, fasting, thinking big, believing in church growth and healing, and even learning to speak with his distinctive south-eastern accent. I appeared at odds with this Full Gospel culture as I asked different questions. I was particularly uncomfortable with the prevailing theological assumption that Christ suffered for all our curses; thus, all that is left for us is good stuff! I suspected that all of us failed to see the tears and struggles that went into the ministry of Cho, as we paid attention only to its fruit. In fact, I often noticed how many books Cho carried in the back seat of his car, which reflected his great devotion to study and prayer, which in turn undergirded his mega ministry. I was querying not only what we believed but also why we did so. Someone has to think, I reckoned. By the time I finished my four-year course in December 1976, most of my classmates were already pastoring! Only a few of us were wondering what came next.

Induction into Mission Without Realizing It

A church that had begun with the remnants of the original Cho congregation in the same vicinity graciously rescued me from my uncertainties. Called Daejo Full Gospel Church, its gentle pastor was known for his reflective thinking, a rarity in our circle. While looking after middle-schoolers, I finally married Julie, whom I had dated for four long years. When I left for the Philippines in 1979 for further study and subsequent teaching there (1983–85), my government, desperate to conserve scarce foreign currency, did not allow my family to travel together. Korean missionaries in this period had a passport valid for only six months, with the travelling country specified, and often valid for a single trip outside of Korea. Julie decided to minister back at Daejo Full Gospel Church, while our son, Woolim, less than a year old, was sent to live with my parents in their city in southern Korea. For one and a half years, all three of us were thus separated from each other in the name of mission.

In spite of my two years in Vietnam, my cultural immersion with a multinational student body in the Philippines took me by surprise. My lonely years away from my family proved to be a rare opportunity to learn to live with other cultures and to acquire the prized language, English. When Julie joined me with Woolim, she struggled greatly to accept a radically changed man as her husband. Although I still refused to be called a missionary, according to her, I was already one through and through! As a woman of prayer, she decided to fast every breakfast and prayed for more than a year to resolve this serious marriage issue. She gave God two choices: to change me to be a "normal" man or convert her to missionary life. God preferred the latter, and Julie eventually became a trained missiologist. What a conversion!

Far East Advanced School of Theology (FEAST) on the outskirts of Manila was a regional Assemblies of God institution for training leaders of national churches and faculty members of Bible colleges. The faculty members were predominantly North American missionaries, with one Filipina who also served as the registrar. In 1983 five of us became the first class of the Master of Divinity degree. At that time, the United States was the only other place where the denomination ran such a programme. The resident faculty was under unbearable stress with the rapid expansion of academic programmes. To meet this particular need, a good number of courses were taught by visiting lecturers. Some of them were world-renowned, such as Gordon D. Fee, William W. Menzies, and Del Tarr. They were never called missionaries, but what they were doing was clearly missional.

Realizing that we may be the first to achieve this academic level in our respective countries, we "Manila Five" carried a sense of burden for the future of Asian Pentecostalism. Immensely grateful as we were, a consensus was reached that Asian Pentecostalism could not be a transplant of an American movement. The group proposed that one of us should become part of the faculty of the alma mater. But who? This was the time when I deeply struggled to figure out what a call to mission meant. The decision-making process brought several vital components into play: a critical evaluation of the "voice" of God, an evaluation of my gifts and desires, and the assessment of the needs of the institution at hand and my potential contribution.[2]

This was also the time when we learned the difference between a missional call and a missionary call. Julie was fully on board in this missionary journey by now, and when I began my teaching at the school, she also began hers at the nearby Bethel Bible College. We made two firsts in this context: I was the first

---

[2] This process and other examples of decision-making through my missionary life are described in Wonsuk Ma, "A Missionary Call? Not Exactly …" in Kiho Park and Wonsuk Ma (eds), *Calling: Here Am I, Send Me Lord* [in Korean] (Seoul: Qumran, 2010), pp. 226–41.

Asian missionary teacher sent by a national Assemblies of God body and the first alumnus who served on the faculty. Later, I became the longest-serving faculty member. But this new life completely changed the whole outlook of our daily living. With meagre financial resources from only one monthly income, our goal was survival; and with our struggling English, our target was passing one course at a time. Though I now stood in front of the students, we felt that our learning continued. Not much changed. But one thing was sure: if it was God who called us to this challenging next stage of life and ministry, it would be the same God who had to make it happen. And God's share of help included finances and English, as we frequently reminded him!

Still Building Mission Foundations

For six years in the next decade (1985–96), we lived and studied in California. Also, our Asian context changed: from Manila to the mountain city of Baguio in the north. One evident focus was our studies, which drastically exposed the whole family to the heart of Western living and to a wide range of church traditions (and learning to accept each of them).

When a noted Pentecostal scholar, William Menzies, became the interim president of FEAST in 1984, he immediately organized a faculty development programme. In 1985 two young American short-term missionaries and I were sent for our PhD studies. This was an audacious undertaking, but he saw the crucial importance of an intentional effort to prepare future faculty members. We later realized that this was a vital turning point and the foundation for the academic excellence of FEAST (which in 1989 changed its name to Asia Pacific Theological Seminary).[3]

When I began to look around for schools, I initially insisted on one in Asia. Having exhausted all my Asian options, I consulted a respected Filipina Christian educator, Mrs Trinidad Seleky, who had earned a Master's from Fuller Theological Seminary in Pasadena, California. Her wise advice was, "If you are going to work with Americans, go there and see how they live. Then you will know how to work with them." This short conversation proved to be the best wisdom I have experienced.

My initial two-year experience in the United States (1985–87) was certainly challenging and enlightening, as was the multi-denominational nature of Fuller. After two years of initial study, our family returned to Baguio, Philippines, as the seminary had moved to this mountain city, known as the nation's summer capital. The city is the hub of six mountain provinces, whose people are known as Igorots. Rarely touched by Spanish colonial power, and thus not by Christianity, the Igorots have preserved their cultural and religious distinctives,

---

[3] Wonsuk Ma, "A Theological Journey of an Institution Through the Eye of an Alumnus-Staff: A Case of Asia Pacific Theological Seminary," *Asian Journal of Pentecostal Studies* 17.1 (2014), pp. 73–84.

along with their languages and severely under-developed society and infrastructure. When we commenced our Baguio life (in 1987), we began our participation in local churches among tribal immigrants to this city, expanding to reach remote mountain villages of Benguet Province.

When we returned to California in 1992 to complete my study, Julie also began her own PhD study. Her research on the Pentecostal ministry among the Igorots drew heavily from our own ministries. We happily graduated together on the same day in 1996.

By this time, the Korean Assemblies of God had organized its Foreign Missions Department, and I was formally appointed as its missionary. However, this new assignment did not result in any lessening of our financial difficulties. During our studies, the Asia Pacific Theological Seminary graciously provided finances, and Inchon Full Gospel Church (pastor Rev. Sung-kyu Choi) in Korea also supported us for our second study leave.

Mission in the Spirit (1996–2006)

During our last ten years in the Philippines, we finally saw the flowering of our mission engagements. Grounded in the preparations, experiences, and exposures of the previous decade, we became more conscious of our identity as Korean Pentecostal missionaries.

Having become the top academic officer (Academic Dean, later called Vice-President for Academic Affairs) of the Seminary, I began two focused efforts. The first was a plan to strengthen Asian members of the faculty, both academically and pastorally. At any given time, the faculty consisted of a dozen members, half Asian and the other half Western. Being a missionary community, everyone came as a missionary gift, and everyone contributed to the institutional life, including finances. There were about ten PhD-degree holders out of twelve faculty members by the time of our departure, and the Asian and non-Asian balance was evenly maintained.

My second emphasis was on the development of Asian Pentecostal studies. It was a milestone in 1998 to organize the Asian Pentecostal Society in Seoul, Korea, to identify those who were engaging in Pentecostal studies in Asia and encourage their research interests. In the following year, the *Asian Journal of Pentecostal Studies* was launched, which required me to learn about journal editing and publication. Then we added new postgraduate programmes in Pentecostal/Charismatic studies at the Seminary. In addition to a strong annual lectureship, occasional Pentecostal lectures brought world-class scholars to the campus, presenting various Pentecostal/Charismatic traditions, theologies, and spiritualities. They included Catholic Charismatics, South African Pentecostalism, Oneness Pentecostalism, European Pentecostalism, and African American Pentecostalism. APTS Press, the publishing arm of the Seminary, was also gaining momentum. The Seminary hosted a PhD programme of the

University of Wales, Bangor, in Pentecostal/Charismatic studies, thus allowing the school to prepare top-level Asian Pentecostal leaders.

Our expanded view of the work of the Spirit impacted not only the institutional life but also our own lives. Julie and I began to represent Asian Pentecostals in wider church networks. This involvement began with an international conference on the globalization of Pentecostalism in 1996 in Costa Rica. Then we participated in various encounters with the World Council of Churches. The newly emerging Global Christian Forum invited strong Pentecostal participation, and we worked closely for the Asian and the first international meetings. The Reformed-Pentecostal Dialogue took us to various parts of the world for an annual theological conversation. As we interacted with different church families, our understanding deepened of the church, God's kingdom, the work of the Spirit, and the locus of modern Pentecostalism. When the first "Towards 2010" (planning for celebrating the centenary of the 1910 Edinburgh World Missionary Conference) meeting was called, Julie and I were invited to join the twenty-member group.

In addition to the journal editing and publishing, which also included the launch in 2000 of the *Journal of Asian Mission*, my passion for publishing began to grow. Julie's and my dissertations were published in this period, and their titles strongly reflect our deep interest in the Holy Spirit and his work today: "When the Spirit Meets the Spirits" (Julie's) and "Until the Spirit Comes: The Spirit of God in the Book of Isaiah" (mine). Two Festschriften appeared in this period, which I used to bring new Asian Pentecostal thinkers to join established (often Western) counterparts in these projects. Similarly, many Asian contributors published their work for the first time in the two journals. When Allan Anderson of the University of Birmingham planned a large conference on Asian Pentecostalism, several other seminary members and we were deeply involved in the conference and the ensuing publication of *Asian and Pentecostal* (2005) works. Several more edited volumes of ours appeared in this period.

Amid this growing academic life, our frontline mission continued. Among many teachers who walked with me closely, one mountain pastor stood out. Tito Inio, a tribal pastor with only an elementary education, excelled in his deep commitment to the gospel, with incredible spiritual gifts.[4] Particularly, his love for those struggling spiritually, economically, socially, or physically was a constant reminder of what the Christian mission is all about. When we left the Philippines, about 160 small congregations had been established throughout the mountain region, functioning as community and social centres. Our roles, however, were strictly secondary, for these ministries were largely the expression of the divine call that each leader in these congregations had received. We learned that a minimal missionary presence made national ministers fully responsible, fostering self-initiated and self-supported ministries.

[4] His role as our mission teacher is described in Chapter 3.

Holistic Mission and Global Christianity (2006–16)

Our decision for a radical transition at the end of our many years in the Philippines came with much struggle and prayer. The Lord was clear, first to Julie, that our time in the Philippines was coming to an end. Sceptical of this "revelation" of hers, I went through an inventory of our work. To my profound surprise, everything we once prayed for the Seminary and for the mountain ministry was in place by 2006. We thanked the Lord that we were leaving the institution in a strong position and the mountain churches in the able hands of national leaders and workers.

Our last ten years of life and work have been with the Oxford Centre for Mission Studies (OCMS) in Oxford, England. This assignment has been a delightful and challenging surprise. OCMS was established in 1983 as an unexpected outcome of the Lausanne Gathering in 1974. The full decade after the congress was marked by the birth of the "holistic mission" movement, championed by radical Evangelicals, especially from the Global South. Thus, from the beginning, the churches in the Majority World have been its main focus, ethos, and mission. Currently, with 120 PhD scholars from the full range of today's Christian families, they bring their daily mission engagements to the highest level of academic reflection.[5] Its publishing arm, Regnum Books, has also become a major mission academic publisher, increasingly known for its focus on research by and on the Global South.

As the OCMS executive director, my work has been the building up of the community and the institution. I inherited a unique ecumenical mission community already exerting unusual influence on the world of Christian mission. Almost all the scholars undertake part-time studies, residing in Oxford for only six weeks per year. A strong spiritual community was therefore essential for them to experience encouraging and nurturing ministry from one another. My primary role has been to make myself available to the community members for conversation, prayer, and fellowship. This call for a caring community has been passionately shared by the staff and scholars. Now, our weekly chapel attracts outsiders from the University and the city.

With a competent and committed academic team, the academic programme of OCMS has steadily grown to become the largest mission PhD programme in Europe.[6] Also, as the institution reached maturity and confidence, OCMS decided to expand its relationship beyond its historic Evangelical circles, offering itself a unique mission gift to any church or community committed to

[5] Its useful history is found in Al Tizon, *Transformation after Lausanne: Radical Evangelical Mission in Global–Local Perspective* (Oxford: Regnum Books, 2008).

[6] Robert J. Priest and Robert DeGeorge, "Doctoral Dissertations on Mission: Ten-Year Update, 2002–2011 (Revised)," *International Bulletin of Missionary Research* 37.4 (October 2013), pp. 195–202. OCMS is ranked as the second largest in Europe after the University of Birmingham. It had a high number because of a merger with Sally Oaks Colleges, whose candidates have by now completed their studies.

mission. It has since engaged with the World Evangelical Alliance, Lausanne Movement, Global Christian Forum, and World Council of Churches. The participation of OCMS in the Edinburgh centenary process was substantial, in the study commissions, the conference, and its publications. My personal participation in the Towards 2010 Conference opened this door to the school. OCMS's Regnum Books is now completing the historic Regnum Edinburgh Centenary Series with thirty-five titles. The small editorial team has also decided to release the full texts for free download as an expression of mission hospitality, manifesting our belief that mission knowledge should be freely available to God's people to advance his kingdom.

My time in Oxford has done more to enrich my understanding of mission than what I have done for the school. The first area has been in grasping more deeply the holistic nature of Christian mission. Our mission engagement in the Philippines was holistic in practice, but it lacked any reflective articulation. "Good works" were viewed either as a means to evangelism or a simple and pragmatic response to human suffering. At OCMS, mission engagement and research areas are wide (from HIV/AIDS to corruption) and deep (through PhD research). A volume on a holistic mission organized by the OCMS network became part of the Edinburgh Centenary Series.[7]

The second area has been in understanding the global picture of Christianity and its mission. Privileging the Global South is the very ethos of OCMS. The radical numerical shift of global Christianity from the North to the South has challenged mission watchers to rethink the very nature of Christian mission seriously.[8] I began to reflect on the new understanding and paradigm of mission for the next era of Christianity.[9] Quite clearly, although many details are still surfacing, (1) a radical new understanding and practice of mission are essential, (2) this will seriously impact all areas of Christian life and mission, including theological education, and (3) the churches in the Global South have a call to lead in this process, maintaining a close partnership with the churches in the North. It appears that these concerns regarding the full understanding of mission in the context of global Christianity will remain my lifelong quest. I thus hope to be able to encourage and challenge the global church to rethink the very nature of being Christian and its mission calling.

Global Pentecostal Mission (2016–)

The move to Oral Roberts University in Tulsa, Oklahoma, USA has set us in the "buckle of the Bible belt". The move from Oxford to Oklahoma was a challenging decision, knowing that it would be the last career change in my life.

---

[7] Brian Woolnough and Wonsuk Ma (eds), *Holistic Mission: God's Plan for God's People*, Regnum Edinburgh Centenary Series (Oxford: Regnum Books, 2010).

[8] Johnson and Ross, *Atlas of Global Christianity*, p.51.

[9] For an example of its implications on theological education, see Chapter 7.

At the same time, I maintained an interest in bringing all my experiences to serve the global Pentecostal-Charismatic movement. I sensed that the earlier work in Asian Pentecostalism and its mission (in the years in Asia), ecumenical activities, holistic mission, and global Christianity (during the OCMS years) could be useful in shaping the future of Pentecostal Christianity. Also with my higher education work, in teaching, research, and management, the next "home" would have a commitment to knowledge production and a global vision. The foundation for the former would be a PhD programme, followed by various research infrastructures. When I was assured of the vision for global reach and a new PhD programme by Dr William Wilson, the president of Oral Roberts University (ORU), I suspected that God might be in this proposition. I also learned that the theology faculty is ecclesially diverse, but united in their belief in and experience with the Holy Spirit. Yes, one perk of this new chapter has been freedom from fundraising!

My immediate task was to plan a PhD programme for the College of Theology and Ministry. Building on the excellent work of the committee, I finalized the planning of a theology PhD programme. In several ways, it proved to be a cutting-edge initiative as it stands on two layers of foundation: global Christianity and the Spirit-empowered movement. My experience at OCMS also allowed us to design the programme to increase the likelihood of completion for each student. As a global programme with international leaders in mind, more than half of the coursework can be taken online, and the remainder in a combination of online and brief residency. In its formative stage, the accrediting organization made a private comment that ours is one of the few theology PhD programmes that intentionally takes global Christianity into its objectives and curriculum. In its four cohorts, so far, the student body is extremely diverse, representing many nations, ethnicities, denominations, and research interests.

While I was searching for reliable publications to learn more about Oral Roberts, the founder of Oral Roberts University, I was disappointed by the lack of research. There were only five PhD dissertations, all comparative studies, dealing with him, among others. Amidst waves of popular reports, mostly critical of him, internal books and promotional publications, and tons of recorded sermons, the lack of scholarly investigation was (negatively) extraordinary.[10] It is especially astonishing that he left a decent university behind with professors whose lives had been profoundly impacted by Roberts' ministry, but that no research was undertaken by his own community! I became quite determined to encourage ORU theologians to undertake studies on him.[11] In addition to internal needs, the university owes American Christianity historical and theological

---

[10] David Edwin Harrell, Jr, *Oral Roberts: An American Life* (San Francisco, CA: Harper & Row, 1987). Another publication is required to cover another two decades of his life.

[11] Wonsuk Ma, "Why Oral Roberts Studies? An Expanded Editorial Marking the Hundredth Year of His Birth," *Spiritus: ORU Journal of Theology* 3.2 (Fall 2018), pp. 157–67.

research on this great evangelist of the twentieth century. This role has been well substantiated in the Five-Year Report of the journal that eight out of ten of the most downloaded studies are on Roberts.[12]

In the building of research infrastructure, I also re-initiated the discussion about an academic journal. By resurrecting the Journal Committee, we made a swift decision to launch one in 2017. Having learned that there was a journal organized by the theology faculty in 1985 that appeared only once, the committee decided to continue this legacy, thus, *Spiritus: ORU Journal of Theology* volume 2. This biennial peer-reviewed and open journal reached 75,000 downloads in five years! It definitely raised the institution's profile, while the college faculty members contributed to it. My wife reminded me that this was my fourth journal! The *Spiritus* journal, also, did something quite remarkable: giving birth to another journal (yes, this is the fifth one)! With the fledgling counselling programmes at ORU, I encouraged its faculty to consider launching a journal for two critical reasons. Firstly, to establish a clear identity for our programmes by taking the role of the Holy Spirit to the centre of counselling study and practice. Secondly, to establish a rallying space for those who are committed to the Christian faith and the work of the Holy Spirit in professional counselling. Thus, the Fall 2021 issue carried studies under the theme, "Counseling and the Spirit." The same contents also formed the launch issue of *Salubritas: International Journal of Spirit-Empowered Counseling*; yes, under a different cover. By the way, in 2020, I resuscitated the inactive journal *Pentecostal Education*, published by the World Alliance for Pentecostal Theological Education, which serves as the Education Commission of the Pentecostal World Fellowship. So, yes, it's the sixth!

Thanks to Wilson's leadership over Empowered21 (and now the Pentecostal World Fellowship, or PWF), I became the co-chair of its annual Scholars Consultation in 2017. This global relational network of Pentecostal-Charismatic-Independent leaders and ministries handily complements the PWF, a global network of (mostly classical) Pentecostal denominations. This delightful role entails organizing and managing the annual Consultations and producing a book from each gathering. The topics are diverse, from human sexuality to COVID-19, but all from Spirit-empowered perspectives. At any given moment, three Consultations are on my plate: producing a book, editing another, and planning the upcoming Consultation. This has become another conducive "space" for ORU faculty and PhD scholars to publish their studies. I found out that editing is a special gift to many emerging scholars as the "creator" of new spaces.[13]

---

[12] Spiritus, "Five Year Report (2017–2021)" (March 2022), p. 5, https://digitalshowcase.oru.edu/spiritus_gallery/10/. Accessed 12 August 2022.

[13] I reflected on this, in part in response to my wife's comment, "Why don't you write your own book?" in Wonsuk Ma, "Publishing as Christian Hospitality: Experiences in Baguio and Oxford," in Stephanie Derrick (ed.), *Chasing Paper: Critical Reflections on Christian Books and Publishing* (Eugene, OR: Cascade, 2021), pp. 27–34.

Within the Consultation insiders, two projects have been on the table for further development: the formation of the Global Network of Spirit-Empowered Scholars; and the publication of the web-based Biographical Dictionary of Global Spirit-Empowered Christianity, which would involve a project proposal for funding.

Another piece of the research infrastructure was the publishing arm of the University. As with a journal, I was well aware of its value in the profile of an institution (such as Regnum Books of OCMS). The University already had an extremely valuable asset in pursuing this enterprise. Dr Mark Roberts, a New Testament scholar, had served as a procurement editor for a major Christian publisher, and he was responsible for securing a major commentary series to add an academic imprint to the publisher. He had been "singing" the same song for some time. Although it took a little bit of convincing and a gentle nudge, the leadership gladly approved the establishment of ORU Press in 2019! With academic and popular imprints, it is slowly establishing itself.[14]

My scholarship is now more focused on global Pentecostal Christianity, while resurrecting my Old Testament training. Thus, I teach two PhD courses each year: Theologization in the Global Christian Context and Old Testament Theology (through the Spirit of God). Various studies I have produced in the ORU years are in these two areas.

All these efforts and foci are to contribute to the bigger picture: to strengthen ORU to "Serve Globally as the Premier University for the Spirit-Empowered Movement."[15] Recent studies show that Pentecostal Christianity in its various forms is growing fastest among denominations. And among the three Pentecostal blocks, Neo-Charismatics are the largest and most diverse, yet lacking resources, such as theological education.[16] If we include the Independents, then there is a vast need to resource them, even for the sake of the future of global Christianity. I found that denominational universities are less capable of reaching out to the full spectrum of Pentecostal-Charismatic-Independent constituencies. Also, Western schools are better prepared, both geopolitically and theologically, to fulfil this role. And I am convinced that ORU is made for this task, with its ecumenical faculty with the Holy Spirit as the common denominator. The student body is equally diverse, ecclesially and ethnically. The university has 126 nations in its student body, with more than 600 going out for short-term missions trips each year. The striking legacy of Oral Roberts has shaped the spiritual direction and ethos, such as serving the whole church.[17]

---

[14] oru.edu/orupress.

[15] Oral Roberts University, "5-Year Adaptive Plan," Goal 8.

[16] See the two studies: Wonsuk Ma, "Global Christianity: Where Are We and How Did We Get Here?," *Pentecostal Education* 6.1 (Spring 2021), pp. 35–59. Wonsuk Ma, "Pentecostalism: A New But Big Kid on the Global Christian Block," *Pentecostal Education* 7.1 (Spring 2022), pp. 73–91.

[17] William M. Wilson, "Oral Roberts and the Spiritual DNA of Oral Roberts University," *Spiritus: ORU Journal of Theology* 3.2 (Fall 2018), pp. 277–84.

I am extremely grateful for these opportunities and privileges at this new "home". I reckon that all the previous experiences are the basis for the current calling. At the same time, the new environment and tasks require another set of learnings. To begin with, the American worldview and lifestyle are unique, and they profoundly influence the shaping of its Christianity. American pragmatism and pioneer spirit produce a new array of innovations. Worshipping at the chapel with thousands of young undergraduate students was a completely new and delightful experience. Mentoring young scholars, both PhD students and young colleagues, through the research path is always rewarding. Although I was finally free from fundraising responsibilities, not so from the administrative life. Reluctantly but also convincingly, I accepted the invitation to lead the College. My portfolio includes external responsibilities, with Empowered21, Pentecostal World Fellowship (by serving in two commissions), Global Christian Forum, and others. I have become a link between the University and the global Christian networks.

In Closing

My missionary life began in the late 1970s and went through three major shifts in three different continents: Asia, Europe, and now North America. I am not ready to "close" my story as yet. Indeed, I may be on the verge of seeing the full flowering of my missionary journey, with many "oops" and "ahas". I also begin to see my Old Testament study heading toward a clearer direction: the life-giving, renewing, flourishing work of the Holy Spirit. The Spirit's empowering work upon individuals and communities is ultimately to consummate God's creation intent: for the whole creation to flourish under the loving lordship of God the Creator and Redeemer. My long-dragged-around Old Testament theology book will carry this message. Its implication for contemporary Christianity and mission may be illustrated in the historic mission document of the World Council of Churches: *Together Towards Life*.[18] As I work with more statistics on global Christianity, my recent interest has been on the implication of global shifts for Christian mission. One of the practical questions I have wrestled with is "How poor churches in the Global South can be bona fide mission players, duly empowered in every sense?" I believe that the radical southward tilt of global Christianity opens up a rare opportunity to correct the power-based mission paradigm as we know it. I also argue that the teaching of Jesus and the early church's understanding of the Great Commission as recorded in the Book of Acts provides a firm foundation for this enterprise.

Thus, I intend to keep my life as an open book as I am still learning about God's mission and my role in it. And I begin to see the latest chapter half unfold as the Holy Spirit takes us forward. What will be the new dimensions and aspects

[18] World Council of Churches, *Together Towards Life: Mission and Evangelism in Changing Landscapes* (Geneva: WCC Publications, 2013).

of mission that I will learn? Who will appear as my unexpected teachers? As I conclude this reflection, I pray that it will particularly encourage rising mission thinkers and activists in the Global South.

3. My Three Mission Teachers

Along my missionary journey, there were "teachers" and "mentors" who shaped, often unknowingly, my understanding of mission and practices. Because I was never formally prepared or trained for mission, I am grateful to God for sending these teachers across my path. Due to this informal formative process, their "teachings" took place so subtly that neither the teacher nor the student may have realized what was happening. Only when I look back and reflect on the journey, do I begin to identify my teachers. Here are three of my unlikely mission teachers.

Manny: "Who is a Missionary?"

Mr Manuel Garcia (or "Manny") is one of the first Filipino Christians from my early missionary days. The early 1980s was a tumultuous period for the country under Marcos's dictatorship. We witnessed two radically different responses of the church, particularly the predominant Catholic Church. The first was political resistance to the autocratic rule, which included armed resistance by forming the New People's Army. This was influenced by the liberation theology of Latin America. The other was a spiritual resurgence, especially among urban Catholics. The Charismatic movement spread like wildfire, and countless prayer groups and Bible study programmes occupied restaurants, public halls, living rooms, and hotels. They rapidly spread among private companies, universities, and military camps and government offices. When the Catholic bishops' conference adopted a "guideline" for such groups, some became "independent" while others remained in the Catholic fold. Although not formally trained theologically, many leaders of the Bible study and prayer movement led several groups each day.[1]

Although born to wealthy Methodist parents in a posh area of Manila, Manny began associating with some of these younger Charismatic leaders. His experiences, insights, and connections in business proved helpful; for example, in securing a worship hall in a five-star hotel for an emerging "fellowship". Being older than many emerging leaders, he naturally appeared as a patron or big brother to them. They frequented his spacious house for fellowship,

[1] For the development of the Philippine Charismatic movement, see Dynnice Rosanny D. Engcoy, "A Reflection of a Missionary to the Philippines: Gary A. Denbow Interview," *Asian Journal of Pentecostal Studies* 8.2 (2005), pp. 315–29.

consultation, or simply relaxation. Manny and his wife were generous in many ways. They also took a radical step to develop their own ministry among prisoners. Muntinlupa housed a large complex of prisons, and Manny took the whole family (including two young daughters) and hundreds of hamburgers each week to different sections of the prison complex.

His Lessons

In two specific ways, Manny contributed to my mission formation. The first was through my participation in his prison ministry. As a Korean Pentecostal minister doing full-time graduate study, I was unsure about my missionary identity. First, it was a new and noble idea in the Korean church. Still under the extended military dictatorship and yet riding an economic boom, the church grew in number and mission awareness. The latter part of the 1970s was the watershed period when the missionary movement of the Korean church began to bud. When I left Korea, many had suggested that I should receive a missionary appointment. But I was going to study, and was not sure about my future after it. Also, my denomination (the Korean Assemblies of God) did not yet have a mission department.[2]

They all added to the stereotypical understanding of a missionary: a formally commissioned and denomination-sponsored long-term intercultural worker. I was none of them. However, when I joined Manny and his whole family – his wife, three teenage daughters, and a young son – in their prison visit, people called it "missionary" work. He had none of the above qualifications; he was not even credentialled! Although he did not care what he was called, he also didn't mind his work being called "missionary". Regardless, his work was extremely impressive. His car was fully loaded with hundreds of hamburgers, drink packs, tee shirts, soaps, and the like. With deep anxiety, we entered the maximum-security prison, the home of hundreds of inmates with long-term sentences, including life and even death sentences. I even saw women and children, suggesting that some families had moved into the prison compound. Against my expectation, everyone roamed freely inside the compound. Thus, the visit of this "civilian" family instantly attracted a large crowd. About a hundred men gathered around the mountain of hamburgers on a sizeably roofed basketball court. Soon a former inmate, now a music minister, began to lead songs, with Manny's children joining the music. This was already a rare entertainment to these incarcerated men. Manny's invited preacher shared a message of hope and salvation. About a dozen indicated their willingness to receive Christ as their Saviour at the end of the sermon. Manny spoke little, but everyone knew he had planned the meeting and made it possible. I soon learned that a missionary is more a functional designation, less a title or office. Through this experience, I became less concerned when people called me a missionary as I often visited

---

[2] I wrote about this initial vagueness of my missionary identity in Ma and Ma, "The Making of Korean Pentecostal Missionaries," pp. 159–76.

small villages to preach. Manny later established a Bible school inside the compound, and many inmates studied to become evangelists inside and outside the prison.

The second experience with him helped me define the missionary's relationship with the nationals as the "art of guesting". Still in the early days of my life in the Philippines, I developed acute pain in my side. As a "poor" student, I waited until the pain reached an intolerable level before asking for help. I was rushed to an emergency room. The doctors concluded that I had a kidney stone. In the middle of the pain, I experienced relief when the doctors decided to keep me for a few more days without a procedure. As the days went by, the pain subsided. However, I began to worry about the hospital bills. Our young family with a two-year-old son lived on a $100 committed monthly support. Illness like this was the exact situation we wanted to avoid. Going through all the potential faces who could help us, Manny was the only one with whom I felt confident in sharing this urgent need. Amazingly, he quickly came by and settled the bills before my discharge. Months later, I brought the money to him, which surprised him! He did not expect this at all. When I later committed our family to missionary work in the Philippines, part of my motivation was a sense of indebtedness to the Filipino brothers and sisters.

This experience shattered my stereotype about a missionary typically coming from a richer country to a poor one, from a "developed" to "developing" or "under-developed" country, and from a lighter complexion to a darker one. I was poorer than Manny, and he had more to teach me (the missionary) and was in a position to help me. Although Jesus came to the world by voluntarily "emptying himself of heavenly glory" (or "incarnation"), I was less capable and resourced than the people whom I was to teach and enlighten! Manny remained a close friend and ministry partner, but more so as my mission teacher, until we concluded our twenty-seven-year life in the Philippines.

Tito: Differently Gifted but All Preciously Called[3]

When Julie and I met Tito Inio for the first time, we had already begun our evangelism and church nurturing among mountain tribes in the northern Philippines. Tito, in his forties at the time, was a Kankana-ey tribesman. As a high school drop-out, he made his daily survival by private gold mining. As a brand-new Christian, he had decided to give one day every week for God's work, away from his daily job. As the head of a family of five, he hardly made enough money by digging ores and refining them to extract gold. He worked about ten

[3] The original and longer text appeared in Wonsuk Ma and Julie Ma, "Spiritualität in der Mission – gelernt vom einheimischen Missionar Tito," in *Mission Erfüllt? Edinburgh 1910 – 100 Jahre Weltmission: Jahrbuch Mission 2009* (Hamburg: Missionshilfe Verlag, 2009), pp. 136–42.

hours a day in private tunnels no higher than one metre. Many lost their lives as these private tunnels collapsed. He decided to move his family to an outskirt of Baguio City, the capital city of the mountain region of the Philippines. That was where we first met him and his family.

He settled among similar tribal immigrants, especially speakers of the Kankana-ey dialect. A few months before the visit, the entire region was shaken by a powerful earthquake that ravaged the region and killed more than 100 in Baguio alone. Many of the casualties were tribal miners buried in makeshift private tunnels. During this depressing time, many people came to hear this simple man, who told them that God is not only more powerful than any spirits they worship, but also far more gracious than their most venerable ancestor spirits.

When we arrived at his "church" under a relative's cocoon house, Tito was preaching in front of a dozen neighbours. Our unannounced appearance surprised him and the people, a missionary couple teaching in a prestigious seminary on the top of the hills. Tito later confessed that it was difficult to continue preaching in the presence of a theologian and a missiologist. But this awkward feeling was broken when they graciously shared their food, and we enjoyed it. So, this is how a mission partnership began between two unlikely parties. One was a new Christian with no theological education and hardly intelligible English, and the other was a career missionary with a doctoral degree and unbelievable resources (at least, to their eyes), but who was equally limited in the Ilocano language. This wonderful partnership and friendship grew stronger and lasted for almost two decades until we left the country. To me, Tito was a true missionary, to the point that we often considered ourselves assistants to him. What lessons did this dear servant of God teach me about mission? Here are a few of them.

Jesus, the Best Thing to Happen to Anyone

Like many fellow tribal groups, Tito's family worshipped many spirits and gods. They range from creator gods and location gods to ancestor spirits and malevolent spirits. We soon learned that their religion bred constant anxiety and terror. This was in stark contrast with Christianity, which preaches peace and assurance. In one case, the grandmother of the household had seen her deceased ancestor in her dreams for three days in a row. According to the common belief, this was a sure sign that the ancestor was now "claiming" her life; her death was sure and imminent. This was almost a self-fulfilling prophecy as she stopped eating, drinking, and sleeping. The whole family and village were waiting for her to die. The village priest and elders already prescribed details of burial rituals, including the specific number of animals she needed to take to her ancestors. Tito arrived in this house on his weekly "holy" day, and only the dogs welcomed him. As the house was virtually empty, he was about to move on to the next house, when he heard a sigh from inside the house. The lady, who had been left to die, told him her story with emotions mixed with anxiety, sadness, fear, and quiet surrender. Tito spoke to her about a God who had dealt a blow to death. He then laid his hand on her head and began praying for God's strengthening. She recovered in a few days, and a Christian gathering was born in her house.

Tito firmly believes that the gospel is not just good news, it's the best news! Recalling his own life, he confessed many times that Jesus drastically turned his life around, making a point between "before" and "after" in his life. To Tito, it is unmistakable that Christian mission cannot be done by hiring unbelieving professionals, but only by everyone whose life was turned upside down by Jesus! His message, therefore, was always the good news of Jesus that could become the best thing one can experience. By the same token, anyone who has experienced this gospel cannot help but share this best news with those who desperately need it.

Believing Perfected by Obedience

Although Tito did not receive formal theological education, his understanding of the gospel was extremely clear and simple. The missional dynamic of his life and ministry may have come from that simplicity. Without diminishing the value of theological sophistication, it is essential to stress that the Christian life is a journey of obedience rather than intellectual enquiry and cognitive acceptance (or believing).

Once, when we were walking through a rugged mountain road, he greeted a farmer passing by us. Having a shovel with him, we suspected that he was returning from his field. To our surprise, he just walked on his way without paying attention to our greeting. Tito went to him and found out that the man was deaf. Moments later, he told me, "I need to pray for him. Who knows what the Lord has for him today, and if it is through me? If I am not obedient, we all lose." He ran and brought the man under a tall pine tree where we were resting. Two tribal men were standing facing each other with a cascade of mountains in their background! I indulged in this beautiful scene for a moment until I heard Tito begin to pray. Thin but tall, Tito put his two fingers on the ears of the short, old farmer and rebuked the spirit of deafness in the name of Jesus! After the first prayer, the man motioned he could hear but not clearly. Before the second prayer, Tito explained that Jesus was the healer. He now said he could hear much better. After leading him to accept Jesus as his Saviour, Tito let him continue his walk home. It now became a sacred moment.

The simple act of obedience sprung out of his firm conviction that he was in God's mission, in season and out of season. Every moment of his life was meant to bring this best news to everyone who passed by him. Indeed, he believed that they were "sent" by God. As we walked for many hours through deep mountains, I often thought of the messenger "whose lovely feet tread many mountains to bring good news" (Isa. 42:7). No wonder many deaf ears are opened, and many sick are healed. Ultimately many lost are led to the saving knowledge of Christ through the act of missional obedience. This continues from generation to generation, and Tito is part of this grand story. A professionally appointed missionary found a brilliant missionary who simply lived his missionary life 24/7!

Sharing the Good News: A Thing of Nature; Less of Nurture

We grew up in Korea with the idea that any missionary work belonged exclusively to the West. When we became missionaries, we struggled to accept that we were called this by others. When we began to work with Tito, to this professionally "trained" and appointed "missionary" he was a novice amateur "mission worker". Tito insisted by action that mission is as innate and instinctive to anyone born to the Kingdom of God as a fish is to swimming. Thus, we learned from him that mission should be a matter of nature, not nurture. I concluded that if we have to teach mission to Christians, the church is in an unfortunate situation. If witnessing is "a beggar telling his fellow beggar where he can find bread", mission is an integral part of any Christian's DNA.

When we began our work in a new Kankana-ey tribal village bordering another mountain tribe, we noticed Tito reminding new Christian youths of their "natural life of mission". They quickly organized a team to visit a Kalangoya village, a four-hour hike away. Before we knew it, the young Kankana-ey church became the mother of the Kalangoya church. In a few years, the "mother" and the "daughter" churches started missionary work in another large Kalangoya village. Within five years, we saw five villages with Christian witnesses and strong communities.

According to him, many Christians try to learn to do mission, while being completely ignorant that their life itself is a missionary testimony. The Spirit, who brought reconciliation with the Father through Christ, is in every believer. Still, the enemy has been highly successful in blinding Christians from recognizing the empowering presence of the Holy Spirit. This is the biggest problem in Christian mission, according to him.

Healing, the Last Piece for the Holistic Mission Puzzle

Healing was the extraordinary gift of the Holy Spirit to Tito. He believes that this was the last piece of the puzzle that was desperately needed for his people. He did not use the expression "holistic mission" that had dominated mission circles for decades. This referred to a mission approach adding the dimension of "life before death" to the traditional mission concern for "life after death". In this way, the whole gospel is for the whole person. His deep concern for suffering was as important as one's eternal life. This comprehensive understanding of mission has been a corrective to liberal theology, which focuses on human needs for earthly life, and to Evangelical thinking, which emphasizes life in heaven. Unaware of this hot academic debate, Tito's mission thinking was inherently holistic and comprehensive. In fact, his holistic mission thinking was more holistic than many mission specialists. For him, healing was a crucial piece lacking in the social works to eliminate human suffering. It was missing in the Evangelical preaching of God's salvation, as it failed to provide an alternative to the ancestor spirits that people could appeal to for healing. He took the gospel in its fullest sense. He fully accepted the scripture, including those records many Western Christians would dismiss as myths. Tito considered, for example, healing and miracle records as a matter of fact, and more amazingly, he took them as "our story for today".

It is sometimes ironic to see foreign missionaries with "selective beliefs" try to evangelize locals, who have strong potential for "comprehensive beliefs". No wonder, once they accept the gospel, the nationals "outperform" the missionaries. Tito is a brilliant illustration; thus, my mission teacher! To honour this powerful yet humble missionary, I will repeat a part of my recently published essay.[4]

During the early 2000s, we travelled to the northern Philippines, where we were to minister in a tiny mountain church. When we arrived, it was already dark, but villagers packed the small church. After a long session of singing and preaching, the prayer time began. My ministry partner Tito started laying his hands on people who came to the front for prayer. Most complained of illness and pain, often rooted in chronic poverty. When Tito approached one older woman, someone standing by her told him that she had been deaf for many years.

Tito rebuked the evil spirit and invited Jesus to come to heal her. By this time, everyone was watching attentively. Tito moved to stand behind her and snapped his fingers near her ears, one at a time. When he asked if she could hear, she affirmed that she could, but also motioned that there were a lot of other noises. The flood of noises after many years of deafness must have been an incredible but delightful experience.

Tito repeated his prayer, placing his hands on her ears. When asked after the second prayer, she joyfully exclaimed that she could now hear clearly. Tito explained to her that Jesus healed her and died for her to have a good life, both in this world and afterward. People shouted their praise to God, who loves his people and is also powerful to protect and bless them. In this woman's context, the Igorot, a Philippine mountain tribal people, regularly offer sacrifices to ancestral spirits for healing, for blessings, and to ward off evil spirits – a practice resulting in heavy debts for many families.

Praying for healing and blessing was not new, but asking Jesus contrasted starkly with asking their usual ancestral spirits. Many mountain churches have been founded as a result of miraculous demonstrations of God's love and power through healing. Pentecostal believers emphasize this extraordinary experience of healing and blessing as their "full gospel".

---

[4] Wonsuk Ma, "More Powerful Than Ancestral Spirits: Prayer, Material Blessing, and Healing," *Christian History* 142 (February 2022), p. 47.

Steve: Still "Who is a Missionary?"

Steve Hong is a Korean American businessman who took mission as his first job and his business as his second one. I need to elaborate on my relationship with him in some detail to preserve this special partnership and encourage aspiring younger BAM (Business as Mission) folks.

Returning to the Philippines

Our meeting with him took place at the conclusion of our doctoral studies in California, against our initial plan to spend several months raising enough funds to travel back to the Philippines, rent a home, and live for at least six months. However, Asia Pacific Theological Seminary asked for an immediate return to teach and begin my Academic Dean's responsibility for the upcoming semester. Leaving our first son for his university study was already an emotional challenge, especially for Julie. As the family head, the whole burden laid heavy on me. Then, I did what I was good at: looking for places to borrow money! My meagre faith informed me that the amount was too big and the time was too short even for God to come up with $20,000! (Yes, that was and still is the state of my faith). To everyone's surprise, the Assemblies of God World Mission was willing to lend the money, thanks to the good words of another teacher, William Menzies. A close friend in Los Angeles hosted a dinner party with a dozen local Christian friends. The host invited Steve; thus, we met for the first time.

He ran a manufacturing business of sporting goods, specifically sports gloves. When he started his business, his plan was to have an office with a fax machine and a secretary. He would secure orders, fax the design to a factory in Indonesia, receive samples, and forward them to his clients. He wanted his business to support his trips to mission locations to strengthen missionaries. He was a minimalist in his business but the opposite in mission. His business was successful, and once, he became the largest supplier of golf gloves to a major global sports company. Yes, and while he spent about half of his time in mission travels! He prayerfully identified (Korean) missionaries whose commitments were tested, but were facing urgent needs. He once shared how he travelled to a missionary who was living and ministering among the Maasais. He packed large travel bags with supplies and spent weeks with the family, encouraging the missionary family while "shadowing" the missionary at every move. His trust in and commitment to these missionaries were beyond imagination. On the other hand, the profile of his missionary contacts made me wonder if Steve maintained a stereotype of an "excellent missionary" in a harder and primitive environment. Someone like us in theological education would not measure up to such expectations.

A few days after our first meeting, he invited us for a lunch meeting in downtown Los Angeles. Over a sushi lunch, he shared his passion for mission. He also asked us about the nature of our missionary work, and we confidently shared our commitment to theological education and tribal ministry among the

Igorots in the northern Philippines. At the end of the meal, he handed us a fat envelope as a missionary gift. Sensing a cash donation, we thanked him and told him my plan to use it toward the loan we had taken out. To his bewildered mind, I briefly explained the amazing provision of God for us to return to the mission field. Indeed, I immediately sent his $5,000 gift to my creditor, reducing my obligation by 25 percent!

Having returned to our "home", our life was more than full: re-settling down in the seminary community, beginning new jobs (first-time teaching in the seminary for Julie and the Academic Dean's job for me). Less than a month into our re-settlement, evidently Steve tried to contact us, and one morning, a fax message arrived from Steve. (He operated with phone and fax machine rather than emails.) In big handwritten words, "What is the account number to send money to your creditor?" Later, I learned about his "conversation" with God. In a dawn prayer time at his church, according to him, the Lord said, "My servant went to the mission field by borrowing money." His response as a businessman was a sort of "so what?" Borrowing is a normal part of his life. Then he heard, "But don't you make money?" He told me that the same "conversation" lasted for three days. He finally asked himself, "Who would borrow money to go on mission?" Thus his near desperate effort to contact me with the fax message. This event served several critical functions: it affirmed that God supplies our needs as we are in his work, and Steve not only "got" it (the words from God) but did it. I now suspected that all the relationships he had built with missionaries were born out of a spiritual process. He remained the largest mission donor throughout our work in the Philippines.

Out of "Mission"

The time came to close our Philippine era, and we decided to work for an established institution. We sent a letter to each mission supporter, thanking them for their faithful partnership and sharing our plan for the next step. Thus, we advised them to discontinue their financial support. This letter was also sent to Steve. During our visit to California, we also travelled to Oxford for an interview with the search committee for the executive director for the Oxford Centre for Mission Studies. The time and experience with the Board were mixed in impression: we were not attracted to the chilly spring rain and equally chilly nineteenth-century neo-Gothic building of the school. However, the school's status among global Evangelicals as the leader of the global holistic mission movement with eighty PhD students was striking. My career in Asia among Pentecostals could be a critical preparation to rejuvenate this community, I thought. When I saw the financial report, I immediately recognized that a large portion of the budget came through donations, mostly from the USA and Europe. A question lingered in my mind: "Where is the meaningful contribution from the Global South, if the school privileges the Majority church?" This task of fundraising loomed heavy when Julie and I sat down in a quaint coffee shop near Gloucester Green in Oxford.

When we returned to California, we decided to speak with Steve. As usual, he took us to a quiet lunch place. We shared our bewilderment and apprehension about my ability to strengthen and grow the school through fundraising. Characteristic of him, he reacted simply, "I don't know when was the last time I completely acted by faith, even if I claimed so. Don't you think you should jump into the challenge by faith, completely trusting him?" He strongly challenged us to decide not based on what we had seen and felt but on the principle of faith. He also committed a large one-off scholarship donation, "should we choose to accept the mission" and move to England. What was later clear and evident was his understanding of mission and a missionary. In his mind, we were continuing our mission call, even if, this time, the support would come in the form of a salary. To this incredible mission leader, we had never left "mission"! We gave ourselves into his challenge of faith and took his donation!

Steve knew all along the unique missional gift that the Lord entrusted to him. His partnership with us also expanded his vision of mission. He invited us to the Grace Mission Church to speak to a large group of several hundred of the church's missionaries.[5] He also arranged for his mission pastor to take a sabbatical in Oxford to produce a book laying a theological foundation for the church's mission.[6] He journeyed through our mission path until he retired, and we moved to the States. He reminded us that mission is not a profession but a vocation for every believer.

Concluding...

Through these and many other teachers, my lifelong learning continues. Through Manny and Tito, my untrained definition of missionary life is "guesting": how to become a good guest. At the same time, we want to be effective witnesses to Christ! It's a tricky balancing act. With better education and more resources, missionaries are quick to teach the nationals. But the real teachers may stand before us in disguise, as Jesus appeared as a village carpenter. Then how should we be good guests or students in mission?

It will require an attitude of gratefulness to the hosts, despite their meagre resources and living standards. Manny made me a lifelong debtor to those we came to minister. In the Philippine culture, once you are indebted, it lasts for your life (*utang na loob*). I also recognized that the nationals are the leading actors in God's mission, with outsiders assisting them to rise to their call. He and Steve also taught me that mission is our life rather than a task. I am in God's mission, even if I am no longer called a missionary. My words, deeds, and life are missionary tools, as our whole life is called to mission. Jesus sent every one

---

[5] Wonsuk Ma, "Grace Korean Church, Fullerton, California: Mission from the Margins," *International Bulletin of Missionary Research* 36.2 (April 2012), pp. 65–71.
[6] Daniel Taechoul Yang, *Called Out for Witness: The Missionary Journey of Grace Korean Church* (Oxford: Regnum Books, 2014).

of us to the world as the Father sent him (John 17:18). Thus, I need to look closely at Stephen Neill's statement, "If everything is mission, nothing is mission."[7] Tito reminded me of the extraordinary missional gift that the Lord had bestowed to Pentecostal-Charismatic churches: manifesting the supernatural power and grace of God. His healing ministry opened many minds previously hardened by their traditional beliefs. His favourite passage was: "When the Holy Spirit comes upon you, you will receive power, and you will be my witnesses … to the uttermost part of the earth" (Acts 1:8). It is "everyone", called, empowered, and sent to witness to the good or best news of Christ. Jargon-crunching minds may use words like the "prophethood of all believers". Tito not only represented this amazing "everyone" but also multiplied himself by discipling a large number of "nameless" missionary heroes.

[7] Neill, *Creative Tension*, p. 81.

4. Rethinking Theological and Missional Formation

The radical shift in world Christianity, elaborated in the third edition of the *World Christian Encyclopedia*,[1] opens up unprecedented possibilities for new theological paradigms. This will affect mission thinking and practices significantly. Tomorrow's theological education will have to be faithful to the message of the scriptures and the context in which people find themselves.

New Theological Paradigms

When we take seriously the context of the Global South, where Christianity has recorded impressive growth in the last century and is expected to continue its dynamism in the foreseeable future, we can observe several paradigms of theologization. First, we need to review top-down theologization seriously. Rooted in the long magisterial tradition, the process of theological formulation has been largely restricted to the learned and properly trained clerical and theological specialists. The majority of Christians, the so-called laity, have been passive recipients. Although this may have ensured the "purity" of theology, the content, language, and the way it is communicated, this theologization paradigm has practically excluded the participation and contribution of the sheer number of total Christians. This will have to be properly balanced, at least by the bottom-up theologization contribution. This "grassroots theology" will be borne of the real context of everyday life, where constant mission engagement takes place. Theologization has to be "democratized" so that every believer participates in this process.

Second, already mentioned above, theology should draw from live mission exercises of practitioners, as much as "specialized theologians" draw from the careful exegesis of the scriptures and the deposit of a long historical development of various theological traditions. Even the categorization of theology suggests that experience is only treated in "Practical Theology". In contrast, proper theology must be produced in libraries or archives, whether dogmatic, biblical, or historical. As we quickly learn from other disciplines, particularly social sciences, experiences are a critical basis for knowledge creation. This theory–practice divide is a superficial outcome of modernist Enlightenment thinking, and Christian viewpoints from the Global South, based on their interpretation of

[1] Johnson and Zurlo, *World Christian Encyclopedia*, p.3.

the gospel and daily interaction with the social environment, will have to take experience seriously in the theological process. For example, living and working with neighbours of other religions as a faithful Christian will be extremely valuable in formulating a theology of religions, and thus, mission practice.

Third, the theologians from the Global South will be more "part-time" theologians, wearing several ministerial hats. They will be denominational or mission leaders involved in pastoral ministries, leading educational institutions, or teaching and mentoring. They will be multitaskers. This engagement will make their theology lively and relevant, enriching theological reflection constantly. However, the downside is equally overwhelming. There are just too many balls to juggle, and more balls are added along the way! The doctoral dissertation may represent the scholarly apex of these individuals' lives, and subsequent research outputs may involve repackaging the dissertation with contextual additions from subsequent experience. This cannot make an expert in one area, but just a generalist "knowing enough to be dangerous". Unless proper attention and intervention are introduced, sooner or later, these theologians will collapse as leaders. But a positive side is that theological product through such a life and work is communicated more in sermons, informal talks, addresses, etc. If carefully grounded in good research, this "ground-friendly" sharing of solid theological thought is very much commended.

Even this shortlist of future theologization presents numerous implications for theological and missional formation. One is the role of the West and the new "Rest". If the leadership of the global theological process is laid primarily on the leaders of the Global South, the role of the Western churches with their theological deposit is critical. Cooperation is a major topic in several global conversations on theological education. Another key topic is certain forms of theological and missional education. If the process and main players of theological formulation have to change, it will have a massive impact on the training of Christian workers and theological thinkers. Furthermore, local congregations will bear more responsibility in theological formation, first informally but in some cases formally. This is where grassroots theological formulation takes place. In that case, the role of a pastor will be significant as the leader of this theological process, as a facilitator to encourage broad participation of parishioners in the process, and one who also sets theologically sound boundaries. This is a very tall order, and that's why sound and contextually sensitive theological and ministerial formation is essential.

Received Legacies

The emerging mission churches in the non-Western world have what is called the "received" missionary paradigm from the West. This perception has been acquired through experience by observing missionary operations in each context and through formal teachings and mission books introduced from the West. At the same time, it is fair to admit that this missionary paradigm has been formulated clearly out of its own social–religious context, namely the Western Christian context. Thus, it was not intended to construct universal missiology or the "rules" of missionary engagement for the world church. Instead, it was a set of best practices informed by the missionaries' best theological judgement and religious contexts to best fulfil the missionary mandate. Nonetheless, for the new missionary churches, they often simply repeat what they have experienced without careful evaluation. Therefore, my intention is to address both sides: for the Western churches to reflect on their missionary thinking and practices in light of the New Testament, and for the new missionary church to critically assess the "received" deposit of knowledge and practices of mission to formulate new missiology that is closer to the life of the early church and effective to mission engagements.

At this point, it is important to clarify that the distance between theology and mission will be much closer than it has been in the past. This closeness or overlap is due to two considerations. First, future theology will take context seriously. Often a theological process will be motivated by a contextual issue. Secondly, I suggest that mission is defined as the introduction of the transforming power of the gospel to every aspect of human life. Here the role of the missioners (or believers) is essential, as they not only introduce the gospel to the world but also foster interaction between the two through their missional life, work, and words.

I will focus on two particular areas that require our urgent attention to formulate future missional thinking and practice as part of the new theological process. One is an epistemological concern, and the other is a set of assumptions that have been steadily built into our subconscious. Both are part of the "received" paradigms requiring critical revisitation.

A Perspective: Centre vs Fringe

The received model of the Christian mission is a movement of the gospel carrier from A to B. As it happened from the Christian West to the "heathen" rest, it was unidirectional; or it was a movement from a Christian "centre" to non-evangelized "fringes". The centre is described not only as Christian but also geopolitically privileged. It is an epistemological issue with the duality of the subject and the object of mission. When Christianity is introduced in a political context, e.g. colonization, it is definitely a power issue to the eyes of the "object" of mission. Unfortunately, the received missionary model was shaped by the "powerful" reality of the Western Christian nations toward the "powerless" objects. This reality has left us with an "established" mission thinking and practice, and several expressions are evident.

First, missionary-sending and receiving are mutually exclusive. A church or nation is either receiving or sending missionaries. The world is missionally divided into two complex parts: missionary-sending subjects and missionary-receiving objects; and, although the division is primarily religious, it is also cultural, political, and, I dare to say, racial. Unfortunately, this perception is not limited to the West, but is also among the new missionary "powers". When I met an African man in a subway in Seoul in the early 1990s, I reacted (within myself) strongly against his claim that he was in Korea as a missionary! I had to spend some time digging into my psyche to conclude that my judgement was based on my own superior-thinking mentality over him. It was basically cultural, economic, and racial! Christianity-wise, his country is over 60 percent Christian, while Korea is less than 25 percent. No wonder the idea of a multicultural church in the West is often faced with the exodus of whites (or "white flight") from the church as immigrants begin to join the church.[2] The biblical model of mission, as we will see below in the case of Antioch, is both sending and receiving missionary gifts. There is no church in the world that does not require missionaries, while no church is too weak to share its missionary gifts. In fact, the serious decline of Western Christianity begs the host churches to recognize God's missionary gifts at their doorsteps. This truth also challenges the immigrant churches to break their own ethnocentric mindset and operation.

Second, mission has been understood as a movement across geographical boundaries, along with cultural and religious ones. Picking up the "go" component of the Great Commission (Matt. 28:19), modern mission history is full of heroic records of missionaries who left the comforts of home and braved all the adverse elements, including hostility from fellow humans. However, this has created an unhealthy understanding that mission takes place strictly outside of one's own geographical location. "Foreign" was one word most frequently used to describe this form of understanding. Consequently, missionaries "at home" are more an exception than the norm, either in deputation or retired. Only recently, "home mission" was added, for example, in North America to refer to ministries among the Native Americans and now gradually includes immigrant communities. Still, an effort to reach the mainstream population in a given country is not considered mission. This further strengthens the notion that mission is not for here but for there. The biblical concept of mission is quite different, perhaps best expressed by the recent phrase, "from everywhere to everywhere".

Third, mission, therefore, is not a call for everyone: it is restricted to a few specialists. Because of the cross-cultural nature of their work, missionaries are specially selected, trained, deployed, and supported. Special cross-cultural training is required in addition to theological study, and some receive further professional training for various works. In fact, historically, the word "mission" was first institutionally used to refer to a person who was commissioned by the church (in this case, the Vatican) to undertake a specific task. This is the term commonly used in the secular world (such as a mission statement for a corporate body). This has an immediate implication: mission is only for trained specialists,

---

[2] Israel Olofinjana, "Multicultural Churches in Britain: The Journey to Crofton Park Baptist Church," in Israel Olofinjana (ed.), *Turning the Tables on Mission: Stories of Christians from the Global South in the UK* (Herts, UK: Instant Apostle, 2013), p. 118.

and the rest of the church is called to pray for them and support their work. More harmfully, mission is viewed as a call for someone else. Unfortunately, this is squarely against the biblical teaching: everyone is called to participate in the great plan of God to bring the whole of humanity into him through the redeeming work of Christ.

This dualistic epistemology of a mission model is not a contemporary development. In fact, this was present at the very beginning of church life. A quick look at two prime early churches, Jerusalem and Antioch, may provide a direction to correct the received paradigm of mission. I am well aware that I am running the risk of characterization. The Jerusalem church continued the aura of its privileged position as the Jewish religious centre. As religious and ethical Jews, early Christians lived with old promises that Jerusalem would be the centre where the nations would gather to worship Yahweh. Into this mindset and expectation, the church was born on the day of Pentecost. Before its birth, the missionary mandate of this new body of Christ's followers was fully assumed, which was earlier given to the disciples. When Christ unfolded the plan of world evangelization, the "centre" nature of Jerusalem must have been further confirmed: "You will be my witnesses in Jerusalem, and all Judea, and Samaria, and to the ends of the earth" (Acts 1:8 NIV). This does not wholly explain why the Jerusalem church did not make any serious attempts to follow this missionary mandate. To be fair, the young church was barely coping with the exponential growth on a daily basis, arising from extremely successful evangelistic activities and a substantial number of returning Jewish diaspora who were attracted to this new revolutionary faith community. It is also possible that the "plan" Jesus revealed to the disciples may have been understood as a programmatic stage of the expansion of Christianity. If that is the case, this four-stage plan may also have assumed that, at the completion of one stage, the next stage would commence, or a progressive expansion would take place. Reversely, until Jerusalem is fully reached, the Judah stage won't begin. Then early Jerusalem Christians were rightly busy reaching fellow Jerusalemites, including those who were constantly drawn to this religious centre.

On the contrary, Antioch Christians must have a radically different orientation: they were not at the centre (Jerusalem) but at the "ends" of the earth. The mission field is not "out there", as they were living right in the outer frontiers of Christian mission. Unlike Jerusalem believers, they were keenly conscious of the social environment: they were already "sent" to the end. From its early days, the Antioch church mobilized its best missionary assets, most likely to present Christ to Antiochians (as they lived in the mission field) and to reach further frontiers. Their understanding might have been that mission is a simultaneous move, with no attention to the possible four-stage plan. Paul and Barnabas, their first missionaries, were a natural extension of their already established missionary life in its immediate locale. The two were not sent to Jerusalem to rebuild and strengthen the centre, but to the West, further away from the centre. Evangelism has to take place at all places at the same time. Antioch Christianity does not represent a power centre to the non-Christian Antioch's majority and to fellow Christians; instead, it was a tiny social minority, looked down upon by Jews and the Gentiles, and sometimes persecuted. They knew they were the social underdog. Their life much reflects the kenotic life of Christ, the author of mission. Thus, mission in Christ's way!

Mission Assumptions

There are assumptions, built slowly and unknowingly, and yet clearly and evidently.[3] The following discussion is to challenge several key mission assumptions slowly accumulated throughout centuries in the West. They are not necessarily adopted as rules or requirements for mission. However, for the emerging churches in the South, they have clearly been present through missionaries in their life and work in mission fields. Although never advocated by missionaries, to the eyes of the "missioned", they have become a practical set of assumptions that soon were perceived as requirements to earn the right of a missionary church. The assumptions and even rules of mission were clearly born and shaped by Western social and religious contexts. These were not seriously questioned for their theological validity, and, unfortunately, this uncritical acceptance is influencing new missionary churches in the Global South. For this reason, several established "missionary myths" need to be challenged in light of the shift in global Christianity and how the early church practised its mission.

Only Christian Nations Do Mission

The 1910 Edinburgh Conference was planned, organized, and run by Western churches, with a small group of delegates and invitees from some mission "fields" or beneficiaries of missionary activities. Although the term Christendom may not have been used during the conference, in the back of everyone's mind it must have been assumed that only after a country has been fully evangelized, or Christianized, does the nation earn the right to be a missionary nation. This seems to just be a natural given as the missionary direction will flow from "gospel rich" to "gospel poor". Only from such centres – Western Europe, North America, and Oceania 100 years ago – would missionaries spread to the heathen lands.

Today, this assumption is challenged by two realities. First, it is no longer 100 percent Christianized nations that send out their missionaries. Many new missionary mega-powers like Korea, China, and India are not "Christian" countries, although countries like Brazil, the Philippines, Nigeria, and others have more Christian populations. In fact, India and China claim less than 10 percent of their populations as Christian. However, they could well be among

[3] This part is taken from Wonsuk Ma, "A Millennial Shift of Global Christianity and Mission: An Initial Reflection," in S. Hun Kim and Wonsuk Ma (eds), *Korean Diaspora and Christian Mission* (Oxford: Regnum Books, 2010), pp. 11–23.

the top five missionary-sending nations if we view it per capita. According to the seventh edition of *Operation World*,[4] several fascinating facts can be extracted. Regardless of the accuracy of the figures, I picked several top missionary-sending countries and calculated how many believers it takes to send a cross-cultural missionary. The US takes 263 (or 93,500 missionaries out of 246,553,000 believers) to send one cross-cultural and international missionary,[5] South Korea takes 698 (or 21,500 missionaries out of 15,011,000 believers),[6] China takes 870 believers (or 120,000 missionaries – both working within and without China – out of 105,382,000 believers),[7] and the United Kingdom takes 5,787 (or 6,405 missionaries out of 37,067,000 believers).[8]

The second, this time a reverse argument, also proves the challenge. Not all Christian nations are missionary entities. Although this notion has much to do with the definition of mission, some African nations, for example, which have more than an impressive 80 percent Christianization success, are not necessarily strong missionary countries. This of course, challenges us with a deep question: what makes a church missional? This comes with an enormous new opportunity as well as challenges. To begin, the understanding of what mission is has to be seriously revisited from the perspective of the new mission players. It will inevitably be holistic in scope, encompassing proclamation and justice with everything in between. As a sign of God's kingdom, the place of a Christian community will be a significant missionary presence in many Christian-minority places. Even if marginalized and sometimes persecuted, the presence of a local congregation itself is a powerful declaration that God is the Lord, and He has an answer to every issue with which society struggles. Consequently, missionary engagement will be profoundly affected as the missioners are now in the field. For instance, issues of other faiths will have a radically different light when those who are surrounded by other religions as a minority set the rules of missionary engagement.

Only Resource-Rich Countries Do Mission

I am sure not even the slightest suggestion has been made that only rich countries can do mission. However, the mission players of the last two hundred years of the previous millennium were all from economically resourceful countries. One may argue that the cause and effect should be reversed; that is, mission commitment has resulted in God's blessings. However, to the eyes of the rest of the world, finance has become an assumed priority requirement for mission, and this has often been the first excuse for Christian-rich countries not engaging in

---

[4] Jason Mandryk, *Operation World: The Definitive Prayer Guide to Every Nation*, 7th ed. (Gerrards Cross, UK: WEC International, 2011).
[5] Mandryk, *Operation World*, p. 862.
[6] Mandryk, *Operation World*, pp. 509–10.
[7] Mandryk, *Operation World*, pp. 215–16.
[8] Mandryk, *Operation World*, pp. 851–52.

mission. This image is often created by the image of a Western, often white and male, missionary, fully "armed" with expensive gadgets, acting as a benefactor to local churches and communities. This has inevitably influenced the understanding of mission and missionaries. This emphasis on resources, even if shaped unintentionally, has serious consequences, as we see today. To be fair, it is important to stress that this was not the intention of the Western church at all. However, when Christian-rich but financially poor churches are asked why they are not engaged in mission, the first answer will likely be the lack of finance. Furthermore, dependency is an ongoing challenge to many emerging nations and their churches.

Today, despite criticism that new missionary churches tend to follow the old "established" Western missionary paradigm, signs suggest that the new emerging churches do not wait to have a certain economic level before they begin missionary engagement. One such example is diaspora. What is encouraging are the creative ways missionaries are deployed and supported by not-so-rich churches. For example, Ethiopian missionaries in South Sudan, India, Pakistan, and Iran have "disappeared" among locals as they live and work with people to whom they minister. This is a forced strategy, as the church does not have the financial resources to sustain its missionaries as Western mission agencies do. However, this is how an "incarnational" missionary presence can be achieved.

The story of the early church's expansion in the first century would be more according to this paradigm, with Galilean fishermen reaching out to Roman citizens. The apostles' emphasis on work-and-preach may indicate their subsistence, as much as their principle of self-support (2 Cor. 11:8). The "nameless" missionaries recorded in Acts 11 may shed light on our discussion. When fleeing the persecution in Jerusalem, some "travelled as far as Phoenicia, Cyprus, and Antioch" (11:19). The impression is that, from Jerusalem, they were reaching the ends of the earth (Acts 1:8). As the three places mentioned are all north of Jerusalem, one can easily assume that these "refugees" were either Jewish diaspora or pilgrims from these regions.[9] As they reached out to the Greek-speaking population, these Jews no longer enjoyed ethnic acceptance among fellow Jews. Their disadvantage could also have been felt in gaps in the social status between these missionaries and the societies such as Antioch, where they preached the gospel. That Paul often debated with local intellectuals, such as in Athens (Acts 17:16-34), serves as an illustration. It is quite clear that, in their missionary context, the missionaries did not come with ready resources to offer assistance to the people in the field, nor did they strengthen their position with material wealth. Rather, they often came with subsistence or out of need.

This paradigm shift has a serious practical implication: the primary resource of mission is a transformed life through the gospel, and not material riches or technology. If a missionary symbol is a satellite-linked communication gadget

---

[9] However, among them were "men from … Cyrene", North Africa (11:20) indicating a more intentional missionary motivation.

in a deep mountain village that does not have electricity, it is quite wrong. If new mission players also continue this trend, this will be hopelessly fatal. But when missionaries, regardless of their national origin, identify themselves with the people they minister to in every aspect of their lives, that is called "incarnational mission" after our Lord.

Mission is by the Developed to the Developing or Under-developed

Related to the preceding points is the notion that the developed, civilized or "first-world" nations do mission to the heathen, uncivilized, or underdeveloped "third-world". At least the last 200 years of Christian mission were undertaken by so-called first-world nations, developed in politics, economics, culture, and education.

This practice and notion of mission are deeply rooted in the racial supremacy of the West and colonial imperialism. Politically, the West took the rest of the world as its subject, while the extremely unbiblical and counter-humanistic claim of a "white man's burden" was viewed as quite natural during the "great [missionary] century". One of the mission aims was to civilize the heathens by introducing medicine, education, and "proper" (that is, Western) ways of living. It is perfectly legitimate to introduce new ways to improve life. Still, this approach often creates a value system that privileges Western paradigms while harshly judging an indigenous culture. This cultural imperialism sometimes produces rather humorous images. One of them is what I encountered in the northern Philippines among the Igorot mountain tribes. An Igorot young man had the "proper" attire of a necktie and a suit for his upper body, but bare feet and a loin cloth, called a G-string, for the lower half of his body. However, there were many serious cases. When Catholicism was first introduced in Korea, the state executed thousands of early believers for refusing ancestor rites and (for men) cutting their long hair. Christianity was misunderstood as requiring a Western lifestyle, with a deep confusion between Christianity and the missionary's culture.

Today, about two-thirds of global Christians live in the Global South or developing or under-developed world countries. As there are more missionaries from these churches than those from the traditional Western churches, mission workers from under-developed countries are now found working in other under-developed or developing countries as well as developed ones. Without much reflection, the flow of mission from relatively developed to less developed is also observed. For instance, the majority of Korean missionaries are concentrated in Asia and Africa, where Korea, in general, can play a "superior" role. Often motivated by pragmatic reasons, this pattern has unfortunately continued the unhealthy and unbiblical notion of mission flowing from civilized to heathen. Missionary movements within the South often ignore cultural and economic differences, as Chinese missionaries are now found in several central Asian nations. However, an increasing number of missionaries from the South are found in the West, and diaspora communities serve as a vanguard of emerging and dynamic Christianity of the Global South in the midst of secular Western societies where Christianity has been weakening. In fact, a large number of Filipino migrants in the Middle East and the West, for example, have demonstrated the possibility of a "reverse" mission, that is, from the developing to the developed. If the flow of mission has to be from the gospel rich to the gospel poor, the "received" notion of mission from the developed to the developing world has been a sheer coincidence for the last two centuries.

As alluded to above, the early church's missionary-centre move from Jerusalem to Antioch was a revolutionary development. When Christian mission moved beyond the Jewish racial framework, Jewish Christians no longer enjoyed their cultural acceptability and privilege in the face of the Gentiles. Some groups may have viewed Jews as racially and culturally inferior to theirs, as often illustrated in Paul's encounters with social elites in various cities. Ultimately, who reached the Roman elite families with the Christian faith? Early missionary forces may have been slaves, merchants, manual workers, and the like, whose life and work manifested the newfound religion. Early Christians did not have, in general, cultural or social advantages over their "mission field".

Conclusion: The Issue of Power

The core of the paradigm shift in Christian mission is the issue of power: is mission achieved by power or powerlessness? In one sense, the gospel is the power of salvation, and this power can be manifested in various ways, as witnessed in the life of Jesus: from the precarious suffering and death to the demonstration of power in healing and exorcism. In fact, many aspects of mission demonstrate this power through the work of the Holy Spirit. However, it is important to note that God's power is manifest through the total obedience of the vessels, often in their weakness. Without the ultimate sacrifice of Christ, through his death, the power of redemption cannot be accomplished. The demonstration of his power and authority over principalities and powers has its place, but not as a substitute for his obedience through total surrender. Paul's understanding of God's power, through his own weakness (2 Cor. 12:10), attests to the same principle.

The established mission paradigm in the nineteenth and twentieth centuries is that of mission with power, be it political, cultural, economic, or military. It also includes "Christian" power. However, mission with superiority, or with an upper hand, is far from the testimony of the life of Jesus. Although the Jerusalem church may have perceived mission in connection with superiority or power, this was quickly replaced by the Antiochian model: mission undertaken with a new paradigm, mission with weakness. This was possible because Antioch was not a "centre" of Christianity but remained a "mission field", surrounded by culture and forces challenging and threatening the Christian presence.

Although hard to verify independently, the argument that the total Muslim converts in the Middle East through the influence of Filipino domestic helpers far outnumber the converts through duly deployed missionaries in the region is revealing.[10] If the two groups of mission players are compared to each other in the places of origin (still predominantly from the West), training, resources, support, and the like, the former cannot outperform the latter. The most striking difference is that the domestic helpers are there to serve but not to instruct and teach. The place of weakness plays such a powerful role in mission, and our observation of the scriptures proves that this is how mission is to be approached. The new mission players from mission fields struggling with resources, and culturally and politically "weak" places, can revitalize Christian mission and restore the right "rules of missionary engagement", as informed by the New Testament. This potential will be realized only if the mission players and their churches know that the "established" or "received" mission paradigm is to be critically evaluated before adoption or rejection, as it was the product of the West's own golden missionary age and socio-political context. They need to avoid the "business as usual" mindset. It requires a serious reflection on the scriptural and historical practices and principles that informed the missionary practices. This is where an entirely new breed of missiologists is needed, as well as the higher education systems that will raise them.

---

[10] Melba Padilla Maggay made this comment during her verbal presentation of her study, although her published chapter does not include this: "Early Protestant Missionary Efforts in the Philippines: Some Intercultural Issues," in Wonsuk Ma and Julie C. Ma (eds), *Asian Church and God's Mission: Studies Presented in the International Symposium on Asian Mission in Manila, January 2002* (Quezon City, Philippines: OMF Lit., 2003), particularly p. 39.

5. The Holy Spirit in the Shaping of Mission Awareness and Practice

The key theological contribution of the modern Pentecostal movement is, without doubt, in pneumatology. As Pentecostalism has theologically challenged the widespread notion that the gifts of the Spirit have ceased, its most significant contribution is the reviving of the dynamic work of the Holy Spirit in Christian life and practice. As a result, the Pentecostal contribution of pneumatological missiology has changed the global Christian landscape in the last century. A recent fine example of pneumatological missiology is *Together Towards Life*, the new mission statement of the World Council of Churches.[1] This ecumenical document definitely reflects changes and challenges in global Christianity and its mission. I also believe that the growth of Charismatic Christianity and its focus on the person and work of the Holy Spirit encouraged the ecumenical process to consider a pneumatological focus in its ecumenical missiology. The role of the Holy Spirit in mission has been a popular subject among theologians, mission leaders, and practitioners, so Pentecostals have no unique claim on the discussion. In its short history, however, Pentecostal insiders have produced a flow of theological reflections significantly enriching this particular discussion.[2]

I have explored the theological basis for Pentecostal mission elsewhere.[3] This study is intended to examine the process of both individual and community Pentecostal mission formation. The question is, therefore, about the process through which Pentecostals individually and cooperatively develop their mission awareness and consciousness. I then wish to consider how this theological formation gives birth to certain mission practices. The role of personal experiences is a hallmark of Pentecostal theologizing, thus taking the audience

---

[1] The leadership of the Commission on World Mission and Evangelism is to be commended for this outstanding achievement; see Jooseop Keum (ed.), *Together Towards Life: Mission and Evangelism in Changing Landscapes, with a Practical Guide* (Geneva: World Council of Churches Publications, 2013). Pentecostals actively participated in the creation of this mission document.

[2] For example, from the previous generation, see Murray W. Dempster, Byron D. Klaus, and Douglas Petersen, (eds), *Called and Empowered: Global Mission in Pentecostal Perspective* (Peabody, MA: Hendrickson, 1991); from the current generation, see Wonsuk Ma, Veli-Matti Kärkkäinen, and J. Kwabena Asamoa-Gyadu (eds), *Pentecostal Mission and Global Christianity* (Oxford: Regnum Books, 2014).

[3] See Chapter 8.

to a very personal, private level.[4] This personal dimension makes the missionary operation of Pentecostal churches and denominations dynamic and effective, albeit with certain weaknesses. The institutional structure evolves only as this grassroots movement develops, requiring administrative and structural support and management. The process of starting from the individual, then moving to communal, and finally institutional and denominational levels is thus true to the Pentecostal ethos.

Pentecostal theology (including pneumatology and missiology) has two fundamental sources: scripture and experience. The relationship between these two is never linear, with one not always preceding the other. For example, an "aha!" moment in a Bible reading is the work of the Holy Spirit, as an aspect of a passage comes alive, generating a powerful conviction. An experience, according to a Pentecostal mind, validates what one reads and understands in the Bible. At the same time, the scripture informs what kind of experience is expected. Pentecostals read the Bible with a set of presumptions or hermeneutical values, which include the sacred value of the Bible, a passion for apostolic restoration, the contribution of the faith community, the role of experience, and the consciousness of the S/spirit(s). [5] Also, Pentecostal interpretations are sometimes different from others and result in a certain type of action or behaviour. Pentecostal mission practice is, therefore, one area where this way of reading the Bible is expressed and lived out. This process is in accordance with the way Pentecostal theology is formed. Because Pentecostal theological formation has a grassroots nature, much takes place at the individual and congregational levels. This study is, therefore, descriptive, reporting on what is taking place in real-life settings. This process is constructive by presenting real experiences in a theological framework.

Because of the nature of the discussion, generalization is inevitable, especially when comparing the West with the rest of the world. Similarly, numbers are used to illustrate the extent of growth or spread. While the precision and basis of statistics can be questioned, they are still useful for drawing trajectories by applying the same methods and criteria at different points of history.

Missionary Formation and the Holy Spirit

As mentioned above, the Pentecostal mission movement begins from a personal rather than from an institutional or denominational level. Therefore, the inner working of one's missionary formation is a logical starting point in this theological probing.

[4] See Chapter 2.
[5] See Chapter 8.

Conversion and Spiritual Formation

The regeneration experience is the foundational building block for Pentecostal spiritual formation. Conversion is often described as a crisis experience. Whether or not every conversion can be characterized objectively as radical, most Pentecostals would perceive it in this manner. Many testify to the experience, which includes a profound emotional sense of one's sinfulness and guilt, and this feeling is attributed to the work of the Holy Spirit convicting of sins (John 16:8). Some report an experience of purging or consuming by the fire of the Holy Spirit (e.g. Isa. 4:4). This encounter is followed by the stage of God's forgiveness, when the redemptive suffering of Christ is experienced. Sensory elements are often expressed, such as "refreshing", "brightness", "bliss", or "cleansing". Again, this aspect of spiritual experience is often attributed to the regenerative work of the Holy Spirit. (Note Jesus' words to Nicodemus about being born again in John 3:3, 5.) Its impact on the ensuing life and work is often profound and long-lasting.

This experience is very personal, with incredible diversity. However, this spiritual struggle and process are often accompanied by a concerned Christian in prayer and in guidance. When the new believer is incorporated into the community of faith (i.e. a local congregation), the individual becomes a new family member. Such a community often serves as a spiritually safe house. In casual settings, stories are freely shared of one's spiritual journey. They can range from a dream, God's intervention in various forms, or simply the daily struggles of life. People are not hesitant to pray for one another's challenges, often laying their hands upon the individual. This physical motion is more than a sign of support. Pentecostals commonly believe that the laying on of hands has a special spiritual significance, with the presence and power of the Holy Spirit being mediated through such an act.

Several important values are shaped through this initial stage of the Christian life. The first is the primacy of inner transformation. Pentecostals share a common belief that every change begins with personal and inner change. The second is the importance of evangelism in every form of ministry, which includes mission. The third is the essential role of a faith community as an alternative family for a newly converted person. However, this intuitive and lived-out work of the Holy Spirit requires more reflection.

Encounters with God

From the time of conversion, Pentecostal religious life is a continuous spiritual journey. Believers are encouraged to actively participate in meetings set by their church, which tends to have more programmes and meetings than non-Pentecostal churches. A Pentecostal gathering, whether a formal worship service at the church or a semi-formal lay-led group meeting in someone's home, is characterized by certain expectations. The most important is a tangible encounter with God. As noted above, a spiritual experience is extremely subjective. Yet there is one commonality: there is no mistaking that life is no longer the same for the believer who encountered God in his power and love.

The focus of Pentecostal worship is this encounter with God. Songs, prayers, preaching, and even offerings are all done to prepare each worshipper to enter into a spiritual space where God's presence is real. Two particular features of Pentecostal worship epitomize this purpose. The first is the sharing of testimonies. Anyone from the congregation is welcome to share one's spiritual experience with the whole congregation. Although the validity of his or her theological interpretation may be questioned, this practice has a powerful effect of spreading the Holy Spirit's work in everyday life. Today, this unique tradition may be practised in different forms, but grassroots participation in communal theological formation continues. The second component is a prayer for divine encounters and interventions. An altar call has been a regular feature of Pentecostal worship. Customarily after preaching, the pastor issues an invitation for special prayers at the front. Such prayers range from accepting Christ as one's Saviour, receiving the baptism in the Holy Spirit, dedicating oneself to God's service, to healing. These prayers are where the presence and work of the Holy Spirit are expected and experienced. Also, utterance gifts may be in operation, such as a word of encouragement in prophecy or a word of knowledge declaring that a specific illness has been healed by God. One more point on the prayer tradition – from the beginning, Pentecostal worship has had a conspicuous place for simultaneous corporate prayers, when everyone joins either in praise (such as singing in tongues) or in a petition (e.g. the Korean practice of people shouting "Juyo" ["Lord"] before a unison congregational prayer). Through this process, personal prayer becomes a community-forming act.

This experience is translated into one's missional life, regardless of the social setting where Pentecostal witnessing takes place. This witness includes courageous Christian living in the midst of marginalization and persecution.

Experience of and Emphasis on Healing and the Miraculous

Stories of healings and the miraculous intervention of God in difficult life situations are part of the Pentecostal experience. They are experienced personally either by Pentecostal believers or by people close to them. These testimonies have a powerful effect on the spiritual shaping of Pentecostal believers. Historically in North America, faith healing was a rich tradition, especially among Holiness circles before the turn of the twentieth century. The newly emerging Pentecostal movement embraced this tradition in full force. It is important to remember that the early Pentecostals firmly believed that the coming of the Holy Spirit was a sure sign of the last day. The increased manifestation of God's power was understood as God's empowerment for the end-time harvest before the return of the Lord. Thus, eschatological urgency strengthened the expectation of God's supernatural work while it provided a theological framework to interpret their experiences of the Holy Spirit.

This openness to the supernatural occurs among Pentecostals due to at least two inherent values and the familiarity mentioned above. The first value is a Pentecostal worldview similar to the typical non-Western worldviews, even among North American Pentecostals. Walter Hollenweger coined the term "Black oral root".[6] In this system, the world consists not only of what is seen, the physical and material, but also of what is unseen, or the spiritual. Indeed, both parts of the world interact constantly, and the latter often causes what happens in the former.[7] The spiritual dimension includes God, angels, spirits, and demons. The modern Pentecostal movement has recovered this lost supernatural world in the Christian worldview. Experience with and belief in the healing and the supernatural have contributed to this restored worldview.

The second is what we could call the Pentecostal collapse of history, that is, the mental linking of Bible times with today.[8] The scripture is not primarily literature to study; it is the living word of God for real engagement with today's issues and needs. Records of healing and miracles are received and believed at face value. Because of this time collapse, the same intervention is expected for Pentecostal believers today. Expectancy, in my view, is one of the primary reasons why we see more supernatural manifestations of God among Pentecostals and the non-Western world.

Calling and Empowerment

In Pentecostal circles, one commonly hears "the Lord spoke to me" or "I heard God". To Pentecostals, God's revelation continues today. A variety of modes are employed in this experience of the Spirit: hearing an audible voice, an inner voice or having a strong impression, a particular scripture "standing out" and "speaking" to one, dreams and visions, a sermon "speaking personally", a prophecy, a message through tongues with an interpretation, a word of knowledge or wisdom, or a simple comment that "speaks to a particular situation". Pentecostal believers expect and accept these experiences as the direct revelation of the Holy Spirit. These personal messages are to be discerned and interpreted in the light of scripture.

In these settings, many will testify that they have received God's call for a specific ministry or a specific location for ministry. Some calls are revealed through a series of particular events. For instance, when Elva Vanderbout was called from Northern California to serve in the northern Philippines in the 1950s, she and her husband were preparing for their missionary work. However, God was specific that she was to go alone. Not long after this revelation, her husband died of a brain illness. As an independent Pentecostal missionary, she became a

---

[6] Walter J. Hollenweger, *Pentecostalism: Origins and Developments Worldwide* (Peabody, MA: Hendrickson, 1997), pp. 18–141.

[7] Paul Hiebert calls the unseen things of this world the "excluded middle": "The Flaw of the Excluded Middle," *Missiology* 10.1 (1982), pp. 35–47.

[8] See Chapter 7.

legend in bringing Christianity to many Igorot tribal areas, significantly using the ministries of healing and evangelism.[9]

Perhaps the most unique and impactful Pentecostal belief in mission is the baptism in the Holy Spirit, empowering believers for witnessing. The primary scriptural basis is Acts 1:8, which is also the most frequently recited passage by Pentecostals: "But you will receive power when the Holy Spirit comes on you, and you will be my witnesses in Jerusalem, and in all Judea and Samaria, and to the ends of the earth" (NIV).

This Acts passage calls all believers to be witnesses (Pentecostals speak of "the prophethood of all believers"), fulfilling, as Peter preached on the day of Pentecost, the promise recorded in Joel 2. This empowerment presumes God's call for witness placed upon each believer and commission to go out to witness. For the Pentecostals, "empowerment" is the mother of this missional pneumatology.

Mission Practice and the Holy Spirit

Mission practice is the direct outcome of the process of Pentecostal mission formation. Accordingly, the four aspects of mission formation result in four distinct and concrete expressions of Pentecostal mission.

Evangelism as the Primary Agenda

The urgency of soul-winning among early Pentecostals was strongly motivated by the eschatological expectation of the Lord's imminent return. They were convinced that the recent advent of the Holy Spirit at the turn of the twentieth century was the "latter rain" following "early rain", which was the coming of the Holy Spirit as recorded in Acts 2. Many early Pentecostals even believed that tongues were, in fact, "missionary languages" for the effective final harvest. For example, *Apostolic Faith*, the publication of the Azusa Street Mission, regularly published columns and sermons strongly urging its members to go to the "ends of the earth" to save souls. Here is an example: "Missionaries for the foreign fields, equipped with several languages, are now on their way, and others are only waiting for the way to open and for the Lord to say: 'Go.' … Awake! Awake! There is but time to dress and be ready, for the cry will soon go forth. 'The Bridegroom cometh.'"[10] This excerpt demonstrates that the primary theological motivation for Pentecostal mission is the empowerment theology through the baptism in the Spirit.

On the mission field, this process nurtures a proactive attitude to believe that one day the whole community will become Christian. At the same time, almost

---

[9] Her moving story is typical of many Pentecostal missionaries. See Inez Sturgeon, *Give Me This Mountain* (Oakland, CA: Hunter Advertising, 1960).

[10] "Fire Still Falling," *The Apostolic Faith* (Los Angeles) 1.3 (October 1906), p. 1, col. 2.

every believer becomes a committed evangelist, following the strong Pentecostal ethos, which includes sharing one's story with neighbours. A study by Julie Ma attests to this dynamic: several entire villages have become Christian, and Pentecostal, as there is only one church in each community.[11]

Establishment of Local Congregations

Forming a local church is a practical necessity to preserve and nurture the (often tiny) fruit of evangelism, as discussed above. Initially, a congregation gradually forms in a home or storefront space. A characteristic of such a group is that the members give more time for church gatherings and programmes than their fellow Christians do in a typical historic or Evangelical church. It is also expected that some, if not most, new members will begin to share ministerial responsibilities. There may be no appointed pastor or leader for the new congregation, especially in rural areas. A mission worker may visit from time to time, but a leader is appointed from among the new believers. I observed that a young congregation in a village deep in the mountains of the northern Philippines planted several daughter churches in a short period. In the meantime, these daughter churches continued giving birth to their own daughter churches. The sense of the Spirit's empowerment is at the heart of this unconventional mobilization of all believers. Pentecostals establish small and large congregations much more than other church traditions. This passion for local churches may have been formed by a local faith community's role in personal spiritual formation.

Signs and Wonders

The supernatural is a vital characteristic of Pentecostal mission. Pentecostal openness to the supernatural comes from experiences (both personal and secondary), a particular way of reading the scripture, and the theological orientation of spiritual empowerment. This combination makes a Pentecostal believer not only an expectant spectator but also an active instrument of the supernatural work of the Holy Spirit.

This recovery of the Holy Spirit in Christian life and mission has impacted two particular groups throughout its history. The first is traditional Christians (or "powerless Christians") who have been "converted" to the power of the Holy Spirit.[12] This need for the power of Christianity is commonly felt among cross-cultural mission workers who face the power orientation of most religions. When the Azusa Street Revival occurred in Los Angeles in 1906–1909, it produced new Spirit-empowered mission workers and missionaries now "converted" to

---

[11] Julie C. Ma, *Mission Possible: The Biblical Strategy for Reaching the Lost*, 2nd ed. (Oxford: Regnum Books, 2016), pp. 23–28.

[12] Charles H. Kraft, *Christianity With Power: Your Worldview and Your Experience of the Supernatural* (Eugene, OR: Wipf & Stock, 2005), contains his personal journey for a powerless evangelical Christian to recover the power of the gospel.

Christianity with power. *The Apostolic Faith* regularly reported such empowered missionaries.[13]

The second group to be touched by the Holy Spirit is the traditional religionists who have become Christians through the message of God's love and the demonstration of his power. In places where historic or Evangelical Christianity has struggled to gain ground, there are reports that Pentecostals have excelled in evangelism and church planting. There is no doubt that Pentecostals later reap the seed sown through hard work. Julie Ma's work demonstrates the attraction of a tribal group to the God who overpowers their traditional spirits and gods as the core reason for Pentecostal success in those regions. Success is not only the result of the verbal presentation of the scripture but also, more importantly, the demonstration of God's power in love through prayer for healing and miracles. The resurgence of Chinese Christianity, especially the house church networks, is regularly attributed to the testimonies of healing.[14] These experiences also explain how two large Ethiopian Protestant denominations officially adopted Pentecostal beliefs into their doctrines: the Kale Heywet Church (with Baptist roots) and the Mekane Yesus Church (with Lutheran and Presbyterian roots). Ethiopia's religious culture has prompted Christianity's awakening to the supernatural dimension of its message and practice. The growth of global Christianity in the last half a century has been led by such Pentecostal and independent church families that are predominantly post-denominational while widely open to the ministry of the Holy Spirit.

Spiritual gifts are exercised and developed in such contexts. I once had the privilege of having a ministry partner with an incredible gift of healing. Over the years, I observed him build his confidence in this gift. The "wow" effect of a healing incident in a tightly knit tribal village is electric. Their resistance to the message of Jesus melts with the appearance of the all-powerful God![15] The whole village gathers with minds open and God's presence anticipated. Soon a church is born, and most, if not all, villagers become believers.[16]

Not all Pentecostal believers are faith-pumping, demon-rebuking, and healing-claiming evangelists. Pentecostals do not have a monopoly on praying for God's healing and miracles. Contextual needs and expectations would also encourage and challenge even non-Pentecostal workers to lay hands upon the sick and pray for healing. The expectations and real needs of the people challenge and motivate hesitant workers to obey God's urge to respond. Some workers may be full of disbelief, but when the Holy Spirit reveals himself in love

---

[13] For example, "Pentecostal Missionary Reports," *The Apostolic Faith* 1.11 (October 1908), p. 1, col. 4.

[14] Caroline Fielder, "The Growth of the Protestant Church in Rural China," *China Study Journal* 23 (Spring/Summer 2008), p. 49.

[15] Ma and Ma, *Mission in the Spirit*, pp. 59–71.

[16] J. Ma, *Mission Possible*, pp. 77–84, records the story of a miracle that led to an entire village turning to the Lord.

and power, the worker becomes open to the new work of God. In the end, these works serve as the signs and wonders of the kingdom, pointing people to Christ the Lord!

Reproducing the Empowerment Cycle

The theological and missiological formation processes in the Pentecostal tradition have two primary outcomes: 1) the expansion of Pentecostal faith through the increase of believers and local faith communities, and 2) the building of a continuing cycle of empowerment in belief and practice. Since the first effect has already been mentioned in several places, this section is devoted to the second point, which is significant to the first.

The first observation in a mission setting is the establishment of missionary congregations that embrace the empowerment theology of the Holy Spirit as their doctrinal foundation. As discussed, this theological formation is the net result of the combination of personal and communal experiences of healing and miracles and the teaching of the empowering presence of the Holy Spirit. When this formation is in place, a young congregation will spring into missionary action by mobilizing new believers.

The second observation is the multiplication of empowered and active mission workers. As we experienced church multiplication during our missionary work in the Philippines, we noticed that the evangelists and church planters were ordinary believers. They were often new and young believers who hiked rugged mountains for hours. Sharing their testimonies and the gospel, and praying for salvation and healing were a natural part of their Christian life. These practices form and strengthen the belief in the prophethood of all believers. On a formal front, Pentecostal mission has been known for its pragmatic training programmes. The Bible institute movement has been best realized in low-level ministerial training programmes that produce pastors, evangelists, and mission workers in a relatively short period of time. Graduate theological education is a relatively late development in the West and the Majority World.

The creativity and entrepreneurial spirit of Pentecostal mission are also observed in the utilization of mass technology and public evangelistic and healing campaigns (often uncritically called crusades). The blast of Western gospel broadcasting is reaching the world's far corners. In Zambia, I noticed at least five out of a dozen available channels were broadcasting Christian programmes on Sundays, with some featuring national preachers. Pentecostal preachers are now flooding radio stations, television channels, YouTube, social media, and Internet television with messages of salvation, healing, and blessing. Unfortunately, an increasing number of them carry sensational types of messages, such as the prosperity gospel. Nonetheless, this use of media is one way in which Pentecostalism is saturating social spaces. Large-scale open-air gatherings are also part of Pentecostal mission. Continuing the camp meeting tradition of Holiness Christianity, Pentecostals and Evangelicals have established urban ministries. Individuals such as T. L. Osborne, Oral Roberts,

Reinhard Bonnke, and David Yonggi Cho became famous because of their large-scale gatherings. Almost all of them highlighted repentance, salvation, divine healing, and practical solutions to life's problems.

Conclusion: A Plea to Broaden Perspectives But to Remain Faithful to Pentecostal Spirituality

In this reflection, I have examined the inner workings and processes of mission formation and their manifestation in actual mission settings. In human eyes, the average Pentecostal missionary lacks proper planning and careful preparation. Claiming God's call to a specific type of ministry in a specific location, he or she is audaciously compulsive and ignorantly courageous. Yes, such missionaries make more mistakes than those sent by highly institutionalized and professional denominational missions and agencies. However, this deeply committed form of Pentecostal faith mission has achieved no less than the unthinkable. Pentecostal-type believers now account for a quarter of world Christians today. As presented above, they have distinguished themselves in several vital areas. Pentecostalism is certainly a special gift to world Christianity if a tree is known by its fruit. However, this high level of mountain-top accomplishment also comes with deep "valleys" with severe inherent challenges. What areas cry out for further examination and exploration in missional pneumatology, broadly shared and practised by Pentecostals? I offer an insider perspective on three.

One is the unbalanced focus on the Charismatic aspect of the Spirit's work. Pentecostals have brought the dynamic work of the Holy Spirit into daily living, church life, and mission. This factor has powerfully impacted the global church, and many cessationist theologies have been seriously challenged. At the same time, Pentecostals' focused attention on the Charismatic work of the Spirit has downplayed the less sensational, even mundane, and yet highly critical, work of the Spirit. The effect of this imbalance is felt on many fronts. For example, in a pastoral setting, prayers for healing have produced fewer cases of healing than those who are not healed. Many faithful believers who have been prayed over for long-term illnesses but have not seen healing should not live with unhealthy disappointment, doubt, or guilt. Instead, they should experience the equally powerful grace of the Spirit in sustaining them through the trial with a victorious attitude. This fascination for Charismatic work may also be responsible for Pentecostals not readily recognizing the long and rich tradition of the Holy Spirit in other churches, which is often less dramatic. In mission settings, Pentecostals have been "evangelizing" many fellow Christians, such as Orthodox believers. Equally problematic is the action orientation of mission, which may not be possible or even legal in some parts of the world. Then the abiding presence of the Holy Spirit as we read in John's gospel will be an important source of balance. In this gospel, the Holy Spirit is not just helping God's people to survive, but he is also empowering them to be powerful witnesses throughout their daily lives. With this caveat, however, I would admonish my fellow

Pentecostals to uphold and strengthen their unique beliefs and practices as a precious gift to the whole church and the world. At the same time, they should do so with a deep consciousness that we are only one part of the body of Christ with many different gifts.

The second area, flowing from the preceding discussion, is the framework of mission shaped by Pentecostal experiences and the unique reading of the scriptures within the prevailing context of Western mission. Immediately evident is the geographic orientation of mission: to be witnesses from one's own place (Jerusalem) to the ends of the earth (Acts 1:8). This command has been taken as the Spirit's map for mission. While this directive resulted in countless formal and informal mission activities among Pentecostals, it is plainly perceived as one-directional: from the West to the rest! In hindsight, we know it is not the whole or right vision of mission: mission flows from and to every place. Also noticeable is a constant emphasis on power and free-flowing "power" language. While the recovery of the dynamic power of the Holy Spirit is the most prominent theological and practical contribution of Pentecostalism, this emphasis can create an unintended conflict, as the world of mission is deeply reflecting on the Western missionary paradigm as part of the colonial expansionist movement. Pentecostals are now called to negotiate between their prized doctrine of empowerment and a careful walk in humility. A closer reading of scripture will provide ample resources for gaining a kenotic (self-emptying) attitude in the face of mission triumphalism.

The third is the crucial relationship between pneumatology and eschatology. Early Pentecostals understandably took the advent of the Holy Spirit as the sign of the last days. Pentecostal pulpits were flooded with the message of the rapture before the horrible tribulation. Except for a momentary resurgence of eschatological expectation around the birth of the State of Israel in 1948, this message steadily lost its place in Pentecostal churches. In a way, the continuing strength of Pentecostal mission proved that pneumatology was the main theological engine for mission. With the rise of the Charismatic movement, the birth of the prosperity gospel, and the church growth movement, the pendulum swung to the other extreme. Perhaps embarrassed by the time-setting eschatological urgency, this-worldly concern fills the theological void. This approach is equally problematic; thus, Pentecostals are urgently called to recover their eschatological heritage and reformulate it so that daily life and mission engagement can still be motivated by the eschatological nature of our life and time. The presence of the Holy Spirit is the sure sign of the end time.

By all accounts, it is clear that Pentecostalism has been and will be a unique gift to the body of Christ, its mission, and the world. Most likely, the continuing growth of world Christianity will largely depend upon the future affairs of this family of Christianity. Most researchers believe that by 2050 Pentecostal Christianity and its incredible variations will constitute one-third of the Christians in the world. It has also become clear that Pentecostalism is not one church but rather a movement of spiritual renewal that can find a home in any church tradition. At the same time, as in all the churches, Pentecostalism is by no means immune from human fallenness. The movement has demonstrated that it is prone to the seduction of fame, mega-size glamour, and the abuse of spiritual power. Such weaknesses have been all-too well known, even in ancient times. Samson and Saul were two Charismatic leaders in the leader board of references to the coming of the Spirit, and both were miserable failures. Let them serve as an encouragement and warning to today's Pentecostals.

6. "When the Poor are Fired Up": Pneumatology in Pentecostal Mission[1]

Introduction

During its 100 years, the modern Pentecostal-Charismatic movement has impacted Christianity in general, but its role in mission is exceptionally significant. The explosive growth of churches, particularly in the non-Western continents, is but one example. As discussed below, several important roles of the Holy Spirit are evident in the mission practices of Pentecostal-Charismatic believers.

However, before we take this journey of discovery, it will be helpful to clarify several issues. The first is the complexity of Pentecostal-Charismatic Christianity in the world today. Many have argued that the "fountainhead" of the movement was found in North America at the turn of the twentieth century, especially at the Azusa Street Mission (1906–1909) under the African American preacher William J. Seymour. However, there is more evidence to contest this theory, with India and Korea being examples. Also, the stunning "discoveries" of the so-called "indigenous Pentecostals" from Africa and Asia appear to support the theory of "multiple fountainheads" for the origin of Pentecostal-Charismatic Christianity.[2] Indeed, we may be arriving at the notion that "the church is Charismatic", after all, from its inception.

As I try to represent this fastest-growing segment of Christianity, I do so with evident limitations. First, Pentecostal-Charismatic Christianity is not homogenous. It encompasses classical (or denominational) Pentecostals, Charismatic (or Neo-) Pentecostals, and indigenous (or Neo-Charismatic) Pentecostals. The last category is particularly problematic because of its diversity and also because some groups in this classification advocate questionable doctrines with which Orthodox Christians are not comfortable. This gives rise to the possibility of having groups that may be "more Pentecostal, but less Christian". Second, the pneumatology of groups broadly classified as Pentecostal or Charismatic is not "standardized". For example, while classical Pentecostals feature a unique experience called "baptism in the Holy Spirit",

---

[1] An earlier version was presented under the same title at the Conference on World Mission and Evangelism, May 2005, in Athens, Greece.

[2] For a good review, see Hwa Yung, "Endued With Power: The Pentecostal-Charismatic Renewal and the Asian Church in the Twenty-First Century," *Asian Journal of Pentecostal Studies* (2003), pp. 63–82.

many other groups may not necessarily subscribe to such a doctrinal statement but are open to the supernatural work of the Holy Spirit.

My reflection comes with two main points: Pentecostal-Charismatics represent the "poor", for whom poverty and sickness are a part of their lives, and the core of Pentecostal-Charismatic pneumatology is "empowerment" for witness.

The Spirit and the "Poor"

"Religion of the Poor"

Early Pentecostals at the turn of the twentieth century were "poor" in many ways. Most participants of the Azusa Street Revival came from the lower socio-economic bracket of society. Urban African Americans and ethnic immigrants, with "sprinkles of whites", made up this controversial epicentre of one of the most significant revivals in modern church history.[3] They were marginalized by society and sometimes by established churches. Thus, they eagerly received the good news of the Messiah, who came "to preach good news to the poor" under the anointing of the Holy Spirit (Luke 4:18). These socially dislocated people forged strong solidarity among themselves, and courageously went against commonly accepted social norms such as racial segregation. As a result, they formed a social and spiritual culture where the hopeless found a space to experience God's grace and power. This "haven for the disinherited" created a powerful drawing force to make Pentecostal Christianity a "religion of the poor".[4] The context of "poor", as the socio-spiritual context of Pentecostal-Charismatic Christianity, has left several unique contributions.

This characterization is essential in Pentecostalism as a religion of the poor, not for the poor. Marginalized by existing churches, this group of people from the lower socio-economic strata found themselves the main players in the church. Their "primal spirituality" is expressed in participatory and expressive worship and testimony times. The fact that the Holy Spirit chose to visit them through powerful experiences such as healings, baptism in the Spirit, prophecy, miracles, and drastic conversion experiences was in itself a social upliftment.

As observed in many non-Western continents, such as Africa, Asia, and Latin America, Pentecostal believers have achieved upward social mobility, which has been viewed as God's special blessing. This is also why the Pentecostal mission

---

[3] E.g. William W. Menzies and Robert P. Menzies, *Spirit and Power: Foundation of Pentecostal Experience: A Call to Evangelical Dialogue* (Grand Rapids, MI: Zondervan, 2000), p. 22 argues, "The uniqueness of the modern Pentecostal revival lies in its very survival, surviving long enough to gain a hearing in the larger church world and to emerge as a significant component of the Christian world."

[4] David Martin, *Pentecostalism: The World Their Parish* (Oxford: Blackwell, 2002), p. 4. Also Robert M. Anderson, *Vision of the Disinherited: The Making of American Pentecostalism* (Peabody, MA: Hendrickson 1992).

has traditionally focused on evangelism (the spiritually lost) and care for the poor and marginalized. While many cultures view women as inappropriate for ministry, the Pentecostal faith has brought "liberation" for them. One such example is the cell system of David Yonggi Cho of Korea. Cho organized, trained, and empowered lay women to exercise their ministry gifts over many cell groups of Yoido Full Gospel Church in this highly male-dominant society.

Immanence of God

The outpouring of the Holy Spirit in the early twentieth century brought several powerful paradigm shifts. First, the Pentecostals' self-understanding changed drastically: from the marginalized to the conspicuously called for God's ministry. Second, it was also seen as a sure eschatological sign of the immediate return of the Lord, and this brought urgency to their divine call to minister. Third, this "apostolic" movement had a strong restoration expectation in the early church. Having inherited the Holiness spiritual traditions, supernatural interventions of God, such as healings and miracles, were regularly expected. Even if "classical Pentecostalism" did begin in North America, its beliefs exhibited a strikingly holistic worldview where the supernatural world intersects with the natural world daily.[5] Fourth, the Pentecostals' unique experience of baptism in the Holy Spirit and other supernatural manifestations made this religion a religion of experience.

This emphasis on God's immanence and the unique religious worldview strongly suggests Pentecostalism's potential for explosive growth in the non-Western world. Testimonies of healings, exorcisms, miracles, and the like are heard daily. Unlike many other Christian traditions, Pentecostal-Charismatic spirituality includes the actual level of daily human existence, including physical and material aspects and spiritual dimensions. This is a "religion with flesh and bones"[6] and compares well with many church traditions where the Holy Spirit and his work are moved to ethical, moral, and spiritual levels, quickly bypassing the physical and material dimensions.

When They Are "Fired Up" for Service

Several critical studies are enumerating distinct characteristics of the Pentecostal mission. One of them, for example, is by Allan Anderson, a South African Pentecostal missiologist. His list includes: 1) pneumato-centric mission, 2) dynamic mission praxis, 3) evangelism: central missiological thrust, 4) contextualization of leadership, 5) mobilization in mission, and 6) contextual

[5] Among others, this may come under the category of the "Black Root" of Pentecostalism. See Hollenweger, *Pentecostalism: Origins and Developments Worldwide*, pp. 18–24, for the Azusa Street Mission.

[6] Wonsuk Ma and Julie C. Ma, "Jesus Christ in Asia: Our Journey with Him as Pentecostal Believers," *International Review of Mission* 94 (2005), pp. 493–506.

missiology.[7] To highlight several essential characteristics of the Holy Spirit's work in Pentecostal mission, I will select several models, including two individuals and several organizations. Not all may overtly identify themselves as "Pentecostal", but their link with Pentecostal Christianity or their unique practices reflect its influence. As any real case is a complex matter, duplication of certain elements is unavoidable.

The Holy Spirit as the Initiator of Mission: "One-way Ticket Missionaries"

The distinct missionary nature of Pentecostal experiences, particularly baptism in the Spirit, is well attested by the stream of missionaries who went out of, and were influenced by, the Azusa Street Mission. Gary McGee argues that, within five years of the Pentecostal revival in Los Angeles, at least 200 Pentecostal missionaries from North America served in various parts of the world.[8] Reinforced by eschatological urgency, many Pentecostal believers, often not adequately trained, clergy and laity, men and women, and young and old, devoted their lives to evangelism. Vinson Synan termed them "missionaries of the one-way ticket", with several helpful examples.[9] He said they were "evangelists and missionaries who went out with little or no institutional or financial support".[10] However, in my opinion, the most crucial genius of this new breed of missionaries lies in their expectation not to return home in their lifetime but work to the end of their lives in mission fields. There is no doubt that their shared eschatological urgency must have contributed to this determination, but equally powerful is their passion for the lost.

Synan has several potent examples, many of whom indeed never returned home but planted a seed that now blossoms powerfully: Ivan Efimovich Veronaev, who introduced the Pentecostal message to his homeland Russia; Willis Collins Hoover, the father of Chilean Pentecostalism; and Daniel Berg and Gunnar Vingren, who began the Brazilian Pentecostal movement. Lillian Trasher (1887–1961), a Spirit-filled, twenty-three-year-old believer, broke her engagement and sailed to Egypt. There she founded the first orphanage in the country and once cared for 1,200 orphans, widows, single mothers, and blind women.[11] Although she received a heroic welcome in her brief 1955 visit to the States after twenty-five years of ministry without a furlough, she was

---

[7] Allan Anderson, "Towards a Pentecostal Missiology for the Majority World," *Asian Journal of Pentecostal Studies* 8.1 (2005), pp. 29–47.

[8] Gary B. McGee, "Mission, Overseas (N. American Pentecostal)," in Stanley M. Burgess and Eduard M. van der Maas (eds), *The New International Dictionary of Pentecostal and Charismatic Movements*, revised and expanded edition (Grand Rapids: Zondervan, 2002), p. 888.

[9] Vinson Synan, *The Spirit Said "Grow": The Astounding Worldwide Expansion of Pentecostal and Charismatic Churches* (Monrovia, CA: MARC, 1992), pp. 39–48.

[10] Synan, *The Spirit Said "Grow,"* p. 39.

[11] The entire issue of *Assemblies of God Heritage* 4.4 (Winter 1984–85) is on Trasher's life and ministry. 26 July 2005.

undoubtedly a missionary with a one-way ticket. Like Trasher, many early Pentecostal missionaries and evangelists exhibited a lifestyle of commitment to mission which is uniquely Pentecostal.

"Prophethood of All Believers": Youth With A Mission (YWAM)

Established by a Pentecostal minister in 1960, this powerful mission group has mobilized Christian youth for mission all over the globe. Loren Cunningham, the founder, once saw "waves on a map", which "turned into young people, going to every continent, sharing the good news about Jesus".[12] YWAM's ministry is focused on evangelism, training, and mercy ministry, with 900 bases (or centres) in over 140 countries, and a staff of over 11,000.[13]

The most significant "Pentecostal" tradition observed in YWAM is the "liberation" of ministry from elite clergy to the hands of every believer. For Pentecostals, one of the most treasured passages is Acts 1:8: "But you will receive power when the Holy Spirit comes on you, and you will be my witnesses in Jerusalem, and in all Judea and Samaria, and to the ends of the earth." The coming of the Holy Spirit (or "baptism in the Spirit", as they call it) is for empowerment, and empowerment is for witnessing. Cunningham had difficulty convincing his own Pentecostal denominational leadership to envision mobilizing youth for mission. Its training programme practically aims to turn the "ministered" into the "ministering" believers. The life-changing testimonies of participants are heard almost daily. To be a "missionary" in this organization, what is required is one's willingness to give time and talent to mission, be it a week or a year. This tradition of "democratization of ministry" is being expressed in various creative ways in many parts of the world. A new expression has been suggested in the academic realm: "prophethood of all believers", possibly becoming an active move from the traditional notion of "priesthood of all believers".[14]

God of Healing and Miracle: David Yonggi Cho

Perhaps best known as the pastor of the largest single congregation in the world, Yoido Full Gospel Church, Cho has changed millions of lives throughout his forty-five years of ministry. Born in 1936 and growing up in Korea under oppressive colonial rule, he went through the difficulties of war and spent a

---

[12] Youth With a Mission, "History of YWAM" (2004), http://www.ywam.org/contents/abo_his_introhistory.htm. Accessed 27 April 2005.

[13] Youth With a Mission, "Introducing YWAM" (2004), http://www.ywam.org/contents/abo_introduction.htm. Accessed 27 April 2005.

[14] Earlier used in James Luther Adams (ed.), *The Prophethood of All Believers* (Boston: Beacon, 1986), the expression is recently appropriated to Pentecostal beliefs by Roger Stronstad in *The Prophethood of All Believers: A Study in Luke's Charismatic Theology* (Sheffield: Sheffield Academic Press, 1999).

hopeless youth with a deadly case of tuberculosis.[15] His encounter with Christianity, particularly a Pentecostal type, is described as follows: on what was thought to be his deathbed, a Christian girl, his sister's friend, visited him. His Buddhist parents had forbidden her to visit their home, but she persisted and gave Cho a Bible, preaching the gospel to him. Soon Cho became a Christian, and his health began to improve dramatically.[16] His radical experience of God's love and power through healing made him an evangelist of a "good God" who heals and blesses those who seek him. Coming from a Buddhist religious tradition and deplorable social conditions, his message has been consistently about a God who loves and cares for the daily needs of his people. Stories of God's miraculous healing, blessing, and restoration (of families, relationships, and the like) filled the pages of the *Shinanggye* (World of Faith), once the most popular monthly magazine (both religious and secular) in the country. It impacted Christians and the entire society as the magazine was read in schools, military camps, prisons, etc.[17] Now he terms this a "ministry of hope".[18]

His ministry and theology demonstrate a holistic worldview, including the physical and material aspects of human life and the spiritual level. A bowl of rice and healing of terminal diseases in a poverty-stricken society are as important as the matter of sin and salvation. In the "majority world", if the most powerful and loving God cannot heal a person, he is not as helpful as the ancestor spirits which many rely on for such needs. God is expected to be the Saviour, not only after this life but also during this earthly existence. This is where the work of the Holy Spirit comes in with "signs and wonders". The demonstration of God's power through the Holy Spirit often triggers a "people's movement" or conversion by groups. It partly explains the phenomenal growth of Pentecostal-Charismatic churches worldwide.

Priority of Inner Change and Evangelism: Teen Challenge

Established by a North American Pentecostal minister, David Wilkerson, in 1958,[19] this drug rehabilitation programme has become the "oldest, largest and most successful program of its kind in the world", with over 170 centres in the

---

[15] Among many biographies of Cho, see Nell L. Kennedy, *Dream Your Way to Success: The Story of Dr Yonggi Cho and Korea* (Plainfield, NJ: Logos International, 1980).
[16] Young-hoon Lee, "The Life and Ministry of David Yonggi Cho and the Yoido Full Gospel Church," *Asian Journal of Pentecostal Studies* 7.1 (2004), pp. 3–20 (4).
[17] Myung Soo Park, "Korean Pentecostal Spirituality as Manifested in the Testimonies of Members of Yoido Full Gospel Church," *Asian Journal of Pentecostal Studies* 7.1 (2004), pp. 35–56.
[18] For example, David Yonggi Cho, *Dr David Yonggi Cho, Ministering Hope for 50 Years* (Alachua, FL: Bridge-Logos, 2008).
[19] David Wilkerson, *Cross and the Switchblade* (New York: B. Geis Associates, 1963) details the story of Teen Challenge.

United States and 250 worldwide.[20] The "National Institute on Drug Abuse Report" found on its website argues that the drug rehabilitation programmes of Teen Challenge record a 70 percent success rate. In comparison, most secular programmes reach a 1–15 percent success rate.[21] The programmes include residential rehabilitation facilities, seminars among youth for education and prevention, and others. The residential programme involves a vital spiritual component that underlines the theological assumption that any transformation of a society begins with individuals. A change in a person begins with his or her inner (in this case, spiritual) being. This internal change involves a conversion experience and an encounter with God's reality, often through baptism in the Holy Spirit. For instance, the first entry in the testimony section reads, "John Melendez was spiritually lost and confused on the streets of New York, as a teen and young man."[22] As human suffering begins with a spiritual loss, the restoration should also start with the spiritual component of a human being.

The practice of Teen Challenge epitomizes two Pentecostal values. The first is the primacy of evangelism as a Pentecostal mission focus. Driven partly by the eschatological conviction that the Holy Spirit was poured upon them for the last-minute harvest before the return of the Lord, many committed their lives to "reaching the lost". They were church planters and evangelists. Be it mercy ministry or training, everything they did was to achieve the ultimate goal of evangelism and church planting.

The second is the Pentecostal pattern of social ministry. Many social ministries were to care for the "poor", such as girls' and boys' homes in India, orphanages in Egypt and many other countries, educational programmes in Latin America, feeding and educational programmes in India, vocational training schools in Korea, etc. This value is aptly expressed in a well-known statement: when asked by a fellow Christian in Latin America if there are any social programmes among Pentecostals, the answer was, "We are social programmes!" Although this "care for victims" is not good enough to remove structural evil in this world, Pentecostals have modelled the ministry of Jesus found in Luke 4:18-19 as their paradigm.

Empowered for Witness: Brother Badol's Story[23]

Brother Badol, as we call him, was a young man who lived in Papasok, a village of the Kankana-ey tribe, deep in the mountains of the northern Philippines. Reachable only by foot, this virtually isolated community had served ancestor

[20] Teen Challenge, "About Us" (2005), http://www.teenchallenge.com/index.cfm?infoID=1&centerID=1194. Accessed 27 April 2005.
[21] Teen Challenge, "National Institute on Drug Abuse Report," http://www.teenchallenge.com/index.cfm?studiesID=3. Accessed 27 April 2005.
[22] Teen Challenge, "Can a Drug Addict Really Change?" (2005), http://www.teenchallenge.com/index.cfm?testimonyID=1. Accessed 27 April 2005.
[23] The full text is available in J. Ma, *Mission Possible*, pp. 18–22.

spirits and many gods for generations. About twenty grass-roofed houses welcome rare visitors, who are by now exhausted from the long mountain hike.

Badol and his wife lost their two young children on the same day. A simple fever took both lives. As advised by village elders, he offered animal sacrifices to appease the angry ancestor spirit who took them. During this time, a Christian worker visited his community once in a while and introduced a God who made pine trees, pigs, and humans. He told them that this God loved everyone dearly and that he also heard prayers, even if there was no animal offering.

Badol and his wife soon had two new children, but they also died young, following another epidemic that took many lives in the village. He decided to try this new God, who seemed to be quite different from the spirits he had served. Of course, this was never easy, as the entire village expected him to be punished by the spirits, but they still began their strange new worship in their house. Very soon, a neighbour quietly asked him if this new God could heal his dying child. Badol laid his hand upon the motionless baby and prayed in the name of Jesus, who had given life to her. The following Sunday, the entire family, with the now recovered baby, joined the "church". Badol believed that the Holy Spirit came to save him from darkness and empower him so that he could share the gospel with effectiveness. The villagers regularly asked him to pray for the sick, and most of them were healed miraculously. About fifteen years later, everyone in Papasok serves this new God who can heal the sick. Badol and his wife had ten more children, and none died. He visited nearby villages and shared this good and powerful God with them. Because of this missionary work, seven villages have their own churches.

This story from our place of ministry epitomizes millions of Pentecostal-Charismatic believers all over the world, who are never adequately recognized as "ministers" or "missionaries", and yet are faithfully and powerfully carrying out God's call for mission. The coming of the Holy Spirit, as promised in Acts 1:8, has been understood as "Pentecostal missiology": the Spirit calls, empowers, and sends his people to the ends of the earth to be his witnesses. The Holy Spirit, whom they experienced through healings, miracles, and empowerment, is also expected to perform miracles and healings. Even the promise of the Lord for supernatural power, as recorded in Mark 16:15-18, is understood in the context of mission: he said to them, "Go into all the world and preach the good news to all creation. Whoever believes and is baptized will be saved, but whoever does not believe will be condemned. And these signs will accompany those who believe: in my name, they will drive out demons; they will speak in new tongues; they will pick up snakes with their hands; and when they drink deadly poison, it will not hurt them at all; they will place their hands on sick people, and they will get well."

"The Spirit Who Makes Us One": Azusa Street Mission

Among the many challenging traditions observed in this renewal movement, the work of the Holy Spirit to remove human barriers is distinct. This incredible anti-cultural phenomenon against the social norm of the day appeared on two fronts. The first was the multi-racial composition of the mission. Under the leadership of an African American Holiness preacher, William Seymour, twelve leaders were an equal mixture of black and white. An observer, who happened to be Seymour's teacher, reported the eruption of this spiritual movement in unpleasant terms:

> Men and women, whites and blacks, knelt together or fell across one another; frequently a white woman, perhaps of wealth and culture, could be seen thrown back in the arms of a big "buck nigger", and held tightly thus as she shivered and shook in freak imitation of Pentecost. Horrible, awful shame! Many of the missions on the Pacific coast are permeated with this foolishness, and in fact, it follows the Azuza [sic!] work everywhere.[24]

However, this congregation where "the color line was washed away in the Blood"[25] is a powerful demonstration of what the Holy Spirit can do in a complex and troubled world. The other was the ecumenical nature of the mission. The participants of the Azusa Street Revival came from a variety of Christian traditions. Stories abound of how a visitor, theologically suspicious, was overwhelmed by the presence of the Holy Spirit, and ecclesial differences suddenly disappeared. This ecumenical potential was again presented during the Charismatic renewal when "Spirit-filled" members of various churches (often from mainline churches, including the Roman Catholic Church) were able to celebrate common faith with genuine Christian love and appreciation.

However, this unique demonstration of the Spirit's work was short-lived, at least in the Azusa Street Revival. Soon, various Pentecostal denominations were organized, often along racial lines. Also, the ever-increasing number of Pentecostal-Charismatic congregations resulting from splits remains a testimony against its spiritual tradition. However, the recent spread of the "Pentecostal" practices (or culture) in singing and worship has reminded us of their potential to bring divided humanity (including the church) together through the Holy Spirit.

Raising the Voice of the Poor: Irene Banda

Irene Mutalima Banda of Zambia is a committed member of a local Pentecostal church in Lusaka, the capital city. She began as a successful banker, but she soon realized that the poor had no access to the services provided by financial institutions. Poverty was rampant in the country, and it produced a destructive cycle. Children of low-income families received less education, health services, and job training. And poverty is inherited by generations.

---

[24] Charles F. Parham, "Free-Love," *The Apostolic Faith* 1.10 (December 1912), pp. 4–5.
[25] Frank Bartleman, *Azusa Street: An Eyewitness Account to the Birth of the Pentecostal Revival* (Plainfield, NJ: Logos International, 1980), p. 54.

Banda's banking knowledge allowed her to work with Western donors to establish a Zambian Christian microfinance work. She observed that a loan of as little as US$20.00 could make a huge difference. Combining her pastoral interest, industry knowledge, and professional relationships, she offered her clients financial assistance, job training, and spiritual care. She also learned that women were creative, diligent, hard-working, and entrepreneurial. Indeed, they are highly motivated to cut the cycle of poverty by all means.

At the same time, she also became aware of the global structure of (Christian) microfinance: Western donors provide capital and impose terms and conditions for recipients (or national microfinance firms). They then create a system according to the requirement of the Western donors and implement the policies, again, required by them. As a frontline leader, Banda often found herself between the needs on the ground and the demands of the Western donors. She thus noticed that, in many Christian microfinance operations, the "mission/ministry" vision was often swallowed up by the number-crunching routine and debt-recovery goals. She understood that the policies were to maintain the integrity of the operation. To her mind, however, they were adaptations of the norms of the Western banking industry. She characterizes this as a top-down business model.[26]

She began to campaign for the critical contribution of the poor. Listening to them and learning their true needs would improve the effectiveness of microfinance. This would also change the perspective of the microfinance beneficiaries from the voiceless poor to partners in the Kingdom of God. Treating her clients as her ministry partners restored their self-esteem, and all the "business" aspects improved: the efficacy of loans, life improvements of the loan recipients, and the loan recovery rates.

Her network drastically expanded when she decided to take her conviction to a PhD study in England. She learned extensively from different microfinance operations and shared her experiences with global microfinance networks. I assume that her campaign for the total well-being of the poor won her a rare invitation by the World Council of Churches in Geneva, Switzerland, to lead its global microfinance programme, Ecumenical Church Loan Fund International.

Although now back in Zambia, Banda is already a global figure, advocating the dignity of every human being and the pattern of the client- or consumer-oriented services. Her research also impacts many mission leaders around the world.[27]

The last question is how Pentecostal are Irene's values, approach, and activities? Her identity with the poor is my primary characterization of

---

[26] Irene Mutalima Banda, "Listening to the Poor in Microfinance," in Brian Woolnough (ed.), *Good News from Africa: Community Transformation Through the Church* (Oxford: Regnum Books, 2013), p. 34.

[27] For example, Irene Mutalima Banda, *Microfinance in Sub-Saharan Africa: Responding to the Voices of Poor People* (Oxford: Regnum Books, forthcoming 2023).

Pentecostals.[28] This makes Pentecostalism a "religion of the poor". Empowering the poor is another aspect of her Pentecostal ethos. As a Pentecostal believer, she was "fired up" by the Holy Spirit to empower the fellow "poor". Also, her passion for the well-being of the whole person aligns with the Pentecostal worldview and mission.

Conclusion

This short presentation is purposefully brief and incorporates Pentecostal narratives. The role of Pentecostal-Charismatic churches and believers in fulfilling God's mission will become increasingly important in the coming years. Particularly significant will be the role of the non-Western churches, which I represent, with their explosive growth and increasing challenges. This will require the active exchange of experiences with world church members.

I presented the strengths unique to Pentecostalism. I did so not to imply that the Pentecostals have at last found the secret formula for world evangelization; but to humbly share with the church community at large that the Lord has brought this movement with its unique gifts to the body of Christ, particularly in fulfilling God's mission mandate. The 100-year history of the Pentecostal-Charismatic movement is an unfortunate combination of the Spirit's empowerment and human shortcomings, and we Pentecostals know this all too well.

As a "new kid on the block", Pentecostals have much to learn from the historic churches with their rich histories and traditions. At the same time, the rise of a new movement (particularly the renewal type) such as this in itself serves as God's reminder to his people of his missionary mandate to the world. If the Pentecostal-Charismatic movement can serve this purpose by strengthening and renewing the body of Christ through its healing and restoration potential, its primary historical calling is fulfilled.

---

[28] See Chapter 6.

7. "Life" in Theological Education and Missional Formation[1]

Introduction

In recent years, at least two global conversations have been attempted in theological education. The first is the Lausanne Consultation on Global Theological Education. Initiated and mediated by several global Evangelical bodies (principally the Langham Partnership International and the Overseas Council International under the umbrella of the Lausanne Movement), it passionately promoted and assisted theological education, particularly for the Global South.. Its first international gathering occurred in 2012 in South Hamilton, Massachusetts, USA. Sixty-three global theological educators participated in this gathering. It is momentous because a serious revision of theological education is imperative when world Christianity is experiencing a significant shift. The theme was "Stronger Partnerships between Western and Majority World Seminaries", reflecting the growing needs in the South with its steady growth, which coincided with the consistent decline of Christianity in the North. The participants were divided approximately evenly by the Global North and South. Its second gathering was held in 2014 in São Paulo with sixty participants under the theme "Towards Biblical Partnership in Global Theological Education". Several others joined the existing two convening bodies: the International Council for Evangelical Theological Education and World Reformed Fellowship. There was no subsequent meeting.

The second is the Global Forum of Theological Educators. It aims to be a "fellowship of leaders in theological education from every Christian tradition who meet to listen to each other and learn from those doing similar work but whose faith traditions might differ from one's own".[2] It began as several Evangelical theological educators engaged with ecumenical counterparts in the early 2010s. The most tangible plan was made in the middle of 2014 to clarify its purpose and strategy. Unlike the Lausanne-hosted network, this initiative has been intentionally inclusive: encompassing historic churches, such as the Catholic and Orthodox churches, as well as Evangelical and Pentecostal ones.

---

[1] This study was inspired by discussions at the Global Ecumenical Theological Institute during the 2013 General Assembly of the World Council of Churches in Busan, Korea.

[2] Global Forum of Theological Educators, "Purpose" (2015), http://www.gfte.org/general-purpose (accessed 24 Feb 2023). For the 2021 virtual meeting, the Association of Theological Schools facilitated the meeting under Lester Ruis's leadership.

How the Evangelicals and the ecumenical partners undertook the serious dialogue and now jointly initiate this inclusive network of theological educators is something to celebrate.

This is where the openness and passion for collaboration of Dietrich Werner, the then director of Ecumenical Theological Education of the World Council of Churches, is warmly noted. Following the main methodology of the Global Christian Forum, providing a neutral and conducive space for theological educators for fellowship, networking, and collaboration is the primary purpose of this new initiative. Its effectiveness has been successfully tested in its two international gatherings in Germany (2016) and Greece (2019). The third gathering, planned to take place in South Korea in 2021, was held virtually due to the pandemic. Ensuring the presence of theological educators from all the major church families was not a small feat. Its koinonic approach has proven successful as natural relationships develop over meals, drinks, casual encounters, worship, and prayer.

While the Lausanne-initiated attempt does not continue, the Global Forum of Theological Educators has been established as an ongoing programme. The appearance of these and perhaps other global programmes may indicate the growing awareness of our changing context and the need for dialogue and collaboration. At the same time, how these global and existing regional and national spaces can promote the future wellness of theological education instead of exposing it to "market competition" is another test.

This chapter will situate the present and future of theological education within the growing focus on the theme of "life". I will explore this development within two particular contexts of today's Christianity: the major numerical and conceptual shift in global Christianity, and the end of the Christendom era that has shaped and influenced theological education and missional formation (or lack thereof) of the church. Within this context, I will identify several major themes that require our attention in re-visioning theological education if it is going to be relevant to its context and truthful to its call.

We live in the early period of the unfolding of a new Christian millennium and its implication for theological education and missional formation. Thus, based on two sources, we will only be able to speculate what the future will be like. They are 1) our observations of the pre-Christendom era, including the life of Jesus and the early church as recorded in the Gospels and Acts, and 2) several critical theological elements that either disappeared or were seriously revised in the development of Christendom. Therefore, we should take seriously contemporary social contexts in the process of theologizing: thus, theological education. This is the context where both old and new Christianity exists and carries out its mission.

This study is intended to be a conversation starter. To a Korean Pentecostal, Christendom is an entirely foreign idea; even if, one way or another, my Christian experience has been seriously impacted by it through Western missionaries. This topic caught my eye only recently as I wrestle with the current state of Western Christianity. At the same time, less attention has been given to this long and deep shadow of Christendom by today's theologization and theological education. The massive *Handbook of Theological Education in World Christianity* (750 pages!) has only one short chapter (out of 80!) that refers to Christendom's legacy on today's theological education.[3] At both of the two gatherings of Evangelical theological educators, time was spent discussing and exploring North–South partnerships. As useful and valuable as it was, the pressing priority would have been digging deeper to discover how today's theological education had been shaped through centuries of development.

Today's Context of Global Christianity: Post-Christendom Era

In defining today's context for exploring tomorrow's theological education tasks, there are two related themes: the global Christian shift in our time as an external phenomenon and the collapse of Christendom, which will impact the identity of church life and mission. For the former, several studies are available.[4]

If the chapter on global Christianity has to do with the spread of global Christian believers, this discussion concerns the nature of present-day Christianity. Undoubtedly the close of the era of Christendom is one of the most researched topics today. A quick Amazon search on "post-Christendom", "after Christendom", and the like produces a long list of books now available on the market. Just as the rise of Christendom in the fourth century radically changed the nature of Christianity, so does the post-Christendom era in the twentieth century.

Christendom as a historical reality may have ended in the sixteenth century at the Reformation. But mini-Christendoms have continued in Europe until recently. Sixteen centuries of Christian domination have shaped all human and social-life sectors, including political, economic, civic, educational, media, and international relations. Throughout its long history, the church as an institution developed, and so did its theology and ministry. Although we now live in a post-Christendom era, and most of today's Christians live in places where Christendom was not a historical experience, we live under its large shadow. Its underlying assumptions and institutional and theological expressions are evident in our Christian life, regardless of location.

---

[3] D. L. Guder, "Theological Formation for Missional Faithfulness After Christendom: A Response to Steven de Gruchy," in D. Werner, D. Esterline, N. Kang, and J. Raja (eds), *Handbook of Theological Education in World Christianity: Theological Perspectives, Ecumenical Trends, Regional Surveys* (Oxford: Regnum Books, 2010), pp. 51–55. It is fair to acknowledge that de Gruchy's chapter, without mentioning "Christendom", wrestles with the issue of Christendom's legacy in today's theological education: S. de Gruchy, "Theological Education and Missional Practice: A Vital Dialogue," in the same *Handbook*, pp. 42–50.

[4] Johnson and Zurlo, *World Christian Encyclopedia*. Ma, "Global Christianity: Where Are We and How Did We Get Here?" pp. 35–53.

According to Stuart Murray, who writes from a British Anabaptist perspective, the "Christendom shifts" radically changed the church's life and the society it served. It is essential to recognize its significant contributions to civil society, intentional missionary operation, the rule of law, etc. It also came with elements that distorted the initial ideals of Christianity. A selection of Murray's points may illustrate the heavy influence of Christendom on today's Christianity as I briefly reflect on them:[5]

- The adoption of Christianity as the official religion has altered the nature of Christianity from a persecuted religion to a privileged one. Becoming Christian comes with recognition and status instead of marginalization and displacement, as we read in the Book of Acts. Christianity is a religion with power; thus, it is for the powerful and not the weak. The hierarchy of clergy symbolizes this.
- An alliance between political power and the church was a strange development once Christianity became the state religion of the Roman Empire. Often, the church authenticated the political establishment, which protected the interests of the church. The power balance fluctuated at times, but the influence of Christianity was undeniable in every aspect of social life. As a result, the church amassed incredible wealth to strengthen its dominance over political and social establishments. Wars were waged in the name of Christ and the church.
- The development of a Christian culture or civilization dramatically impacts the world. This is to the point that Western civilization is viewed as a direct result of Christianization. For example, a recent report argues that some Chinese now view Christianity as "the roots of Western strength [and] the force behind the development of social justice, civil society and the rule of law, all things they hope to see in China".[6]
- The world is divided between Christendom and "heathendom". This Eurocentric value system has persisted in various other concepts, such as "developed" and "developing" or "under-developed". "Barbarian", a Roman political term, was effectively "Christianized" to refer to non-Christian people beyond Christendom territories. Consequently, everything outside Christendom became an object of subjugation, conquest, and conversion. They included religions, cultures, and social

---

[5] S. Murray, *Post-Christendom: Church and Mission in a Strange New World* (Milton Keynes: Paternoster, 2004), pp. 83–84. Since the publication of this groundbreaking title, the revised (reduced) edition has appeared as part of the After Christendom Series (Cascade Books).

[6] "Cracks in the Atheist Edifice: The Rapid Spread of Christianity Is Forcing an Official Rethink on Religion," *The Economist*, 1 November 2014. Available at: http://www.economist.com/news/ briefing/21629218-rapid-spread-christianity-forcing-official-rethink-religion-cracks. Accessed 22 November 2014.

systems. This attitude of superiority had a severely adverse effect on missionary work.

If theological education was primarily to prepare leaders (that is, clergy) of the church to fulfil its mission in a given time and context, these and other Christendom traits seriously impacted the objectives and goals of theological education. Therefore, the modern-day reflection on theological education will require:

1. Keeping the biblical vision of theological education.
2. Carefully assessing its development in the long Christendom centuries.
3. Critical revision of theological education in today's global Christian context.

New Era, New World, and New Theological Education

The two contextual considerations are essential for exploring theological education for two reasons. Firstly, theological education is, by nature, one of the church's most structured and institutionalized operations. This is also closely related to how the church understands itself and its mission in a given time and context. For this reason, the long development of Christendom as an institution has impacted the content, process, and methods of formal theological education and broader theological formation. This impact is regardless of location, whether in the West or the rest. For the former, theological education is the product of a long development of Christianity, including Christendom. For the latter, Christianity and all its components, including theological education, were handed down by Western churches. Christianity is considered a Western religion in many parts of the world, not just because it is the West who introduced it, but because its form, structure, and components were all shaped through the long Western Christian history.

Secondly, the recent southward shift of global Christianity for the second time in its history is a powerful reminder of the birth context of Christian mission. Today, churches in the Global South face various challenges. This contrasts with the church's position during the Christendom era but shares many similarities with the early and pre-Christendom church. To begin with, many churches struggle to survive in religiously and socially hostile environments. Take, for example, churches in Pakistan, Northern Iraq, and Syria. Even in Christian-majority nations, Christians face enormous challenges. In November 2014, more than twenty Christians were murdered in northern Kenya by al-Shabab terrorists in a bus raid simply because they were non-Muslims, many being most likely

Christian.[7] In places where freedom of worship is upheld, Christianity no longer exercises the kind of influence that it used to exert on society. Today, churches in Christian-majority nations do not have the political or financial dominance to influence other religions and nations.

Yes, post-Christendom is not pre-Christendom. Nonetheless, there are several key components from the pre-Christendom era, including the life of Jesus and the early church, which can serve us in the shaping of theological education in the new generation and context. This list is highly provisional, and it is only an initial attempt. It is also essential to add a strong disclaimer that Christendom is not all negative, nor do the following distortions find their origin in Christendom alone.

What Happened to the "World"?

One significant outcome of the Christendom shift is a radical change in the perception of the "world" by the church. In a sense, the world disappeared in the church's life and theological discourse in Christendom. As the church gained increasing influence, it, directly and indirectly, controlled almost every aspect of "secular" life. This included political, economic, civic, and judicial systems, education, arts, and the media. This "filled gap" between the sacred and the secular had several impacts on Christian life and thoughts.

The first is a close alliance between the church and the state. While the church authenticated the political power (the church influenced the succession of powers), the state looked after the church's affairs. Regardless of the balance of power, this closing gap between the two powers had a severe consequence. When the political power was viewed as an extension of the church or even God, the sacralization of the secular took place. Social affairs, then, were handily divided, and the state functioned to govern the "world" on behalf of the church. This dynamic was exemplified during the maritime expeditions to conquer the world in the name of God and the king. The Spanish fleet of the Portuguese explorer Ferdinand Magellan first circumnavigated the Pacific in the sixteenth century. When they reached the Philippines, it was quickly annexed to Spanish power and "Christianized" to the Catholic faith by the Catholic priests on board the ships.

The second is the disappearance of the "world" in theological discourse. The world had been effectively "reached" by the church. The prayer of Jesus for his disciples became no longer applicable: "As the Father has sent me [to the world], so I am sending you" (John 20:21). As the world was practically controlled by the church through the agency of the state, at least in the Christian world, "Thy Kingdom has come on earth!" The "disappearance" of the world has seriously altered the church's identity, since it can understand itself only in the context of

---

[7] "Al-Shabab massacres 28 Kenyan bus passengers," *Al Jazeera*, 23 November 2014. Available at: http:// www.aljazeera.com/news/africa/2014/11/killed-kenya-bus-attack-201411226446296802.html. Accessed 26 November 2014.

the world it sent to. For example, religions (here, non-Christian) are part of the world. In the Christendom West, an encounter with another religion was rare, as any religion except Judaism was illegal. If there was such an encounter, it was an object of annihilation or conquest, either by imposition or cohesion. Other religions were found in a far land in such a theological mind: civilized Christians were not expected to engage with them, let alone live with them.

In such a dynamic power environment, theology occupied prime position in the world of learning (e.g. universities). Theological education was driven to maintain the church's dominant status quo in a given social context. It relegated any engagement with the "world" to secular power or non-theological disciplines. This is a radical departure from the significant pre-Christendom literature on apologetics. Unfortunately, this created a gap between theological education and the ordinary daily lives of the people in the pews.

One of the most dramatic shifts in theology (away from the long Christendom shadow) we have witnessed in our lifetime is Vatican Council II of the Catholic Church, as S. Bevans summarizes.[8] The Council now acknowledges the rightful place of the world. Missionaries (Christ's church as defined in *Gaudium et Spes*) are encouraged to discover treasures embedded in foreign cultures as a gift of a generous God distributed among the nations of the earth.[9] The Council even includes people of other faiths participating in Christ's truth and "other" churches.[10] The appreciation of culture (or the "world") influences the priestly formation of the church, especially in Africa, Asia, Latin America, and Oceania.[11] The theologizing process is also encouraged to be intentionally contextual or enculturated. How this institutional change in perspective is faithfully fulfilled in local settings is an open question. However, this intentional process taken by the church to disavow its long Christendom legacy is admirable.

Today, in Africa, Asia, and Latin America, Christianity thrives and grows, and the "world" surrounds the church. To begin with, in many settings, Christianity is a minority newcomer in the plethora of religions, sometimes making it illegal and persecuted. In a typical daily life, a Christian may have to negotiate the challenges that the "world" poses: corruption, poverty, gender issues, health matters (such as sanitation, Ebola, or HIV/AIDS), and racial

---

[8] S. Bevans, "From Roman Catholic Church to World Church: Roman Catholic Theological Education," in *Handbook of Theological Education in World Christianity*, pp. 3–12.

[9] Second Vatican Council, "*Decree Ad Gentes* on the Mission Activity of the Church" https://www.vatican.va/archive/hist_councils/ii_vatican_council/documents/vat-ii_decree_19651207_ad-gentes_en.html, accessed April 13, 2023.

[10] Second Vatican Council, "Dogmatic Constitution on the Church," *Lumen Gentium*, https://www.vatican.va/archive/hist_councils/ii_vatican_council/documents/vat-ii_const_19641121_lumen-gentium_en.html, accessed on April 13, 2023.

[11] Second Vatican Council, "Decree on Priestly Training," *Optatam Totius*, https://www.vatican.va/archive/hist_councils/ii_vatican_council/documents/vat-ii_decree_19651028_optatam-totius_en.html, accessed on April 13, 2023.

conflicts, including civil war and others. All of these need to be considered in the theologizing process and theological construct. How a racial conflict can be theologically, culturally, and politically understood, for example, must be part of theological formation. If this reality is agreed to be a raw material of the theological process, then this should affect the mode, curriculum, and delivery of theological education. In this way, the world helps us to shape our theological identity as we are designed to remain in the world (John 17:15).

Place of Mission

The significant alteration or disappearance of the world in the theological vocabulary had the most significant impact on the concept of mission. Its consequence set the church further apart from the biblical vision of mission, as its status moved from the margins to the power centre. In the Christendom setting, the development of mission, or lack thereof, resulted in much of today's mission understanding and practice. Some of them are as follows.

First, mission was taken from the hand of local congregations to special orders or societies. As the "world" was no longer present in the language of church life, the church's identity as the body of Christ sent to the world for witness underwent a theological change. Consequently, believers were devoid of their daily missionary witnessing in work and life in the "world." With the mission destination no longer in existence, a mission "field" was pushed to either the geographical margin of Christian territories or the outer world, called "heathendom". The former was often "Christianized" by forces as empires continued military expansion, some of which the church also sanctioned as "holy wars". In such cases, mission was carried out either by imposition or coercion.

Secondly, related to the above, when the church began to implement mission more intentionally, special missionary arms of the church were instituted. Such a move was natural as the "field" is culturally and geographically distant and different from the Christian "home". The rise of the Jesuit order in the Catholic Church and Protestant mission societies in the later centuries is a good example. They were followed by an ever-increasing number of mission organizations, often voluntary. This move is rather praiseworthy, as mission was taken intentionally and seriously despite the enormous resources required to recruit, train, commission, support, and look after them in distant lands. Advancement in knowledge in mission of different cultures, customs, languages, and religions was equally noteworthy. Missionary heroism was born, and children in the church grew up with their admiration for these heroes and a commitment by many to follow their paths. On the other hand, because mission was pushed to geographical edges or hinterlands, it was theologically established as something only a small number of specialized experts (mainly clergy) were to carry out. Even among Protestant Christians, the (in)famous phrase reveals this theological distortion: "Go or send." This elitization of mission is now a grave distortion of the vision of mission as understood and obeyed by the early church and the pre-Christendom church.

Thirdly, although many other forces shaped this specialization of mission through a long process, the net theological outcome is undeniably distorting. As S. Murray points out, the world was divided between Christendom and "heathendom" or, more popularly, "the West and the Rest". A new generation was effectively "missionized" through institutionalized infant baptism to the point that the state punished anyone who refused to baptize their infants. In such a setting, being a Christian meant belonging to a society.

In theological education, understandably, mission was an exotic subject designed only for a few who would go to the "ends of the earth". It was not for every future Christian worker. When a study of mission was brought back to theological education in the twentieth century, it was not without controversy.[12]

The Edinburgh Missionary Conference of 1910 was a watershed moment, despite its perspective being predominantly Western and imperialistic, as much discussion was on how more "natives" could be evangelized. The subsequent theological development through the meetings of the International Missionary Council, and subsequently of the Commission on World Mission and Evangelism of the World Council of Churches, has brought mission back to church life and theology and a radical revision of mission thinking. The creation of the Theological Education Fund in 1958 greatly assisted theological institutions in the Global South in several areas. They are: training national theological educators to replace Western missionary teachers, radically reforming theological curricula, networking among institutions through various associations, and identifying critical issues in theological education that are contextually pressing.[13]

If theology is to be contextual by nature, despite key "universalizing" dogmas, it should be "mission as theology" instead of "mission in theology". This shift will require a redefinition of mission, away from the Christendom framework.

Just as mission was intended for every believer in every social circumstance, it should be all-emphasizing in theological construct and thus, in theological education. Those trained in theology are expected to prepare the church and people in the pew for daily missionary engagement in the world. Ott's proposal for missiologically motivated theological education is based on missiology and theology's interdependent nature: missiology being both the "intention" and "dimension" of theology. His chart, outlined in Table I, is constructive.[14]

---

[12] For instance, a paragraph on "mission" was added to the Westminster Confession by the Presbyterian Church USA only in 1903 under the heading, "Of the Love of God and Mission."

[13] D. Esterline, "From Western Church to World Christianity: Developments in Theological Education in the Ecumenical Movement," in *Handbook of Theological Education in World Christianity*, pp. 16–19.

[14] B. Ott, "Mission Oriented Theological Education: Moving Beyond Traditional Models of Theological Education," *Transformation* 18.2 (2001), p. 82.

Table I. Process of theological education.

	Dimension	Intention
Missio Dei	God's missionary nature	God's act of sending God's Son and the Spirit
Ecclesiology	The missionary nature of the church	The church's specific missionary actions
Theology	The missionary nature of theology	Specific reflection of the church in mission
Theological education	The missionary centre of all theological education	Specific mission-oriented training

Many churches in the Global South do not have to cross an ocean to reach a mission "field": they are already at the "ends of the earth". Christianity is but one of several long-existing religions in a given society, or, in places, it is even marginalized, illegal, and persecuted. Right in their neighbourhoods, there are plenty of people who, Christians believe, should be reached by the good news of Christ. Many social systems are oppressive, corrupt, or simply evil, reminding us that God's kingdom is yet to shine through every layer of human life. Widespread suffering is a constant reminder to Christians of their life sent to the world. Geographical "ends" of the earth are only an extension of the "ends" that Christians live every day. Decades ago, the study undertaken by the Theological Education Fund contended that the "Third World would have a decisive word to speak to the West" in this matter.[15] The efforts of the ecumenical missiological circles over the last century should be warmly acknowledged.[16] Still, its effect has not been as strong as that of the Catholic Church through Vatican II. Some of its radical missiological expressions embracing the world, such as liberation theology, have been viewed by more conservative eyes as more "relevant" to the world but simply less Christian. Also, any form of theological formation must take this reality as an essential component, along with the revelation of God. Thus, theologization is fundamentally missiological. The recovery of mission in

[15] Theological Education Fund, Ministry in Context: The Third Mandate Programme of the Theological Education Fund (1970–77) (Bromley: Theological Education Fund, 1973), p. 9.

[16] See for example, Kenneth R. Ross, Jooseop Keum, Kyriaki Avtzi, and Roderick R. Hewitt (eds), *Ecumenical Missiology: Changing Landscapes and New Conceptions of Mission* (Oxford: Regnum Books, 2016).

theological construct and theological education will impact curricula, qualifications of teachers, kinds of textbooks and instructional materials, and assessment of the educational outcome. This is a radical vision, and we do not know what it will be like when this vision is fully realized. It is too early to predict or prescribe. But one thing is clear: it will take more than adding more mission courses: it will take a total transformation of content and process.[17]

Issue of Life in Mission and Theology

The close alliance and sharing of responsibilities between the church and state during the Christendom centuries produced a dichotomy of human and social life between sacred and secular, spiritual, and everything else. The former was the church's domain and the latter the state's. Thus, most of the non-spiritual affairs of daily life were not what the church was much involved in, perhaps except for life's milestones such as birth (baptism), confirmation, marriage, and death. In addition to the unhealthy divides of human and social life, this "allocated" domain between the church and the state resulted in the relegation of issues that belong to "life before death" to the state. The church's resort to the spiritual and religious domain away from real-life issues made its theology more otherworldly, that is, of "life after death".

The biggest assumption that Christendom is Christian, individually and collectively, was a fragile notion. Everyone was Christian either by birth or by belonging to a specific territory. In this total "Christian" environment, other religions were either illegal, marginalized, or persecuted. Followers of these religions were not real people to be understood or to live as our neighbours, but an object of destruction or conversion, often by force or coercion. Over centuries of such Christendom-living, the church soon lost its willingness to understand and ability to engage with them. When Christianity found itself in a new land, where dominant religions were already operating, a typical Christian mission transplanted the Christendom attitude: non-Christian religions should be isolated or eradicated. This is an absurd response for a newly arrived religion.

Here is a case of Korean Christianity (or, more accurately, Protestantism) according to a 2014 survey undertaken by a Buddhist think tank in Korea. First of all, the study uses the following religious distribution (presumably according to the latest government census): Catholic (10.9 percent), Protestant (18.3 percent), Buddhist (24.5 percent), Won Buddhist (0.3 percent), Other Religions (0.7 percent), and No Religion (45.3 percent).[18] According to these numbers, the combination of Catholic and Protestant believers forms the largest religious

---

[17] B. Edgar, "The Theology of Theological Education," *Evangelical Review of Theology* 29.3 (2005), p. 212.

[18] Institute for the Study of Buddhism and Society, *A Survey of Attitudes towards Social, Political, and Religious Issues in Korea* [in Korean] (Seoul: Jogye Order Institute for the Study of Buddhism and Society, 2014), p. 4.

group in Korea (29.2 percent), but by no means is it a majority.[19] In attitudes towards religions in Korea, 32.9 percent of the population "distrust" or "distrust strongly" Protestantism, while only 11.2 percent feel the same towards Catholicism and 23.7 percent towards Buddhism.[20] We need to take this negative perception toward Protestantism in the context that only 16.2 percent of the population refuses the social contribution of Protestants.[21] More seriously, 59.2 percent blame Protestant Christianity as the primary source of religious tensions and conflicts in Korean society, but only 38 percent of Protestants admit their responsibility. Although Muslims are relatively minimal in number in Korea, only 6.8 percent believe that Islam is a source of religious conflict.[22]

It is also essential to recognize that many non-Christian religions that came into contact with Christianity have become more self-aware and more "missionary" for inter-religious matters. For example, indigenous Won Buddhism in Korea opened its temples in urban centres and residential areas to the public. It contrasts with the traditional temples in deep mountains. It has adopted singing Buddhist hymns (unlike traditional chanting), provides social services, engages in relief work, and actively participates in inter-religious conversations and initiatives.

The same survey shows that urgent social issues are: parity in resource distribution (or poverty) (44.3 percent), corruption (24.9 percent), political instability (24.1 percent), crime (22.4 percent), aged population (14.2 percent), education (10.8 percent), and dissolution of families (10.1 percent).[23] Religions are expected to increase their contribution to reducing these social challenges. Catholics (46.2 percent) and Protestants (45.1 percent) believe their religion's role in society has grown.[24] This case clearly illustrates that the church takes every individual and social issue as its mission agenda. Although there is a role for every social entity (including state and religious and civic groups), the church and its theology must take them as part of its thinking, action, and education. As life is holistic, so are the gospel and Christian mission. The vision of God's rulership or kingdom is the overarching context in which life flourishes. And the "life" encompasses the whole: of this life or life after, of human and the whole creation.

Steven de Gruchy makes a passionate plea for theological education to take missional practice as its inseparable partner. In his view, missional practice keeps theological education adequately oriented toward the world that the church is called to serve.[25] He further argues that the close engagement with missional

---

[19] In Korea, like in China, Catholicism and Protestantism are treated as separate religions.

[20] *A Survey of Attitudes*, p. 18.

[21] *A Survey of Attitudes*, p. 17.

[22] *A Survey of Attitudes*, p. 19.

[23] *A Survey of Attitudes*, p. 11.

[24] *A Survey of Attitudes*, p. 17.

[25] de Gruchy, "Theological Education and Missional Practice," p. 42.

practice provides theological education with "a sense of telos, of purpose or direction, for that engagement". It is because *missio Dei* is a "statement of faith about God's redemptive intention in a world struggling with injustice, sickness, alienation, corruption, violence, oppression, and dislocation". He sums up this telos as "shalom, kingdom, life".[26] He further asserts that this will require theological education to be intentionally interdisciplinary, as the reality of life cannot be explained and responded to by theology alone.[27]

The pre-Christendom evidence and many new social environments for Christianity suggest many religions and daily social challenges will surround it. Theology must bring the gospel's response to them today and present a more holistic view of the church's ministry, life, and the gospel. So will be the case for theological formation in formal theological institutions, local congregation settings, and family. Preserving, protecting, and helping to flourish life will be an immediate and essential concern for Christian mission. For example, if a family has both Muslims and Christians, it is critical to accept the social reality and respect one another, and thus their religions, in the same family.

The Otherness of the Gospel

As we discuss the legacy of Christendom here of a more negative sort, it is essential to recognize that various movements and groups rose to challenge and counter the Christendom process. S. Murray's book highlights some of them in multiple periods and social contexts. Evangelicalism, in a sense, stands in this counter-Christendom tradition, especially detesting the close state–church collaboration. Although my previous exemplars of new initiatives are drawn from Catholic and ecumenical traditions, the place of Evangelicalism is unique in this engagement between a new Christian landscape and post-Christian thoughts.

Experience since the Edinburgh Missionary Conference in 1910 provides essential data, especially among the Protestant churches. In the first half of the twentieth century, they developed a missiology that is consciously ecumenical and contextual. The incorporation of the International Missionary Council with the World Council of Churches in 1958 symbolizes this missiological trend. It committed to fostering contextual and local theologies, so its theological education was systematically carried out through the creation of the Theological Education Fund. As discussed above, its efforts to move away from Christendom mission thinking and practice are admirable. The second half of the century witnessed a split in Protestant mission between Evangelical and ecumenical. The Lausanne Movement represents the former and the Commission of World Mission and Evangelism the latter, which we discussed above. Evangelical mission, especially with heavy influence from North American churches, has

---

[26] de Gruchy, "Theological Education and Missional Practice," p. 43.
[27] de Gruchy, "Theological Education and Missional Practice," p. 45.

maintained the primary focus on evangelism and church planting, or the expansion of Christianity.[28] The rise of Pentecostal Christianity as a missionary movement worldwide further strengthened this emphasis. Some approaches can easily be branded as "proselytism" or "evangelism by coercion" as part of the Christendom or colonial mission legacy. The growth of global Evangelicalism is the outcome of this theological and missional priority.

This changing mission landscape poses several critical questions, as this stands squarely on the opposite side of the de-Christendom process of mainline (including Catholic) missiology. First, what is the result of this rigorous process to reshape Christian mission away from Christendom's legacy? The *Atlas of Global Christianity*, a volume published to celebrate the centenary of the Edinburgh Conference, informs us that 1910 might have been the glorious moment of Christianity in terms of its worldwide reach. The unprecedented 34.8 percent of the world as Christian was perhaps the highest in a two-millennia history. Serious efforts have been exerted over the hundred years since the Conference to make the Christian message and mission less "foreign" but more relevant to cultures and contemporary contexts. The question is how much these efforts have contributed to the expansion of global Christianity in the last century, especially in the Global South. Considering that it is Evangelicals and Pentecostals, and also Evangelical wings of mainline churches, that led the growth, this question begs a thoughtful pondering. Equally important is that in a hundred years since the Conference, the gross number of Christians has increased drastically. Still, the proportion of Christianity against the world population has decreased to 33.2 percent. If the mainline churches have been losing their members globally, we should investigate the effect of their contextualizing efforts.

Of course, one can question the validity of this argument: quantitative vs authentic witnessing. Do the numbers matter? Yes, by all means. (This may be a feeling of a Southern Christian.) Historically, many ancient homes of Christianity have only signs of their presence in history. For example, see Turkey today: the home of the seven churches in Asia that the Apostle John addressed. From a missional viewpoint, are we confident there can be a Christian witness without a Christian? Or should we be content with today's close-to-nil Christian presence, with its brilliant history? Is it all right that Western Europe is thoroughly secularized and Islamized, with churches steadily closing or being sold? Certainly not. The number matters, as it is a critical part of Christian presence.

We also need to take one reality critically in Christian mission: most of today's Christians live in a multi-religious context, where each religion contends with the rest for their "market-" or "heart-share". Thanks to the increasing missional activities of the church, especially in the last two centuries, other

[28] L. Dahle, M. S. Dahle, and K. Jorgensen (eds), *The Lausanne Movement: A Range of Perspectives* (Oxford: Regnum Books, 2014).

religions have also learned to become missional. In this context, the numerical growth of Christianity is a foundation for other worthy activities, including theological education, contextualization, and mission.

Then one place to look at may be the "otherness" of the gospel. The core of the Christian message is the introduction of a radically different kingdom with an equally foreign lifestyle. This otherness or foreignness will create a sharp tension with an existing life order. That is exactly where the alternative world and its life are introduced as a countercultural force. The missional calling of Christianity to the world is to be priestly as well as to be prophetic. I wonder if the concerted effort to take the context seriously may have unwittingly side-lined the "text" or the message of God's rule in every life. Consequently, the approach may have reduced the recipients' resistance, but the message did not reach them fully.

Here are some illustrations. The first is substantial field research undertaken by D. Miller and T. Yamamori. Their search for "growing churches in the developing world that are involved in significant social ministry" with indigenous initiatives and resources led to a surprising discovery that nearly 85 percent of the nominated churches are Pentecostal in their orientation.[29] Their focus is on caring for and empowering the suffering ones, be it the poor, the addicted, the sick, the oppressed, the marginalized, or the under-educated. The research maintains that the churches are "progressive" as they were "growing" numerically while responding to the daily struggles of their communities. Thus, their priority is to respond to their spiritual, physical, material, and communal (including family) needs. A Korean theologian makes a similar observation by comparing Minjung theology (the Korean version of liberation theology, Minjung being an ordinary or even oppressed mass) and Pentecostal Christianity represented by *kibock sinang* (the Korean version of prosperity preaching).[30] Both are legitimate responses to the reality of poverty. I suspect that more people have been affected by the Pentecostal response than by Minjung theology, albeit with challenging theological problems that the former has manifested over the decades.

Now, this does not negate the validity of the contextual emphasis on and its contribution to the reshaping of Christian mission and theological education. But it also implies that the complete picture of Christian mission and theological formation is much larger than one network of churches can claim to have found. This is one foundational reason for churches working together.[31] It simply

[29] D. E. Miller and T. Yamamori, *Global Pentecostalism: The New Face of Christian Social Engagement* (Berkeley: University of California Press, 2007), pp. 5–6.
[30] Sebastian C. H. Kim, "The Problem of Poverty in Post-War Korean Christianity: *Kibock Sinang* or Minjung Theology?" *Transformation* 24.1 (2007), pp. 43–50.
[31] The publication of an Edinburgh Centenary volume on church unity is timely and its title telling: J. Gibaut and K. Jorgensen (eds), *Called to Unity: For the Sake of Mission*, Regnum Edinburgh Centenary Series 25 (Oxford: Regnum Books, 2014).

illustrates the complexity of human life in the world and the rich and multi-faceted nature of the gospel. Diversity in Christianity is thus a profound gift for mission to the world. We are indeed called to unity for the sake of mission.

Conclusion

This initial reflection is motivated by the ongoing shift in global Christianity. As a Korean Protestant Christian with a relatively short Christian history, taking up Christendom in discussion proves to be daunting. Two elements are particularly challenging: 1) Christendom was a long and complex process, and 2) Protestantism, in general, includes continuities and discontinuities of Christendom's legacy. Therefore, how Christendom affects "new" Christianities will significantly vary from one setting to another. For this reason, this reflection has been highly simplistic, with overgeneralizations. Nonetheless, I felt it worthwhile to take up this enormous subject for consideration.

It is essential to clarify that not all the ills and goods of Christianity (especially in the Global South) are to be blamed or attributed to Christendom's paradigms. For example, the "absence" of the world in current Evangelical mission thinking is due to its reaction to the overly this-worldly emphasis of ecumenical missiology. Another example is the never-ending divides and splits among churches, in the North and particularly in the South. Nonetheless, we cannot deny the effect of the long legacy of Western Christianity, especially that of Christendom, on today's Christianity. More seriously, many mission churches have received forms and contents of Christianity without much critical reflection. This is where the drastic southward shift of the gravity of global Christianity opens up a unique opportunity to examine closely what has been transmitted and its origin. The tradition is now to be scrutinized through the evidence of the scripture and the context.

In this study, two critical elements practically disappeared in the theological vocabulary of the church by the end of the Christendom era: when the "world" was eliminated from theology, soon also was "mission" in the church's thinking and life. Implications of their absence were far-reaching, and I picked up only one concept that was also taken away from the church's concern: life. The centre of the church's identity is bringing God's gift of life to individuals, families, society, the state, and the whole of creation. So should be its theological life; thus, theological formation.

Two things may be mentioned before closing. The first is that the global church is called to assess Christendom's legacy critically. Murray suggests several possible "d-" responses: denying, defending, dismissing, dissociating, demonizing, disavowing, disentangling, deconstructing, and disembarking.[32] He

[32] Murray, *Post-Christendom*, pp. 206–16.

prefers Nigel Wright's "disavowal" approach:[33] it is more nuanced. This approach is also charitable towards those who endorsed the Christendom shift and found treasures in Christendom. It assesses the shift and the system it created as fundamentally flawed; thus, decides not to defend, justify or maintain it. Disavowal requires repentance and humility.

The second is the role of the global church in undertaking this process of the disavowal of Christendom legacies, which will be essential in charting the new future of global Christianity. Murray speaks primarily to the Western church, but the non-West is not exempted from this vital process. In undertaking this critical assessment, there are several essential resources. In addition to the complex historical process of Christendom and its effects on the church, mission, and society, Murray identifies the church of pre-Christendom and various anti-Christendom movements. To these historical assessments, we need to add the scriptures, especially the life and teachings of Jesus, and the records of the early church.

Furthermore, we have present-day churches not directly affected (at least historically), namely in the Global South. This list implies that the whole church (both in the South and in the North) takes all these resources to heart and works closely to forge the joint future together. More than ever before, we face common challenges. For example, religious plurality is experienced both in the South and the North. As much as the emerging churches in the South have to chart their theological path away from Christendom vestiges as much as possible, the churches in the West have a vital role to play in this endeavour. They are best prepared to provide an assessment of, and reflection on, Christendom to the whole church.

Now, exactly what form the future theological education will take is anybody's guess. We are only among the first generation of the third Christian millennium. A further challenge is that formal theological education is an institutionalized and structured reality. It can range from a radically new perspective while maintaining much of the current structure, fresh perspective and new form altogether. Various models may emerge in different social contexts.[34] This is where the recently published handbooks of theological education can be a rich mine to explore.[35] Experiences of anti-Christendom may

---

[33] Murray, *Post-Christendom*, pp. 212–13; N. Wright, *Disavowing Constantine: Mission, Church and the Social Order in the Theologies of John Howard Yoder and Jürgen Moltmann* (Carlisle: Paternoster, 2000).

[34] Power-sensitive discourses may be one direction to consider. See for example Namsoon Kang, "Envisioning Postcolonial Theological Education: Dilemmas and Possibilities," in *Handbook of Theological Education in World Christianity*, pp. 30–41.

[35] In addition to the aforementioned *Handbook*, see the equally massive I. A. Phiri and D. Werner (eds), *Handbook of Theological Education in Africa* (Oxford: Regnum Books, 2013); H. Antone, W. Longchar, H. Bae H. et al. (eds), *Asian Handbook for Theological Education and Ecumenism* (Oxford: Regnum Books, 2013); P. Kalaitzidis,

also provide helpful examples. While many things are uncertain, I can say that one thing is clear: we are all in this together, both North and South, both historic and new churches, both left and right, with everyone in between, and we have to do it together. After all, we are in the one body of Christ, serving one another, but ultimately serving Christ, the head of the church.

T. Fitzgerald, C. Hovorun et al (eds), *Orthodox Handbook on Ecumenism: Resources for Theological Education* (Oxford: Regnum Books, 2013).

8. The Theological Motivations for Pentecostal Mission

Introduction

The Growth of Global Pentecostalism

The growth of the modern Pentecostal movement is a remarkable story. During the century of its existence, it has grown from a "fringe" group congregating daily in a run-down warehouse in downtown Los Angeles, whose members were branded as religious fanatics, to a worldwide movement which has influenced other church traditions. Its followers now number close to 650 million in 2020, predicted to rise to 1,031.5 million by 2050 across the globe. This growing Christian family encompasses various forms and practices, including Charismatics and Neo-Charismatics. [1] This chapter charts the developing missiology, demonstrating the complex interplay of the Bible, experience, and theology as it does so.

The significance of Pentecostal expansion was evident as the world church celebrated the centenary of the Edinburgh Missionary Conference. At its original 1910 conference, Pentecostals were in their infancy. The disappearance of the Azusa Street Mission in 1909, perhaps the most visible expression of Pentecostal Christianity after a three-year controversial existence, may have been a relief to some Christian leaders who felt embarrassed by this "tongue-babbling cultish group".[2] So, the Edinburgh Conference did not need to worry about them, as they were already struggling with issues surrounding the Catholic Church. However, Pentecostals did not "die out". The dramatic expansion of Christianity owes much to the exponential growth of Pentecostal churches and their variants.[3] The African Independent Churches, most Chinese house church networks, and most Latin American Evangelicals are defined as Pentecostal in a broader sense.

By the time the world church came to celebrate the centenary of the Edinburgh Conference in June 2010, the radical shift of the landscape of global Christianity was crystal clear, as reviewed in Chapter 2. The widening gap between the Global South and North is an observable trend. A steady decline of Western Christianity and a corresponding growth of Christianity in the Global South

---

[1] Johnson and Zurlo, *World Christian Encyclopedia*, p.26.

[2] Cecil M. Robeck, Jr, *The Azusa Street Mission and Revival: The Birth of the Global Pentecostal Movement* (Nashville, TN: Thomas Nelson, 2006), p. 134.

[3] Philip Jenkins, *The Next Christendom: The Coming of Global Christianity* (Oxford: Oxford University Press, 2002), p. 63.

occurred between the two conferences. As much of the new Christianity in the South is Pentecostal or its variation, it is noteworthy that in the West, growing segments of the church are Pentecostal-Charismatic. For example, amid a rapid decline of Christians in Great Britain, the annual New Wine conferences among Charismatic churches are refreshing. In the 2010 Somerset conference, I witnessed about 15,000 participants of all ages savouring expositions of the word, praises, and various seminars.

The expectation is that the growth of Christianity in the South will continue, and with it Pentecostal worship and spirituality. The exponential growth of African Christianity marked the twentieth century, and the continent would continue its leading role in the growth of global Christianity. Also, Asia holds another possibility. In 2020, Christianity reached only 8.2 percent of its vast population of 4.6 billion (more than half of the world's population). The prospect is bright as the 2020 annual growth rate of overall Christianity was 1.52 percent, and every Christian tradition, except Orthodox, recorded higher than the growth rate of the population (1.08 percent). The combination of Pentecostal-Charismatics and Independents amounted to 5.4 percent of the vast population, and the share of Pentecostals in the growth of Christianity in Asia will be significant.[4]

While evangelism and church expansion have been the focus of Pentecostal mission, it is also important to note that so-called "mercy ministry" has been an integral part of Pentecostal mission practice, although it took a while before appearing in formal statements.[5] Countless orphanages, various levels of educational institutions, relief work, and others have been deeply ingrained in "soul-saving" activities. Often without theological reflection, Pentecostals exercise instinctive solidarity with the poor and suffering, perhaps as they are from a lower social strata. Two recent publications may serve as valuable illustrations. *Not by Might, Nor by Power*[6] looks into the Latin American ChildCare programme of the US Assemblies of God World Mission. It records the growth of the educational programme for low-income families throughout the continent and its impact on societies. The author constructs a Pentecostal mission theology of social engagement from this success. *Global Pentecostalism* by Miller and Yamamori[7] is a summary of a four-year field study of growing congregations in the Global South that engage with issues facing societies and communities. It found that most of the congregations meeting these requirements were Pentecostal. This sociological study reveals that Pentecostal mission

[4] Johnson and Zurlo, *World Christian Encyclopedia*, p. 10.

[5] Article III, "Constitution of the Assemblies of God," revised 8–11 August 2007, Indianapolis. http://agchurches.org/Sitefiles/Default/RSS/AG.org%20T0P/2007ConstitutionandBylaws.pdf. Accessed 21 July 2011.

[6] Doug Petersen, *Not by Might, Nor by Power: A Pentecostal Theology of Social Concern in Latin America* (Oxford: Regnum Books, 1996).

[7] Miller and Yamamori, *Global Pentecostalism.*

thinking and practice include care for the suffering. The book, however, challenges Pentecostals on two fronts: to move beyond the dimension of evangelism and church planting and to construct an appropriate theology to provide Pentecostals with a valid conceptual ground for social engagement, including justice as a mission agenda.[8]

Enquiry at Hand

This study probes the theological motivation for such exponential growth. Considering that such expansion requires the agency of Pentecostal believers, the study looks at the hermeneutical roots and missional theology of Pentecostalism. This two-stage enquiry is appropriate for the "grassroots" nature of Pentecostal theologization, a process that is often participatory and context-based: it is undertaken by people in the pews and responds to immediate human needs. Therefore, at the crux of this process are not trained academic theologians but preacher-pastors.[9] Consequently, Pentecostal theology is deeply embedded in prayers, sermons, songs, and non-verbal expressions of its spirituality. This makes a theologian's first work a description, articulation, and analysis of embedded theological assumptions and arguments.

Hermeneutical values are a set of orientations inherent in Pentecostal spirituality and theology. These characteristics have critically contributed to the identity of Pentecostal believers and their theological framework, although implicitly expressed. These values also guide Pentecostals in interpreting the scriptures and their religious experiences. Although they have evolved throughout history and are expressed in various forms in different contexts, they remain constants among Pentecostal believers. They may provide clues to defining Pentecostalism.

Pentecostal Hermeneutical Values

Any theological investigation needs to consider the hermeneutical strategies of a particular group seriously. Pentecostal's hermeneutical approach influences how to read the scriptures and interpret one's life according to their theological construct. Much of Pentecostalism's unique hermeneutical ethos emerged in the nineteenth century. The following discussion is intended to be a brief presentation of crucial hermeneutical sources for Pentecostal mission theology.

---

[8] Wonsuk Ma and Julie C. Ma, "Missiology: Evangelization, Holistic Ministry, and Social Justice," in Wolfgang Vondey (ed.), *Routledge Handbook of Pentecostal Theology* (London: Routledge, 2020), pp. 279–89.

[9] Ma and Ma, *Mission in the Spirit*, pp. 227–41, under the title "Local Church, Worship, and Theological Formation."

"People of the Book": Scripture and Life

Pentecostals have been called the "people of the book" due to their unquestioned acceptance of the authority of the Bible and their literalistic reading of it. The first characteristic is the non-critical reading of the Bible or, perhaps more accurately, the post-critical reading by Pentecostal academics and the pre-critical reading by Pentecostals in the pew. Like their conservative Evangelical cousins, early Pentecostals had a firm belief in the (almost mechanical) inspiration of the scriptures. This was part of the general trend against intellectual enquiries and the critical reading of the Bible, originating in nineteenth-century German scholarship and gradually spreading to Europe and North America. Hence, any attempt to critically study the scriptures used to be viewed as a theologically "liberal" practice. This attitude has been further reinforced among the majority of non-Western Pentecostals who live in places where sacred scriptures are never questioned. They are objects of reverence and obedience, and this "Evangelical" attitude toward the Bible is believed to be the basis for the Christian dynamic of the Global South.[10]

Pentecostals have maintained a notion that the more literally one takes the scripture, the more faithful they become to the word of God and, thus, the will of God. Triggered by their reading of narratives in the Gospels and Acts, the narratives' historicity is never questioned. Furthermore, certain narratives in the scriptures were also taken as proof of a normative pattern. Speaking in tongues as "the initial physical evidence" of baptism in the Holy Spirit is based on the recurrence of Spirit-filled tongue-speaking in Acts. Pentecostals naturally subscribe to the historicity and authenticity of supernatural events recorded in the scripture. Their unique view of scripture and the Holy Spirit allows Pentecostals to collapse the time gap between biblical times and the present, establishing a link between the early church and the Azusa Street Mission. They assume that miracles included in the biblical narratives are repeatable today. This comes with advantages and disadvantages.

The Bible to the Pentecostals is not an ancient book at all. The temporal truncation also collapses the distance between God and humans, or the sacred and the secular. The transcendental God is now imminent. They expect to "hear the voice of God" from the book. Narratives have a particular appeal as the process of reading will soon become the process of participation: the readers find themselves in the story, be it of healing or miracles. This ability to "time travel" provides live religious experiences. The God of Exodus, for example, is expected to appear here and now, allowing the believers to have a similar experience of God's intervention. Thus, the interplay of such a Bible reading and experience-oriented religious life creates a spiral effect to enhance a highly engaged Christian life with God's reality. A Pentecostal's pre-critical reading of the Bible naturally results in a literal reading, leaving little room for the spiritualization or demythologization of the "irrational" contents of the Bible.

---

[10] Jenkins, *The New Faces of Christianity*, p.11.

Restorational Impulse: Apostolic Vision

As the twentieth century approached, there was a heightened interest in eschatology. One stream was the expectation of the early church restored with the manifestation of the spiritual gifts of prophecy, healing, and an outpouring of the Holy Spirit as recorded in Acts and 1 Corinthians. Camp meetings were a common annual feature for devout believers and their families to experience personal revival. One of the most popular words among the late nineteenth-century Holiness and early twentieth-century Pentecostal believers was "apostolic", reflecting the expectation and yearning for the restoration of church life as is recorded in the Book of Acts. The dawning of the new century reinforced their eager anticipation of the "latter rain" to mark the end of the end time.

The modern Pentecostal movement has developed its unique mission-oriented theology of the Holy Spirit and Christian life. With their unique experiences, such as baptism in the Holy Spirit and tongues as its accompanying sign, early Pentecostals understood themselves as people called for a specific task. Considering that the advent of the Spirit gave birth to the church, the very foundation of its existence is missional. Accordingly, spiritual baptism has been closely linked to witnessing (Acts 1:8), and some early Pentecostal leaders advocated tongues as a practical missionary tool.[11] This unique theological understanding shaped a peculiar self-identity as a people empowered for God's mission. Pentecostals were countercultural both in the church and in society and courageously endured ridicule and marginalization. Yet throughout its history, Pentecostalism has flourished where Christian presence had been in existence, instead of "virgin" Christian frontiers. In this sense, Pentecostalism is a revival and renewal movement, challenging and energizing the church to recover its "apostolic" authority and call to witness Christ to the ends of the earth. Evangelism and church planting have been at the core of Pentecostal mission, partly due to its eschatological orientation and early twentieth-century Evangelical Christianity.

Participatory Process: Place of Community

The role of community is the focal point of religious life and the hermeneutical process. The work of the Holy Spirit in community formation is experienced at least on two fronts: bringing people together around common spiritual experiences and breaking barriers that divide God's people. In the Azusa Street Mission, the shared experience of the Spirit baptism brought together people of different races, social strata, and denominational affiliations. At the turn of the twentieth century, white and Afro-Americans worshipping together was a radical countercultural departure from the norm. The division of the movement along

---

[11] James R. Goff, Jr, "Initial Tongues in the Theology of Charles Fox Parham," in Gary B. McGee (ed.), *Initial Evidence: Historical and Biblical Perspectives on the Pentecostal Doctrine of Spirit Baptism* (Peabody, MA: Hendrickson, 1991), pp. 57–71.

racial lines has become a stark reminder of human sinfulness and failure against the Spirit's intention and work. However, this extraordinary potential continued to appear throughout its history. In the 1980s, a sociologist discovered close relationships between Pentecostals and Charismatic Catholics in the Philippines, despite the hostility between Protestants and Catholics.[12]

At the centre of Pentecostal community formation is worship. It provides a space and time for religious experiences, theological formation, and the shared process of theology-making. Worship is incredibly participatory, often blurring the boundary between the pulpit and the pews. One excellent example is the "testimony" time, where anyone can be the "main speaker". By publicly sharing one's religious experience "to praise the Lord" or "to plea to the Lord", any member of the community contributes to the corporate deposit of theology. It is also a chance for the community to exercise the "gift" of discernment, evaluation, and shared ownership of the presented experience and its interpretation. Pentecostal spirituality's "democratic" nature significantly enhances the community formation process. The exercise of spiritual gifts also takes place in a community setting, often a prophecy or a message in tongues, ideally accompanied by an interpretation.

Even seemingly individualistic matters are experienced in the community context among Pentecostals. My yearning for baptism in the Spirit became the subject of community prayer. I walked through this process together with many fellow Pentecostal believers. When I finally "got it", we celebrated in praise and worship together. In Korea, it is usual that a family's prayer becomes the prayer of the entire cell group. Sometimes the cell leader will bring the family to a prayer mountain for prayer and fasting for several days while the whole cell group intercedes. In various dimensions, people experience the community-forming work of the Holy Spirit.

Experience: Lived-Out Spirituality

Another essential aspect of restorational thinking is the recovery of religious experience. From the Pentecostal view of scripture, it follows that Bible stories are read to experience an encounter with God and show the miracles that contemporary readers can experience.[13] Pentecostals never "demythologize" the miracle stories of the Bible. The Pentecostal appropriation of biblical narratives occurs in two ways: they transport the ancient stories to contemporary life (existentialization) and "slip" themselves into the old story of action (identification). The logic is simple: if the God of the Bible acted then, he could

[12] Koichi Kitano, "Socio-Religious Distance Between Charismatics and Other Religious Group Members: A Case Study of the Philippines in the 1980s," *Journal of Asian Mission* 5.2 (2003), pp. 231–42.

[13] Keith Warrington, *Pentecostal Theology: A Theology of Encounter* (London: T. & T. Clark, 2008).

do the same today. For this reason, Pentecostals love to affirm that God is "the same yesterday, today, and forever" (Heb. 13:8).

This mindset promotes an expectation of having a tangible encounter with God through worship, prayer, sermons, Bible reading, and the like. The nature of such encounters varies, but Pentecostals expect to "hear from the Lord". Hearing from God is a common feature of Christianity. The distinctiveness of the Pentecostal experience of hearing is rather concrete and tangible, even if one can argue that tangibility is a subjective notion. Pentecostals are pretty open to various channels of such revelation, including dreams, visions, audible or "inner" voices, mental impressions, or a passage "being lifted from the page". Such "voices" are not limited to matters of spirituality but apply almost to any issue in life. The other area of encounter is the "touch of the Lord". This expression often refers to various experiences of God's reality, be it divine healing, an overwhelming sense of God's presence, relief from physical, emotional, or circumstantial difficulties, a deep conviction of God's truth, and the like.

Unlike the Reformers' notion of the Holy Spirit as a shy member of the Trinity, Pentecostals, based on their reading of Luke-Acts, have re-profiled the Holy Spirit. He is now the active executor in birthing the church, initiating mission, and overseeing the spread of the gospel through empowerment.[14] Whether supernatural or circumstantial, many experiences are carefully undertaken by the Holy Spirit. This has led Pentecostals to two important theological conclusions: 1) The Holy Spirit interacts with God's people through a wide range of religious experiences, including prophecy (11:22-23; 19:6; 21:9), dreams and visions (9:10; 10:3), hearing voices (10:19;16:9; 18:9), healings (3:1-8; 4:30), and the like; and 2) such experiences embolden believers in their faith and lead them into opportunities to witness of the risen Lord. However, the role of experience in biblical interpretation is a controversial issue. Ideally, the word should guide, inform, and set a parameter to religious experience, while experience affirms the word. Pentecostals are called to guard themselves against the danger of placing experience over the word. Nonetheless, with their literalistic reading of the Bible, religious experiences have a definite role in strengthening their sense of call and commitment to sacred vocation, as baptism in the Spirit will illustrate below.

People of the Spirit(s)

Pentecostals assume a worldview distinct from many contemporary Western Christians but closer to a non-Western understanding of life and the world. For example, Pentecostals are conscious of spiritual beings: benevolent and malevolent spirits, angels, and demons, at work in human lives. For this reason, Pentecostals are the people of the S/spirit(s). With their literal reading of the

[14] Roger Stronstad, *The Charismatic Theology of St Luke* (Peabody, MA: Hendrickson, 1984) and Robert P. Menzies, *Empowered for Witness: The Spirit in Luke-Acts* (London: T. & T. Clark, 2004).

Bible and emphasis on the experiential dimension of religious life, Pentecostals gravitate to the unseen yet active world of the supernatural.

Two particular areas may be noteworthy. As noted briefly above, the first is the development of a dynamic theology of the Holy Spirit. Pneumatology that is born out of one's radical experience of the Holy Spirit – be it baptism in the Spirit, healing, exorcism, "hearing" him, or "seeing" his work – will be explosive. The Holy Spirit has become a miracle-working member of the Trinity. He empowers the church to be victorious in the middle of a hostile world, providing signs and wonders as part of the Christian witness. This orientation gives a shape of empowerment theology that is unique to Pentecostalism. The second area is the similarity between the Pentecostal worldview and that of many non-Western cultures, where diverse spirits are perceived to operate daily, generating a clash of the (supernatural) forces. Only the most powerful Spirit (or God) earns a right to be worshipped, and the contest of such spiritual forces has become the basis for mass conversions.[15] The explosion of Pentecostal-type Christianity in Africa, Asia, and Latin America is partly attributed to these worldview similarities[16] and common interests in life, such as healings, blessings, and curses.[17] Pentecostalism can supply functional substitutes to the felt and perceived religious needs because the worldviews have corresponding categories. This helps the missionary recognize the needs of the recipient.

Theological Resources for Pentecostal Mission

This section traces the historical development of the mission implications of four theological beliefs unique to Pentecostalism. The nineteenth-century Holiness movement of North America is the root of the modern Pentecostal movement.[18] Thus, Charles Parham and William J. Seymour, the two most renowned Pentecostal "fathers", began as Holiness preachers. To illustrate the beliefs and practices of early Pentecostals, we will use reports published in *The Apostolic Faith* of the Azusa Street Mission of Los Angeles (1906–1909), the most representative Pentecostal periodical of the formative years of its theological construction. Several key components, as mentioned above, play a vital role in Pentecostal theological construction: scripture, the Holy Spirit interacting with scripture, the community of believers,[19] the Pentecostal experience, and the

---

[15] Alan P. Tippett, *People Movements in Southern Polynesia: A Study in Church Growth* (Chicago: Moody, 1971).

[16] Walter J. Hollenweger, *Pentecostalism: Origins and Developments Worldwide* (Peabody, MA: Hendrickson, 1997), pp. 18–80.

[17] Julie C. Ma, *When the Spirit Meets the Spirits: Pentecostal Mission to an Animistic Tribe of the Northern Philippines* (Frankfurt: Peter Lang, 2000).

[18] I am aware of arguments on multiple "springheads" of the movement. For this reason I use the qualifier "organized" theological and spiritual tradition.

[19] Kenneth J. Archer, *A Pentecostal Hermeneutics for the Twenty-First Century: Spirit, Scripture and Community* (London: T. & T. Clark, 2004), pp. 156–91.

broader social context. As we observe in the Global South, the context has been prominent in Pentecostal development.

Baptism in the Spirit

This cardinal doctrine makes (classical) Pentecostals distinct from the rest of Christianity. Understood as an experience distinct from and subsequent to regeneration, belief in the baptism in the Holy Spirit has caused a continuing debate between Pentecostals and Evangelicals. Based on the post-resurrection promise of the Lord that his followers would be baptized in the Holy Spirit, Pentecostals took it as a sign of the restoration of early church spirituality, especially the experience on the day of Pentecost (Acts 2).[20] For the present discussion, three aspects of this belief will be explored, with mission as proclamation in mind: experience, interpretation, and consequences.

As discussed above, Pentecostalism has brought back the significant role of religious experiences. Testimonies abound to the powerful impact of experiences loosely termed "the baptism in the Holy Spirit". Various life-changing stories are shared, although most North American classical Pentecostal churches insist on speaking in tongues as "the physical and initial evidence". The sense of God's overwhelming presence is a common element of these experiences, as recorded in the first issue of *The Apostolic Faith*:

> Proud, well-dressed preachers come in to "investigate". Soon their high looks are replaced with wonder, then conviction comes, and very often, you will find them in a short time wallowing on the dirty floor, asking God to forgive them and make them as little children. It would be impossible to state how many have been converted, sanctified, and filled with the Holy Ghost. They have been and are daily going out to all compass points to spread this wonderful Gospel.[21]

Speaking in tongues also brought tangible impact to the recipients of the Spirit baptism and those who witnessed them. It is no wonder that Pentecostalism spread like wildfire. Therefore, Spirit baptism serves as the sign of the restoration of early church spirituality and shapes the self-identity of Pentecostals as people called and commissioned to bring the news of salvation to the ends of the earth. It is also interpreted as the reception of power from above for witnessing in the context of Acts 1:8. The early Pentecostal literature made it clear that "the baptism with the Holy Spirit is not a work of grace but a gift of power. The baptism in the Holy Ghost makes you a witness unto the uttermost parts of the earth. It gives you power to speak in the languages of the nations."[22] Its biblical

---

[20] Frank D. Macchia, *Baptized in the Spirit: A Global Pentecostal Theology* (Grand Rapids: Zondervan, 2006).

[21] "Pentecostal Has Come: Los Angeles Being Visited by a Revival of Bible Salvation and Pentecost as Recorded in the Book of Acts," *The Apostolic Faith* 1 (September 1906), p. 1, col. 1.

[22] "The Enduement of Power," *The Apostolic Faith* 4 (December 1906), p. 2, col. 2.

illustrations are often taken from Peter's bold preaching in Acts 2:14-40 and Stephen's courageous sermon in Acts 7:2-53. Lastly, especially at a popular level, baptism in the Spirit is understood as the "floodgate" of spiritual gifts, including healing and miracles.

The consequences of this doctrine are evident in an unbending commitment to mission. With a strong sense of calling to be witnesses "to the end of the earth", this revival movement quickly turned into a missionary movement. Despite little or no training or support, a catalogue of heroic missionary achievements is attributed to this sense of call. Another consequence is a zeal for preaching the "full gospel", in which tongue-speaking often functions as a reinforcement. Some early Pentecostals expected tongues to enable them to bypass laborious language learning.[23] Third, after the pattern of Acts, signs and wonders are expected in the mission context. This power orientation makes Pentecostals bold witnesses with claims of healings and miracles, albeit with many controversies surrounding them. The net result is the fast spread of the Pentecostal message and the expansion of the Pentecostal movement globally. This pneumatologically shaped missiology is well attested in *The Apostolic Faith* report of an Azusa missionary in the Revival's early days:

> A Pentecostal missionary has left for foreign lands, Bro. Thos P. Mahler, a young man of German nationality. He has the gift of tongues besides the knowledge of several. He left here for San Bernardino. He may go by way of Alaska, Russia, Norway, Germany and to his destination in Africa. As our brother was leaving, Bro. Post spoke of his call and gave a message in tongues in regard to Bro. Mahler which he interpreted as follows: "I have anointed this dear one with my Spirit, and he is a chosen vessel to me to preach the gospel to many, and to suffer martyrdom in Africa."[24]

The Prophethood of All Believers

This theological tradition is closely related to the previous discussion on baptism in the Spirit. However, a separate discussion is deemed necessary because of its significance in Pentecostal mission. This is almost a natural and logical outgrowth of the belief in the baptism in the Holy Spirit. Peter's interpretation of the advent of the Holy Spirit on the day of Pentecost is essential. In the Old Testament period, only a handful of leaders experienced the coming of the Spirit of God, such as the seventy elders (Num. 11), selected judges, the first two kings of United Israel, and selected prophets. However, an eschatological expectation of the Old Testament is to break this exclusivity of the Spirit: everyone in God's community will experience the coming of the Spirit. This is the prophecy by Joel (2:28-29), which has its root in Moses' desire for the whole of Israel (Num.

---

[23] "Russians Hear in Their Own Tongue," *The Apostolic Faith* 1 (September 1906), p. 4, col. 3.

[24] "The Lord Sends Him," *The Apostolic Faith* 1 (September 1906), p. 4, col. 1.

11:29). This democratization of the Spirit is the gist of Peter's sermon in presenting the coming of the Holy Spirit on the day of Pentecost (Acts 2:16-21).

Anyone in God's community is baptized in the Holy Spirit, regardless of age, gender, and social status. The calling, empowerment, and commission for God's work are for every believer, thus, the "prophethood of all believers". This theological paradigm contrasted with the long-standing clergy-oriented professionalism of (Western) church life.

Of particular note is the significant contribution of women to Pentecostal mission. Later, this is expressed in Korea through the mobilization of lay women leaders in David Yonggi Cho's well-known cell group system. Young people are also mobilized for mission in networks, such as Youth With A Mission. This liberates ministry from the exclusive hands of the elite clergy. Often advocating short-term missionary service, YWAM and others have "democratized" ministry and mission for every believer. Thirdly, an extension of this radical mission thinking is the establishment and empowerment of, and transfer to, national and local leadership at the earliest opportunity,[25] a practice that has made Pentecostalism the fastest-growing religious movement in our day.

Eschatology

Early Pentecostals shared their eschatology with the late-nineteenth-century, conservative, pre-millennial orientation. The turn of the century provided a native expectation of the end of human history. Here is an example found in *The Apostolic Faith*:

> All these 6,000 years, we have been fighting against sin and Satan. Soon we shall have a rest of 1,000 years ... We must go on to perfection and holiness, and get the baptism with the Holy Ghost and not stop there, but go on to perfection and maturity.[26]

The outpouring of the Holy Spirit was a sure sign of the end time, the last opportunity for the greatest harvest of souls before the return of the Lord. This created an incongruent theological system for Pentecostals, adopting the dispensational scheme of human history. As the church age or the age of grace moves fast toward a closure, they believed that God would take the church to heaven before the new dispensation would begin. It's the time when God would deal with Jews through tribulation. This eschatology formed the awareness of living at the "five-to midnight" moment, giving a tiny window of opportunity to save as many souls as possible. "One-way ticket missionaries" were strongly motivated by the eschatological urgency. It was not unusual that engaged young

---

[25] Melvin L. Hodges, *The Indigenous Church* (Springfield, MO: Gospel Publishing House, 1963).

[26] "Toe [sic!] Millennium," *The Apostolic Faith* 1 (September 1906), p. 3, col. 3.

women broke their engagements and left for their mission field.[27] This eschatological consciousness made them other-world-oriented. Coupled with the religious consciousness of call and empowerment for witness, they are the best ingredients for the significant mission movement we have seen in the last hundred years.

Despite the powerful and positive contribution of this pre-millennialism with the expectation of the imminent return of the Lord, such clock-setting eschatology must expire sooner or later. As the movement enters the third generation, eschatological messages from Pentecostal pulpits have gradually disappeared to be replaced by this-worldly concerns, such as church growth and the message of blessing and health.[28] Fortunately, the pneumatological interpretation rather than the temporal eschatological expectation serves the dynamic motive of Pentecostal mission. The global Pentecostal movement has continued its growth even after the waning of an imminent eschatology.

The Primacy of "Soul" Matter

Pentecostalism has all the crucial ingredients to become an unprecedented "religion to travel", well-evidenced by its exponential growth and spread worldwide in its wild diversity and creativity. The consequence of its Evangelical heritage and the temporally oriented eschatology has been the focus of Pentecostal missiology on evangelism and church planting. The rise of the social gospel in the middle of the twentieth century may have further encouraged the already narrowly focused attention. Mission impetus was also taken from the mission roadmap found in their favourite passage: "from Jerusalem, all Judea, Samaria and (finally) to the ends of the earth" (Acts 1:8). Crossing geographical boundaries, therefore, has been part of the Pentecostal mission paradigm. Many brilliant social programmes have soul-winning as their ultimate goal.[29]

This, however, may reveal the Pentecostal understanding of humans, sin, and salvation. Every evil, be it personal or corporate, is traced to sin and to Genesis 3, where separation from God resulted in spiritual damnation, physical suffering, broken society, and a cursed environment. Therefore, the Pentecostal view of restoration reverses the order, beginning with the spiritual regeneration, and expanding to personal (including the physical level, such as healing), communal

---

[27] For one example see S. Shemeth, "Trasher, Lillian Hunt," in Burgess and van der Maas, *New International Dictionary of Pentecostal and Charismatic Movements*, p. 1153.

[28] See Chapter. 9.

[29] See for example, Calcutta Mercy Ministries, "History," http://www.buntain.org/about.html. Accessed 15 March 2010.

(social), and even environmental dimensions.[30] For example, the upward social mobility of Pentecostals has been attributed to this paradigm.[31]

Naturally, "revival" or "renewal" is a crucial concept in Pentecostal thinking. The Pentecostal movement itself is often classified as a revival movement. The January 1907 issue of *The Apostolic Faith* reveals a glimpse of the Azusa Street Revival:

> From morning till late at night the meetings continue with about three altar services a day. We have made no record of souls saved, sanctified and baptized with the Holy Ghost, but a brother said last week he counted about fifty in all that had been baptized with the Holy Ghost during the week.[32]

As Pentecostal missiology matures, an argument seems to gain ground that spiritual dynamism, evangelism, church growth, and social service are not mutually exclusive.[33]

Conclusion

If this short study leaves an impression that Pentecostals have finally unlocked the secret of Christian mission, the reality is precisely the opposite. In the name of God's kingdom and renewal, church divisions were caused by this movement, and unfortunately, they have been part of its growth "strategy". Some of its serious blind spots, such as its eschatological expectation, are already presented. While they are praised for their creativity in contextualization, Pentecostals are also criticized for the ugly "prosperity gospel"[34] and their extremely "Western" outlook and ethos. All in all, there is much for further reflection and study.

In the subsequent decades, the progress of Pentecostal mission will depend on how Pentecostals preserve and strengthen their unique spiritual values and understand their changing contexts so that their theological constructs will respond to their missional call and contextual needs. The Bible will continue to play a significant role as the movement spreads increasingly in the Global South.

---

[30] Teen Challenge, the successful drug rehabilitation programme, emphasizes regeneration and baptism in the Spirit. David Batty and Ethan Campbell, "Teen Challenge: 50 Years of Miracles," *Assemblies of God Heritage* 28 (2008), pp. 14–21.

[31] David Martin, *Tongues of Fire: The Explosion of Protestantism in Latin America* (Oxford: Blackwell, 1990).

[32] "The Pentecostal Baptism Restored," *The Apostolic Faith* 2 (October, 1906), p. 1, cols. 1-2.

[33] Young-hoon Lee, *The Holy Spirit Movement in Korea* (Oxford: Regnum Books, 2009), pp. 126–27.

[34] See Hwa Yung, "The Missiological Challenge of David Yonggi Cho's Theology," in Wonsuk Ma, et al. (eds), *David Yonggi Cho: A Close Look at His Theology and Ministry* (Baguio, Philippines: APTS Press, 2004), pp. 85–90; Wonsuk Ma, "David Yonggi Cho's Theology of Blessing: Basis, Legitimacy and Limitations," *Evangelical Review of Theology* 35.2 (April 2011), pp. 140–59.

The expectation of the supernatural dimension of Christianity, the role of community and experience, and a more holistic worldview will continue to play critical roles in Pentecostal religious life. Serious challenges and new opportunities will arise on the theological front, and any good theology will need to be locally grounded and relevant. This requires the conscious engagement of Pentecostal values and context. If frontline workers such as pastors, evangelists, and missionaries continue their critical role in popular theological construction, theological formation will be essential. Aided by Pentecostal theologians, frontline leaders can protect Pentecostal communities from consumerism-driven, self-serving popular religion and become relevant to their context. As seen in the past, Pentecostal eschatology have played a substantial role in the beginning, along with the belief in the baptism in the Spirit. However, the latter's empowerment theology, incorporated in the prophethood of all believers, will remain high in Pentecostal theological agendas if the theology is to remain "Pentecostal". The primary purpose of soul-winning is expected to continue, although the Pentecostal horizon in mission thinking and practice has become more holistic and inclusive. At the same time, more locally motivated theological agendas should surface, such as reconciliation in places where religious and racial conflicts raise tensions.

Classical Pentecostals have the most theological and institutional resources. In non-Western lands, they look radically different from their North American or European "mothers", who are not necessarily growing. This is a formidable challenge to their century-old theology and constantly institutionalizing ethos. Yet, they may also empower the rest of the Pentecostal-Charismatic churches. Together they should continue their engagement in new mission frontiers because, to remain faithful to the scriptures and Pentecostal spiritual heritage, and yet be relevant to the immediate context will pose a significant challenge to emerging Pentecostal mission communities worldwide.

9. Eschatology and Mission: What Happened When the Wave Hit the West End of the Ocean?

Introduction

As the world's Pentecostal-Charismatic movement enjoys sustained growth, Asia has reason to be thankful to the Lord and early Pentecostal pioneers in North America and Asia. As the spiritual eruption made waves across the Pacific Ocean, its power generated varying effects in different parts of Asia, just like the destructive tsunami force that devastated the eastern coast of Japan more than a decade ago.

It is reasonable to expect continuity and discontinuity between the Azusa Street spirituality and what is found among Asian Pentecostals today. The unique spiritual and theological tradition of the Azusa Street Mission continues, but the temporal and spatial gaps between the extreme ends of the Pacific Ocean resulted in marked differences. These are often creative modifications of existing traditions or even the emergence of something entirely new in Asia.

How much direct correlation can one trace between these two entities is another challenging question. There is no doubt that the early Pentecostal movement began as a powerful missionary force, and many Pentecostal missionaries reached parts of Asia and preached the Pentecostal message. However, an increasing number of studies, primarily based on Asian evidence, have challenged the "one fountainhead" theory of the movement: the Azusa Street Mission as the mother of all Pentecostal churches.[1]

Asian Pentecostalism has come a long way and is now at a critical juncture for its growth and development. According to the latest edition of the *World Christian Encyclopedia*, the size of Pentecostal Christianity in Asia, around 214.5 million followers projected for 2050, trails behind Africa (450.7 million) and Latin America (243.2 million).[2] Despite the struggle of Asian Christianity, overwhelmed by the traditional religions, Pentecostalism shows its resilience and significant presence. The proportion of Pentecostals to the total Christian population is encouraging (20.8 percent in Asia in 2050, in comparison with 43.7

---

[1] E.g. Yung Hwa, "'Endued with Power': The Pentecostal-Charismatic Renewal and the Asian Church in the Twenty-First Century," *Asian Journal of Pentecostal Studies* 6.1 (2003), p. 66; and Allan Anderson, *To the Ends of the Earth: Pentecostalism and the Transformation of World Christianity*, Oxford Studies in World Christianity (Oxford: Oxford University Press, 2013).

[2] Johnson and Zurlo, *World Christian Encyclopedia*, p. 26.

percent and 23.6 percent in Africa and Latin America, respectively). More importantly, Asian Pentecostalism, as Christianity in Asia, has a large "growth room", as it will account for only 4.1 percent of Asia's vast population. By contrast, in Latin America, with its high Christian population (90.2 percent in 2050), much of the Pentecostal growth must come from transfers from other churches, especially the Catholic Church. Africa, also with more than half of its population evangelized (and more for the Sub-Saharan regions), the future growth of Pentecostalism will be more likely through church transfers. Particularly noteworthy is the emergence and growth of the house church networks in China, a large portion of which are considered Pentecostal-Charismatic.[3] As the African Independent (or Instituted) Churches have led the fast Pentecostal growth in Africa, these Chinese churches may blaze the trail for the continent.

Then, how did the early theological orientations of the Azusa Street Mission impact Asian Pentecostalism? My reflection is intentionally theological, and this focus comes from a few assumptions: 1) theological conviction directly influences behaviour, and 2) theology is shaped through constant interaction between the (imported, thus, foreign) message and the real-life situation where the message should be received as the word of God by receptors. Using hindsight, many suspect that Asian Pentecostal theology has been shaped not through intentional reflections but often by default; that is, by the lack of deliberate action in preserving Azusa theological traditions and bringing these to an active dialogue with a given socio-cultural context.

This discussion focuses on one theological issue, eschatology, which shaped the Pentecostal ethos in the early days. The enquiry has four aspects: 1) how did eschatology impact early Pentecostal theology; 2) how was this transmitted to Asians (as it crossed the ocean); 3) how does this Asian version of Pentecostal eschatology give birth to unique spiritual traditions that we see in Asia, and 4) in what areas do Asian Pentecostals need to exert an intentional theological assessment and reflection for the sound future of the Asian Pentecostal movement? In the discussion, the contextual elements will constantly interact with the "message".

This discussion also centres on classical Pentecostals, although, due to the ambiguous nature of Asian Pentecostalism, Charismatic Pentecostalism will naturally be considered when needed. An equally important consideration for the reader is to keep in mind the complexity and diversity of Asian countries in their history, society, culture, religion, economy, and political systems.

---

[3] Luke Wesley, *The Church in China: Persecuted, Pentecostal and Powerful* (Baguio, Philippines: AJPS Books, 2004).

Pentecostal Eschatology: Then, Now, and Future

One Hundred Years Ago, There...

Scholars agree that an urgent eschatological expectation was the backbone of early Pentecostal spirituality. Although this may appear less prominent than other cardinal Pentecostal doctrines such as baptism in the Holy Spirit with speaking in tongues as the "initial physical evidence",[4] the eschatological framework enhanced Pentecostal distinctives. Anderson forcefully argues that the primary message among early Pentecostals was "Jesus is coming soon".[5] This early Pentecostal eschatology had several unique expressions.

The first is what may be termed as "realized eschatological urgency". Mainline Christianity in North America at the turn of the twentieth century was a middle-class phenomenon, with the pious anti-cultural Holiness movement balancing the Christian world. Interestingly, however, eschatological urgency was not found in either camp. Initially based on John Darby's dispensationalism, the Keswick movement proposed a sweeping revival to usher in the eschatological climax, the return of the Lord.[6]

Thus, Pentecostalism was born as an eschatological movement by interpreting the outbreak of the unprecedented revival as the prerequisite for the imminent return of the Lord in their lifetime. The experience of the Holy Spirit among them was quickly labelled the "latter rain", assuming that the original advent of the Holy Spirit recorded in Acts 2 was the "former rain".[7] In the pre-millennial framework, this also signals the last hour of the great harvest before the tribulation. That was where the baptism in the Holy Spirit to empower believers to witness found its eschatological and missionary impetus. Acts 1:8 has become the motto for Pentecostal believers: "But you will receive power when the Holy Spirit comes on you; and you will be my witnesses in Jerusalem, and in all Judea and Samaria, and to the ends of the earth" (NIV). The only other passage which has attained a similar status is Zechariah 4:6: ""Not by might, nor by power, but by my Spirit, saith the Lord of hosts" (KJV). This eschatological urgency was evident in many early testimonies. The very first issue of *The Apostolic Faith* (Los Angeles) reports:

---

[4] Robert M. Anderson, *Vision of the Disinherited: The Making of American Pentecostalism* (Peabody, MA: Hendrickson, 1979), pp. 44–45. As Anderson puts it, "In short, the Pentecostal movement was as much a departure from the Wesleyan tradition as a development from it" (p. 43).

[5] Anderson, *Vision of the Disinherited*, Chapter 5, entitled "The Pentecostal Message," pp. 79–97.

[6] E.g. Frank Macchia, "The Struggle for Global Witness: Shifting Paradigms in Pentecostal Theology," in Murray Dempster, Byron Klaus and Doug Petersen (eds), *The Globalization of Pentecostalism: A Religion Made to Travel* (Oxford: Regnum Books, 1999), pp. 8–9.

[7] E.g. Joel 2:23 where the "former rain" is to be moderate (KJV).

> The gift of languages is given with the commission, "Go ye into all the world and preach the gospel to every creature." An early Pentecostal record claimed that the Lord gave languages to the "unlearned Greek, Latin, Hebrew, French, German, Italian, Chinese, Japanese, Zulu and languages of Africa, Hindu and Bengali and dialects of India, Chippewa and other languages of the Indians, Esquimaux, the deaf mute language and, in fact, the Holy Ghost speaks all the languages of the world through His children."[8]

This eschatological urgency led naturally to the missionary focus of the Pentecostal movement.

The second expression is the resultant other-worldly orientation and missionary impetus. Almost all authors agree that the early Pentecostal expectation of the imminent return of the Lord fuelled missionary zeal. Their pre-millennial eschatology conditioned them to view the world as the object of God's judgement for the seven-year tribulation. At the same time, the church would be taken to heaven to meet the Bride. Because of this theological orientation, they were preoccupied with "soul-winning", leaving little room for anything else. The first issue of *The Apostolic Faith* also reports, "Hundreds of dollars have been laid down for the sending of missionaries and thousands will be laid down."[9]

Early Pentecostals expressed this commitment to mission with eschatological urgency in various ways.[10] Theological education comprised strictly practical and short-term ministerial training. Unlike established divinity schools, this programme aimed to produce pastors, evangelists, and missionaries in a minimum amount of time. Their summer activities consisted primarily of evangelistic tours. The most noteworthy development was the deployment of zealous missionaries, appropriately called "missionaries with one-way tickets".[11] They left for mission fields without any intention or expectation to return home due to their commitment to mission and their eschatological conviction. With the experience of the baptism in the Spirit, they were experientially and theologically convinced that they were called, empowered, and were now being sent. Eschatological urgency "put a pair of wings to a tiger", as Koreans would say.

The third is a "revision by default". It is perfectly reasonable to expect that the eschatological urgency, which the Pentecostal pioneers held, would face some revisions as the second generation slowly came into leadership. Various signs appeared, such as "spiritual dryness and a lack of God's presence", as early as the 1940s. Then, the Latter Rain movement brought back much of the early Pentecostal emphases, including the "imminence of the pre-millennial return of

---

[8] *The Apostolic Faith* 1 (September 1906), p. 1.

[9] *The Apostolic Faith* 1 (September 1906), p. 1.

[10] By the printing of the second issue of *The Apostolic Faith* (October 1906), p. 3, "Eight missionaries have started to the foreign field since this movement began at Los Angeles a few months ago. About thirty workers have gone out into the field."

[11] Synan, in *The Spirit Said "Grow,"* pp. 39–48, coined this term.

Jesus Christ, preceded by an outpouring of God's Spirit".[12] A theological revision was not unfamiliar to early Pentecostals. Parham's contention that tongues were meant to be a missionary gift that bypassed the language learning process[13] was quickly revised.[14] Pentecostal theology has been intuitively and experientially shaped; thus, the function of tongues was revised through experiential observations. Worse yet, the revision of the Pentecostal notion of eschatological urgency took place by default; that is, without any explicit or intentional process. The consequence of this seemingly irresponsible silence on the eschatological belief of the Pentecostal pioneers has been rather negative. It took until the 60s, but the message of the Lord's return began to disappear slowly but steadily from Pentecostal pulpits. This vacuum was quickly filled by the exact-opposite message of this-worldly concerns, such as blessing, church growth, and others. This second- and third-generation phenomenon coincided with the advent of the Charismatic movement, which by nature had more of this-worldly concern due to the mainline churches' established social and theological state.

One Hundred Years Later, Here...

It is important to note that Pentecostal Christianity in Asia began to make its presence known to its constituents in the 1960s and onwards. New Pentecostal missionaries of the second and later third generations from North America and Europe came with the revised version of eschatology. This was also when many Asian nations gained independence, coming out of their painful colonial past. But some countries, such as Vietnam, China, and Korea, remained divided. Establishing their self-identity often took ideological struggles and consequent bloodshed through civil wars (e.g. Indonesia, Malaysia, Myanmar, and Cambodia) and even all-out wars (Vietnam and Korea).

---

[12] R. M. Riss, "Latter Rain Movement," in Burgess and van der Maas, *The New International Dictionary of Pentecostal and Charismatic Movements*, p. 830.

[13] *The Apostolic Faith* 1.2 (October 1906), p. 1, recounts Charles Parham's experience suggesting that tongues were a "language of preaching": "Instantly the Lord took his [Parham's] vocal organs, and he was preaching the Word in another language. This man has preached in different languages over the United States, and men and women of that nationality have come to the altar and sought God." Under the title "Fire Still Falling," in the same issue of *The Apostolic Faith*, p. 2, a more explicit reference is found, "Missionaries for the foreign fields, equipped with several languages, are now on their way." Also under "Testimonies of Outgoing Missionaries" in the same issue, p. 6, it is plainly reported one "received the baptism with the Holy Ghost and the gift of the Uganda language." These quick surveys prove that the notion of tongues as the missionary language was widespread.

[14] By 1909, this popular notion of tongues as a Pentecostal missionary tool was simply abandoned as "many Pentecostals were becoming skeptical." James R. Goff, Jr, *Fields White Unto Harvest: Charles F. Parham and the Missionary Origins of Pentecostalism* (Fayetteville, AR: University of Arkansas Press, 1988), p. 16.

Asia presented more challenges to Pentecostal Christianity than Los Angeles did at the beginning of the twentieth century. It is essential to remind the reader that, during the 1920s and 30s, when the wave of the Azusa missionaries hit this continent, most Asian countries were still under colonial rules, the majority by Christian colonizers, but some (particularly East Asia) by non-Christian, thus often anti-Christian, colonial forces. In the former cases, already established Christian traditions (e.g. Reformed Christianity in Indonesia or the East Indies) posed a challenge to Pentecostal pioneers. In the latter, such as Korea and China, the challenge was more severe as Christianity, in general, was viewed as an anti-Japanese force; thus, a threat against the colonial authorities. Pentecostalism began to establish its presence after World War II, and we may observe the following characteristics.

The first is the revised version of Pentecostal eschatology. Until the 1950s, Pentecostal missionaries had a strong eschatological orientation.[15] For example, some Filipino balikbayan[16] missionaries from North America returned to the Philippines in the 1940s to preach their newfound Pentecostal message to their people. They gave up their American dream and returned to their own provinces in the Philippines to propagate the Pentecostal faith. Their new experience with the Holy Spirit gave them zeal and commitment, and the eschatological urgency of the imminent return of the Lord caused them to return to the Philippines.[17]

The waning eschatological expectation among Western Pentecostals and the arrival of the message of hope "for here and now" through the Charismatic movement from the 1960s quickly affected the theological orientation of many Pentecostal churches in Asia. Unlike the first half of the twentieth century, the second half witnessed the influx of Western (often North American) evangelists holding mass evangelistic crusades, crowding radio and later TV channels with their messages. The speed with which the "Charismatic" version of the Pentecostal message spread heavily influenced Asian Pentecostal churches whose theological foundations were not yet solid.

For several decades, "Christ Is the Answer" was the most popular theme song among Pentecostals. Many churches were named after this title. Currently, the lyric reads,

> Christ is the answer to all my longing.
> Christ is the answer to all my needs,
> Saviour, Baptizer, the great Physician,
> Oh, hallelujah, He's all I need.

---

[15] In the 1960s and the early 70s, eschatological expectation was widespread in my own Christian experience in Korea.

[16] Returning Filipinos from overseas residency.

[17] Trinidad E. Seleky, "The Organization of the Philippines Assemblies of God and the Role of Early Missionaries," *Asian Journal of Pentecostal Studies* 8.2 (2005), pp. 271–82 (273), "They anticipated the early return of Christ and were constrained to spread the gospel to every tribe."

However, as some still remember, the last line originally read: "He is coming soon". If this popular contention is correct, all the experiences with Christ, such as salvation, the Spirit baptism, and healing, were originally understood as being with the end time. However, with this revision, the same experiences are perceived to mean life here and now. Today, Asian Pentecostal theology, in many places, is more accurately "Charismatic" with a good dose of influence from the prosperity gospel and the faith movement. The animistic orientation of Asian minds is a highly fertile ground for such "good news", with welcome supernatural help.

The second characteristic is this-worldly attention. This revised version of Pentecostal eschatology, with the resulting lack of major eschatological components, began to direct the attention of Christian life from the "other world" to this world. In a sense, the eschatological immediacy was replaced by the immediacy of God's action in daily life.

As briefly observed above, this "here and now" relevancy of the Pentecostal message found a suitable audience in Asia, as daily suffering was the immediate context. In addition to the political struggles Asian nations faced in the latter part of the twentieth century, simple daily survival was Asia's greatest challenge. Regardless of the sources of poverty in different parts of Asia, economic hardship was compounded by a rising population, to the point that, for example, China imposed the one-child policy per family. Depleted natural resources by the colonial powers, deeply rooted structural corruption, social unrest, and an inefficient socialist or communist system in some parts of Asia have driven many Asian societies to the extreme edge for survival. The preaching of the Pentecostal message, by this time fully revised through Charismatic influences, was indeed good news for everyone.

For instance, David Yonggi Cho, who grew up under the harsh Japanese colonial rule and the devastation of the Korean War, received a Christian message that was much different from what was being preached in existing churches.[18] This gospel introduced him to the God who heals and performs miracles "here and now". This God is good, not only after death but also now. Although his theology was initially shaped under classical Pentecostal missionaries, theological influences also came from Charismatic sources. His Yoido era (1973–2008) saw pulpit guests such as Robert Schuller, Oral Roberts, and other popular Charismatic preachers. His *Fourth Dimension*,[19] a million-seller throughout the world, proves that his theology has a strong Charismatic character. The high expectation of God's supernatural intervention in human life is the central message of Cho, often punctuated with testimonies of healing and miracles. We can sum up his message as a theology of blessing through the

---

[18] E.g. Young-hoon Lee, "Life and Ministry of David Yonggi Cho," in *David Yonggi Cho: A Close Look at His Theology and Ministry*, pp. 3–23 (3–4).

[19] *The Fourth Dimension*, vols 1–2 (South Plainfield, NJ: Bridge Publishing, 1979 and 1983).

supernatural intervention of God. This explains why 3 John 2 has been the most popular passage in his church: "Dear friend, I pray that you may enjoy good health and that all may go well with you, even as your soul is getting along well" (NIV).

However, it is unfair to give all the credit for Cho's theological shaping to Charismatic influences. His theology also bears the distinct mark that Christian (in this case, Pentecostal-Charismatic) theology has wrestled with the context of suffering. If we borrow Cox's theory, deprivation in human life and eschatological hope have been the main context and causes for Pentecostal churches' growth throughout the world.[20] Like Latin America, Asia's Pentecostal growth can, in part, be attributed to the sheer challenges of life. The fact that most Pentecostal believers in Asia come from the lower social strata proves this point. Only recently, Pentecostal congregations have begun to attain respectability in some Asian societies, thus attracting the more educated and established in social and economic aspects.

This revised version of eschatology also came with some surprising positive contributions. Attention to social issues and environmental concerns among some Asian Pentecostals has been possible because of this-worldly orientation. The growing awareness of the potential of socio-political influence was clearly brought about during the 2004 presidential election in the Philippines. A Charismatic minister among the presidential candidates[21] and the nine-million-strong Catholic Charismatic group publicly endorsed a candidate. The recent Indonesian election also witnessed many Pentecostal ministers running for public posts. Aside from the question of whether these decisions were right or not, both incidents indicate Pentecostal-Charismatic believers' awareness of the potential of their socio-political influence, as well as their determination to exercise it. The Korean Pentecostals included their prayer for the environment, beginning in the 1980s. During the World Assemblies of God Conference in Seoul, Korea (1994), the published prayer for the gathering listed environmental concerns among the first four prayer topics.

Another surprising development is the social service area. Malaysian Pentecostal-Charismatic churches, for example, have pioneered social service programmes for the neglected. Homes for orphans, single mothers, the elderly, and drug addicts have become a regular feature of many Pentecostal churches.

---

[20] E.g. Harvey Cox, *Fire From Heaven: The Rise of Pentecostal Spirituality and the Reshaping of Religion in the Twenty-First Century* (Reading, MA: Addison-Wesley, 1995), p. 58, for the Azusa Street Mission.

[21] "Brother" Eddie Villanueva, the founder (in 1978) of the Jesus Is Lord, the "biggest born-again Christian group" with its claim of five million members, was the presidential candidate. He once held a prayer rally for the nation, attracting not only one million participants (according to the organizer) but also Catholic bishops, religious leaders, and many politicians. Leslie Ann Aquino and Raymund Antonio, "Thousands Join JIL Anniversary Rites, Prayer Rally at Rizal Park," *Manila Bulletin* 3 (October 2005), p. 1, 6.

This began as a creative evangelistic strategy because Muslim law prohibits public evangelistic activities to Muslim Malays. Also, we have seen the formation of a growing number of non-governmental organizations (NGOs) among Asian Pentecostal churches. Equally unexpected are the ecumenical initiatives of some Asian Pentecostal leaders and churches. The exponential growth of Pentecostal churches has increased their influence among Christian communities. They cooperate in local and national ecumenical initiatives and have started to lead ecumenical movements. The Korean Assemblies of God, which joined the Korean National Council of Churches (KNCC) in 1996, had one of their Pentecostal ministers become the general secretary of the ecumenical body. He set a goal to merge the KNCC with its Evangelical counterpart in Korea. Malaysia is another case in point. Early Pentecostal churches had traditionally kept interchurch activities at arm's length, sometimes by choice but more often by external forces. On the other hand, Malaysian Pentecostal leaders have actively cooperated with other Evangelical churches to the point that more than half of the current executive members of the National Evangelical Christian Fellowship Malaysia are Pentecostal-Charismatic.[22] Also, the chairman of the board of the Philippine Council of Evangelical Churches is a Pentecostal minister. However, it is critical to note that these encouraging signs are still far from widespread.

Third, this radical shift of attention from other-worldly to this-worldly concerns has become an enormous challenge to Christianity in Asia. Asia has birthed many of the world's religions and animistic religious beliefs. Traditional gods have been used, even exploited, for the worshipper's benefit. Spiritual power without an eschatological goal and moral commitment can easily fall into religious utilitarianism. And this would make the Christian faith not much different from animism and shamanism. Also, church growth seems to have replaced (cross-cultural) mission as the ultimate goal of the church. Admittedly, church growth has been a positive influence in making Christianity known in predominantly non- or often anti-Christian societies. However, the church growth movement has evolved into a shape representing the this-worldly orientation of Pentecostal Christianity. More seriously, this attention to the growth of local churches may have taken place at the expense of global mission, an essential theological tradition of Pentecostalism. Recently, a needed reflection on the megachurch movement has taken place with suggested alternative approaches.[23]

---

[22] Yeu Chuen Lim, "Malaysian Evangelical Fellowship" (email message to the author, 3 October 2005). More information about the organization is available at http://www.necf.org.my. Accessed 3 October 2005.

[23] E.g. David Lim, "A Missiological Evaluation of David Yonggi Cho's Church Growth," in *David Yonggi Cho: A Close Look at His Theology and Ministry*, pp. 181–207, strongly advocates church multiplication.

A careful examination of the record of Pentecostal expansion seems to suggest that, unlike the common notion that Pentecostalism is predominantly a missionary movement, it has an equally, if not more substantial, renewal potential among existing churches. One can quickly point to the advent of the Charismatic movement, which literally "renewed" existing churches. Perhaps even more critical is an observation that Pentecostalism seems to flourish more in already Christianized areas than in "virgin" territories.[24] If the primary missionary character of the movement is to be proven, there must be growing Pentecostal churches in places where there is little Christian witness. However, that is rarely the case.[25] Latin America and some parts of Africa are good examples. This has caused a debate on proselytism in existing churches.[26] The only exception known to the author may be China. Most of the house church networks in rural China are indeed characteristically Pentecostal in belief and worship;[27] yet, this phenomenon is more "indigenous" in nature and origin than the result of Pentecostal missionary efforts.

This calls for a recovery of the early Pentecostal commitment to soul-winning, especially the cross-cultural variety. The history of the Western Pentecostal movement has already demonstrated that the expansion of missionary work is not solely fuelled by eschatological urgency. Even among second- and third-generation Pentecostals, the missionary movement continues to flourish. For example, in US Assemblies of God (2,729,000 adherents), only 5.2 percent of the world Assemblies of God family (52,811,000) has sent 33 percent (or 2,590) of the global Assemblies of God missionary force (7,796).[28] The Pentecostal mission has been known to be triumphalist in its attitude, partly due to its success but also its "power missiology". Their aggressive approach to "converting" even believers, under the pretext that they are nominal, has been viewed as a sign of spiritual arrogance. As the Edinburgh Conference's centenary approached, the

---

[24] This observation was made by Alan Johnson, a Pentecostal missionary to Thailand, in February 2005 in Baguio, Philippines. In his follow-up, he argues, "… my gut impression is that you are hard pressed to find a place where Pentecostals went that was a resistant hard to reach group and they either a) were the first ones there or b) had a breakthrough. Instead, what you tend to see is that where the church among every stripe has grown greatly, Pentecostals have grown greatly. Where the church is small, Pentecostals are small." Allan Johnson, "On Chapel Service" (email message to the author, 6 October 2005).

[25] This does not mean that in "difficult" areas such as Thailand and Japan, there are no large Pentecostal-Charismatic churches, but their overall impact on the larger church world and to society has not been felt.

[26] The 1997 joint statement of the fourth phase of the international Catholic–Pentecostal dialogue (1990–1997) was titled "Evangelization, Proselytism and Common Witness." For the full text, see *Asian Journal of Pentecostal Studies* 2.1 (1999), pp. 105–51.

[27] See Luke Wesley, *The Church in China: Persecuted, Pentecostal, and Powerful* (Baguio, Philippines: AJPS Books, 2005), esp. pp. 35–67.

[28] Assemblies of God World Missions, "Current Facts and Highlights: As of December 31, 2004" (Springfield, MO: Assemblies of God World Mission, 2005).

Western church called for the new shaping of Christian mission in humility and hope.[29] As a movement of the poor fired up by the Holy Spirit,[30] Pentecostal mission needs to recover its trademark of power mission and, more importantly, its humble attitude.

There is more reason to be mindful of the triumphalist attitude of Pentecostal mission. We cannot dismiss the reality of human suffering with simple faith statements. Asians, including Pentecostal believers, are living in a constant struggle for survival. It is simply impossible to list all the factors contributing to suffering. The magnitude of natural and "(hu)man-made" disasters claims thousands of lives, as seen in the tsunami incident in the Indian Ocean in December 2004 and the earthquake in Pakistan in 2005. Many terrorist attacks have been staged in Asia, be it in Iraq, the southern Philippines, or Bali, Indonesia. Turning to the Christian scene, for about three years since 1996, 275 Christian churches were closed, vandalized, destroyed, or burned by Muslims in Indonesia. Close to one half (121 churches) were Pentecostal churches, and next on the list were Catholic churches (18).[31] In many countries, gathering for Christian worship is still illegal, and subject to state punishment, including death. An average first-generation Christian in Asia has to overcome much marginalization and even persecution from family and society.[32] Perhaps the highest proportion of modem martyrdom occurs in Asia, partly due to the highly volatile religious context. A triumphalist pronouncement of miracles and healings will not resolve this very real challenge. It will take far more than a band-aid treatment; this is where a proper understanding of Christian life from a balanced eschatological perspective becomes critical.[33]

Equally urgent is a proper understanding of blessing. Due to the dire situation, God's blessing – supernatural, economic, or social – will continue to be the main focus of Asian Christianity. For Asian Pentecostals to avoid the grave theological

---

[29] Towards 2010, "Edinburgh 2010 – Mission in Humility and Hope" (2005), www.towards2010.org.uk. Accessed 15 October 2005.

[30] See Chapter 6.

[31] Paul Tahalele, *The Church and Human Rights in Indonesia* (Surabaya, Indonesia: Indonesia Christian Communication Forum, 1998), pp. 7–20; Gani Wiyono, "Pentecostalism in Indonesia," in Allan Anderson and Edmond Tang (eds), *Asian and Pentecostal: The Charismatic Face of Christianity in Asia* (Oxford: Regnum Books; Baguio, Philippines: APTS Books, 2005), p. 320, points out the aggressive evangelistic activities as the main cause; thus, in a sense, self-invited.

[32] One less drastic and yet common example is found in Wonsuk Ma and Julie C. Ma, "Jesus Christ in Asia: Our Journey With Him as Pentecostal Believers," *International Review of Mission* 94 (October 2005), pp. 493–506.

[33] David Yonggi Cho, at a monthly prayer meeting of the Korean Evangelical Fellowship on 8 April 2005, publicly repented of his preaching of [God's] "cheap grace" which more accurately refers to [physical and material] "blessing", while ignoring human suffering. Keun-young Kim, "Korean Church Leaders Repent" [in Korean], *Christian Today*, 9 April 2005, http://www.chtoday.co.kr/news/rs 6269.htm. Accessed 7 October 2005.

mistakes of the prosperity gospel, refining the popular theology blessing with the theological and eschatological understanding of Christian life in mind is urgent. The Spirit of God is the source of life, sustenance, rejuvenation, and restoration.[34] Thus, it is legitimate to expect the Holy Spirit to "bless" lives for their material, physical, emotional, social, and spiritual daily needs.[35] Here I stress "needs" (versus "desires"), as God's blessing is interpreted as God's gracious means for human sustenance. This may be called a "theology of blessing" compared to a "prosperity gospel".

What is more critical is the proper theological purpose of blessing. One valid Pentecostal interpretation is to subordinate blessings under God's empowerment for witnessing (Acts 1:8). Unlike the common supernatural perception of empowerment among Pentecostals, the "power" that the Holy Spirit endows can be understood broadly. Thus, elements seemingly less than supernatural, such as circumstances, should also be viewed as part of the Spirit's empowerment. The record in the Book of Acts, such as Paul's missionary journeys, seems to suggest this point repeatedly. If we follow this interpretation, the "blessing" attains its new missionary purpose and eschatological significance.[36] This would safely keep the theology of blessing from the dangerous utilitarian trap.

Ultimately, formulating a sound Pentecostal mission theology will be the goal of Pentecostal theological enquiries. It is fascinating that Pentecostal mission did not decline along with its early eschatological urgency. This perhaps explains that eschatology was not the sole or primary driving force for Pentecostal mission. By the time Pentecostalism reached the Asian shores, the "power" came, but "mission" was no longer in the boat. Much of the emphasis of early Pentecostal preaching was indeed on the power of God. The relative silence of mission can be explained in two ways: 1) Western Pentecostal missionaries were already doing mission,[37] and 2) given the "pagan" state of Asian nations, evangelism (versus "foreign" mission) was a more urgent task. However, even after the substantial growth of Pentecostal Christianity in many Asian countries, there is little evidence that the unique missionary theology of Pentecostalism distinguished itself from the rest of the churches in crossing cultural barriers to

---

[34] For a contextual argument, see Wonsuk Ma, "Asian (Classical) Pentecostal Theology in Context," in Anderson and Tang, *Asian and Pentecostal*, pp. 65–66.

[35] This is based on the creation-spirit tradition of the Old Testament, e.g. as found in Isaiah 32:14ff. Wonsuk Ma, *Until the Spirit Comes: The Spirit of God in the Book of Isaiah* (Sheffield: Sheffield Academic Press, 1999), pp. 25–32.

[36] For an elaborate treatment of this point, see Ma, "David Yonggi Cho's Theology of Blessing," pp. 140–59.

[37] It is also plausible that the early Western Pentecostal missionaries, like their colleagues, may not have had the "full-circle mission" understanding as advocated by C. Peter Wagner, *On the Crest of the Wave: Becoming a World Christian* (Ventura, CA: Regal Books, 1983), Chapter 9. For a Pentecostal reflection and possibility, see Wonsuk Ma, "Full Circle Mission: A Possibility of Pentecostal Missiology," *Asian Journal of Pentecostal Studies* 8.1 (2005), pp. 5–27.

be witnesses. For example, despite its robust growth in Korea, the rate of cross-cultural missionary growth is not the highest among denominations. The issue boils down to the theological foundation of how faithfully the missionary nature of Pentecostal theology was transmitted to Asians by Western missionaries. It is, therefore, surprisingly encouraging to see the steady and sometimes explosive growth of Asian Pentecostal missionary forces.[38] However, the question remains: what distinguishes Asian Pentecostal missionaries from the rest in their conviction and practices? There is no doubt that a healthy eschatology with the Pentecostal theology of empowerment will equip them to be a significant missionary force in the coming decades.

Toward Tomorrow

My suggestions are limited to the revision of Pentecostal eschatology, particularly in Asia. As Western Pentecostal scholarship continues its quest for revision,[39] Asians need to participate in this global journey by keeping in mind that every generation needs to hear the same message but often in a revised or re-cased form, and such collaborative work will benefit everyone.

Eschatology has at least two dimensions: the time of the Lord's return and the nature of the church and Christian life. Eschatological expectation involves the specific time of his return, as we have seen in early Pentecostal thought. Although no one knows when the urgency of the Lord's return was modified to an ambiguous future time ("soon"). This can be explained through the church's journey in history, as sandwiched between the Lord's ascension and the second coming. The end has begun, and history is moving toward the end of the end time. However, this does not always generate the kind of eschatological urgency which would create a "crisis mode" of life. For eschatology to be more relevant, it has to relate on a personal level. By looking at our life experiences, there are sufficient signs that Pentecostals yearn to "rediscover the original eschatological fervor that allowed them in the early years of the movement to swim against the stream of the spirit of the age and to advocate female participation in the ministry

---

[38] The new "Back to Jerusalem" missionary movement of the Chinese house church networks is an example. David Aikman, *Jesus in Beijing: How Christianity Is Transforming China and Changing the Global Balance of Power* (Washington, DC: Salem Books, 2006), pp. 103–205. Also, Paul Hattaway, *Back to Jerusalem: Three Chinese House Church Leaders Share Their Vision to Complete the Great Commission* (Waynesboro, GA: Authentic Media, 2003). An insider's voice provides a biblical rationale: Mingri Jin, *Back to Jerusalem with All Nations: A Biblical Foundation* (Oxford: Regnum Books, 2016).

[39] E.g. Daniel D. Isgrigg, *Imagining the Future : The Origin, Development, and Future of Assemblies of God Eschatology* (Tulsa, OK: ORU Press, 2021); Robert P. Menzies, *The End of History: Pentecostals and a Fresh Approach to the Apocalypse* (Springfield, MO: ACPT Press, 2022).

and interracial fellowship".[40] Its shape may not be identical to the early Pentecostal days, but the impetus is here. After all, we are people of the end time; either the Lord returns, or we go to him soon. Even though the Lord's return may not occur in our generation, this should not keep us from maintaining the eschatological urgency. Life's uncertainty and unpredictability, yet the certainty of the closure itself, are sure signs of our eschatological life.

The more critical aspect of eschatology is the nature of Christian life. We are in the world but not of the world. Asian Christians, including Pentecostal believers, are keenly aware that Christians bring "foreignness" to their context not because of its Western outlook but because of its radically "other" kingdom character.

We should bring the pilgrim identity of our life to the primary focus of Pentecostal Christianity, which will put the powerful experiential Christian life in the proper perspective, with eternity in sight. From the same eschatological perspective, we can interpret miracles and healing not as the manifestation of the "kingdom now" but as the token "invasion" of God's reign. Christ had inaugurated the kingdom, yet we anticipate its fulfilment in the unknown near future. Thus, any supernatural manifestation is to be taken as a reminder or "sign" of God's reign that has begun but has not been fully recognized. Donald Gee may be theologically sound when he argued that the gift of healing has its true value when it occurs with evangelism as the ultimate goal.[41]

The good news for Asian Pentecostals is that this is not the first revision of eschatology; church history attests well that every generation has struggled with this challenge, and there are sufficient examples from which we can learn.

Conclusion

Going back to the beginning of this reflection, it is not true that eschatology has been the only determinant in shaping Asian Pentecostal thinking and ethos to its present form. Yet the major shift in Pentecostal eschatology in the West has undeniably impacted Asian Pentecostalism.

The group that began as an anti-intellectual movement has come a long way as it crossed the Pacific Ocean in the past 100 years. Now Asia boasts more than two dozen graduate-level Pentecostal institutions, with at least four offering

[40] Macchia, "The Struggle for Global Witness," 23.

[41] Donald Gee, *Spiritual Gifts in the Work of Ministry Today* (Springfield, MO: Gospel Publishing House, 1963), pp. 72–73.

doctoral-level programmes.[42] The appearance of three international[43] and at least three vernacular Pentecostal journals in Asia attests to the rising interest in higher learning.

The revision of Pentecostal eschatology is inevitable. With the explosive growth on the one hand and the ever-changing social situations on the other, Asian Pentecostals are called to engage in the constant process of theological reflection. This is the only way the powerful spiritual tradition can appeal to ever-changing generations in this diverse continent. A proactive and intentional theological undertaking is the key to the future of healthy Pentecostalism. With much history behind us, Asian Pentecostals must demonstrate that we have learned an important lesson. Instead of blaming Western Pentecostal missionaries who unintentionally brought a revised eschatology to this most populated continent, we must evaluate whether we made intentional choices with proper evaluation of what was introduced to us. This may be the only way to renew this renewal movement and to keep Asian Pentecostalism from falling into the trap of a modernist pop religion or an extremely self-centred utilitarian religion.

---

[42] A recent survey includes six schools in Korea, one in Japan, three in the Philippines, three in Indonesia, three in Singapore, two in Malaysia, one in Hong Kong and at least five in India. If Oceania is included, at least two more schools are added.

[43] *Asian Journal of Pentecostal Studies* (Philippines), *The Spirit and Church* (Korea), and *Australasian Pentecostal Studies* (Australia). Also, *Journal of Youngsan Theology* by Hansei University, Korea.

10. Evangelism and Church Planting

In its epoch-making gathering in 1910, the Edinburgh Missionary Conference prayed to achieve the "evangelization of the world in our [their] generation". The Conference was clear and correct in believing that evangelism is the heart of Christian mission. There will be no Christianity without Christians, just as there is no church without believers. Unfortunately, theological sophistication, over-consciousness of political correctness, and the presence of other faiths, especially in the West, have put evangelism in the backseat of mission discussion. It is high time to restore evangelism to the centre of Christian mission. However, the approaches used will need to be "as wise as a serpent" in the delicate religious context. "Saving soul" has been the foundation for Pentecostal mission. Indeed, for so long, evangelism, church planting, and ministerial training were the sum and definition of mission for many Pentecostal organizations. For example, the US Assemblies of God and its World Mission added care for the suffering in 2009 as part of its understanding of mission. Others argue that Christian mission should expand to include the "justice" dimension, such as social justice, public theology, reconciliation, and environmental care.[1] Within the Pentecostal circles, addressing immediate social issues has been a long-held tradition. For example, David Yonggi Cho took God's goodness and power to the centre of his message to the poverty-stricken, post-war Korean population. And I also argue elsewhere that Pentecostals are to expand their mission understanding and activities to include both "caring" and "justice".[2] However, even though one takes the pressing circumstance as the starting point, Pentecostals always end with saving souls for eternal life. It is the pattern of Jesus: his ministry may begin with feeding the hungry and healing the sick, but he always drives home the proclamation of God's kingdom.

Changes in Global Christianity and Its Future Prospects

Statistics agree on the radical shifts of global Christianity from the second half of the twentieth century. Today, more than two-thirds of Christians live in the southern continents (or the Global South): Africa, Asia, and Latin America. This

---

[1] Ecumenical missiology has developed this aspect for decades. See Jooseop Keum (ed.), *Together Towards Life: Mission and Evangelism in Changing Landscapes* (Geneva: WCC Publications, 2013).

[2] Ma and Ma, "Missiology: Evangelization, Holistic Ministry, and Social Justice," pp. 279–89.

change is the celebrated fruit of centuries of Western Christian mission, beginning with the sixteenth-century Catholic mission to Latin America, parts of Africa, and Asia to the modern Protestant mission in the nineteenth and twentieth centuries. The rising of Pentecostal/Charismatic Christianity, initially in the West, quickly spread in the South and gave birth to countless forms of "spiritual" churches in all the southern continents. The rise of the African Independent Churches and the Chinese house church networks represents how this particular form of the Christian faith adapts to local spiritual/religious and social contexts. Unfortunately, this exceptional gain has been dwarfed by the steady decline of churches in the modern Christian heartland – the West. This partly explains why Christianity has receded in the last 100 years by 2.6 percent (from 34.8 percent in 1910 to 33.2 percent of the world's population).[3]

This recent shift, however, should be understood in the larger context of changes in global Christianity. The *Atlas of Global Christianity* reveals the North–South shifts of global Christianity in each millennium of church history.[4] In the first millennium of church history, the concentration of Christianity was in Asia Minor and North Africa until the rise and expansion of Islam marked the end of this era.[5] The second era is the flourishing of Christianity in what is called the "West". The golden period of the second era is between 1400 and 1910, coinciding with the colonial expansion of Western power.

What the Change Implies

It is immediately clear that several points are emerging from this global and historical survey. The first is the tremendous missionary achievement in the last 100-year period, which saw, in fact, the largest gain in the entirety of Christian history. A staggering net of 1,680.5 million new Christians was added, from 613 million (in 1910) to 2,292.5 million (in 2010), a growth of 3.75 times. The increase in Africa is most dazzling: from 11.7 million (in 1910) to 494.7 million (in 2010), a 42.3-fold growth.[6] In addition to the work of Western missionaries, this tremendous expansion can be attributed to several significant factors: a series of revivals, the rise and spread of Pentecostal/Charismatic Christianity, the strengthening of local leadership, and the appearance of indigenous forms of Christianity, among others.

Second, despite this historical spread, Christianity's share of the world's population in the same period dropped from 34.8 percent to 33.2 percent: thus, a recession. As mentioned above, while the South accomplished a tremendous gain, the North lost its Christian ground, cancelling the net gains. During the

---

[3] Johnson and Ross, *Atlas of Global Christianity*, p.11.

[4] Todd Johnson and Sun Young Chung, "Christianity's Centre of Gravity, AD 33–2100," in *Atlas of Global Christianity*, pp. 50–51.

[5] Johnson and Chung, "Christianity's Centre of Gravity," p. 50.

[6] Unless stated otherwise, all the statistics are taken from *Atlas of Global Christianity*.

same period, Islam, another global and increasingly missionary religion, recorded a substantial increase: from 12.5 percent of the world's population (in 1910) to 22.4 percent (in 2010), an almost two-fold growth. Its gain in the actual number of believers leaves all other religions, including Christianity, far behind. It is perhaps helpful to remind ourselves that, except for a short period around 1910, world Christianity has never crossed the one-third line of the world's population throughout its two-millennium history. We will pick up on this point later.

Third, the onus of future mission lies heavily on the shoulders of the churches in the Global South. Much of the exponential spread of Christianity in the last century results from committed work by nationals, often without outsiders' involvement. The shape of Christianity due to these national initiatives is closer to the cultural context of the people the church serves, although sometimes theological questions can be raised. All the Central and Latin American nations are "Christian", and many African Sub-Saharan countries have Christian majorities. Some of these churches are emerging as new missionary forces. Also, the northward influx of immigration has changed many Western nations' racial and religious landscape, where Christianity has been dwindling. This missionary potential, however, meets with formidable challenges, and they are primarily theological and practical. Again, we will pick up on this point later.

Fourth, along with the fast de-Christianization of Western Europe and North America and "strongholds" of non-Christian organized religions, the last frontier for Christian mission is Asia. With a sheer 53 percent of the world's population scattered in this vast continent (2010 figure), how Christianity fares here will have the most significant implication on the future of world Christianity. Currently, the evangelization rate in Asia is 8.5 percent, only a quarter of the world's average. Knowing that this is the very birth continent of Christianity, the trace of the recent growth trajectory of the Christian movement in Asia provides a glimmer of hope for tomorrow's global landscape.

Evangelistic Possibility of the One-Third Wall!

One historic mission question we can ask is the following: can global Christianity break the one-third barrier in our lifetime? It is a relatively modest ambition compared to the record of 100 years ago. Nonetheless, the goal is exceptionally formidable, as this has never been achieved throughout church history. Admittedly, although in 1910 Christianity reached a record 34.8 percent of the world's population, it did not sustain that growth, and the accuracy of specific numbers is often in question. The 1910 Conference must have had genuine faith or expectation that the complete evangelization of the world was within their reach.

100 years forward, we now cautiously revisit this audacious aspiration. There are several convincing reasons why this belief is plausible. One is the concentration of the Christian population and its growth. The three southern

continents hold close to 84 percent of today's world population, and their Christian rate was 61 percent (compared to the 33.2 percent global rate) in 2010. Latin America has remained a Christian continent (92.5 percent evangelization rate) for centuries, although its composition has significantly changed in recent years. Africa's ascension to become a Christian continent is a twentieth-century missionary marvel. Today, 47.9 percent of its 1,032 million are Christians, and the rate will be much higher for Sub-Sahara alone.

But Asia, the largest continent and the home of 4,623.5 million in 2020, holds the key to the historical realization of Christianity's advancement beyond the one-third barrier of the world's population. There are several critical reasons to believe that the future growth of Asian Christianity can be expected. First, the recent growth of energy in many Asian countries is impressive. For example, the development of indigenous Christianity in China after the Cultural Revolution is nothing short of a miracle. The expansion of Indian and Indonesian Christianity is also encouraging.

Second, there is a strong missionary consciousness leading to the formation of a missionary movement. Korea, the Philippines, India, Malaysia, and Indonesia have emerged as critical missionary-sending forces. China's missionary zeal is popularized in the "Back to Jerusalem" movement. Third, in Asia, almost half of Christians are categorized as Pentecostal/Charismatic, the segment that has fuelled global growth. Although this claim is subject to verification, spiritual dynamism characterizes Asian Christianity. These and other factors reasonably suggest the continuing growth of Christianity in Asia.

However, this rational construction of Christianity's future is always precarious, as the same mistake was made 100 years ago. With all political, cultural, economic, and religious powers at their disposal, and standing at the highest vista point of the entire church history, Western mission leaders were confident that the world's evangelization could be a true reality in their lifetime. With the same dose of faith and strategy, this good judgement was quickly shattered by the two world wars in their generation, fought among Christian nations, except for one. There is no guarantee that we are not making the same mistake this time. Therefore, it is critical to admit that mission belongs to God, and we have been graciously invited to partner in God's plan for restoration.

Pentecostal Gift of Evangelization

If Pentecostalism holds the key to the continuing expansion and growth of global Christianity, in what ways can we expect it to play such a pivotal role? Several unique features of the Pentecostal faith contribute to this expectation.

Empowered Evangelists

In several places, I have discussed the unique strength of Pentecostals as evangelists. Baptism in the Holy Spirit represents well the process of Pentecostal formation for witnessing. It provides at least two theological grounds for evangelism: 1) Every believer's call and commission to witness to Christ, and 2) empowerment through the Holy Spirit.[7] And this strong spiritual motivation is further enhanced by believers' encounters with God, often supernatural in nature. In addition to often radical conversion experience and Spirit baptism, many Pentecostal believers either experienced their own healing or of someone close to them. Thus, they are story-bearers. The combination is already explosive: powerful motivation and an experiential dimension, resulting in a unique and dynamic message to share. In the Pentecostal tradition, the sharing of testimonies has been a regular part of worship or prayer meetings. The members are invited to tell their experiences with God. The home cell meetings, popularized by David Yonggi Cho's Yoido Full Gospel Church in Korea, open a wide space for such experiences to be shared with the cell members and non-believing visitors. In this semi-formal setting, people interact with one another through questions, input, and encouragement. With their enthusiasm and mobility, this story-telling evangelism continues in their neighbourhoods and workplaces. It is also common for Pentecostal churches to mobilize their members for short-term and long-term missionary programmes. Women's empowerment in evangelism is particularly significant. In many cultures, women are socially marginalized, and this value is generally shared in church structures. But women are natural communicators; thus, good evangelists. The sphere of their social engagement also creates a natural space for evangelism. As fellow women are reached, their secondary evangelistic influence can spread to the entire family. This can also result in the social empowerment of women.

In missionary settings, evangelism is a low-cost or no-cost ministry, enabling any church to send missionaries to the next town or to a neighbouring tribe or country, even if they are poverty-stricken. This has an important implication for forming a new missionary paradigm: mission in the position of weakness, without requiring superior power or an advanced economy.

Sustained Growth

The presence of a vibrant Christian community in society is a "sign and portent" of God's kingdom in their midst. It is especially true where Christianity as a minority religion is present in the context of dominant religion(s). This unique gift of Pentecostalism is expressed in several areas. Statistics attest to the saturated state of Pentecostal churches, especially in the growing Global South. The 2017 statistics reveal that 63 percent of 2,479.6 million world Christians now live in the South. Among them are 669.2 million Pentecostals, or 27 percent

---

[7] Wonsuk Ma, "Pentecostal Theological Formation: Serving the Future of Global Christianity and the Movement (sec 1)," *Pentecostal Education* 7.2 (Fall 2022), pp. 265–73.

of world Christians. [8] However, in the Global South, the proportion of Pentecostal believers is much higher at 35.7 percent, while in the North, the rate was only 12.9 percent in 2010.

The growth of Pentecostal Christian families in the last 100 years is unprecedented. Its spread in the Global South is particularly compelling. In the 2010 report, in Africa, where Christianity grew 42-fold in a century, about 32.9 percent of Christians were Pentecostal in various forms. In Latin America, the rate was 28.4 percent, but in Asia, it is a whopping 51 percent!

More significantly, the annual growth rate in the year 2000 of Pentecostal Christianity (2.22 percent) is the highest among Christian groups (1.33 percent) and all religions. The highest among non-Christian religions is Islam, at 1.91 percent. Independents record the next highest growth at 2.21 percent, many of which groups are considered leaning toward Pentecostal beliefs and ethos. These two categories (669.1 million Pentecostals and 437.4 million Independents in 2017) make the second-largest Christian group after Catholics (1,231 million in 2017). Pentecostal Christianity has not only grown but is also expected to grow continually. By 2050, this combined group (1,791.5 million) will outgrow the Catholics (1,268.6 million).[9]

Saturated Presence of Pentecostal Congregations

Pentecostal evangelism, as a rule, aims at the establishment of a believing community or a local church. The presence of Pentecostal believers and communities is almost ubiquitous. Statistics again attest to this saturated presence.

According to *Operation World* (2010 edition), in Burkina Faso, the 1.1 million (Pentecostal) Assemblies of God denomination has 7,100 congregations, while the 1.9 million Catholic Church has 2,420 churches. This means the Assemblies of God adds a new congregation with just 155 people, while the Catholic Church would add one congregation where there are 785 people. The number of Spirit-filled believers in the country is 2.55 million, combining denominational Pentecostals and Charismatic believers in Evangelical and Catholic churches.[10]

In Brazil, there are 103.8 million Catholics scattered in 9,250 churches, while the Assemblies of God has 15.7 million in 116,000 churches. In other words, it takes the Catholic Church 11,221 people before a new local church is opened, while for the Assemblies of God, only 135 people will result in a new

---

[8] The statistics are from Todd M. Johnson, Gina A. Zurio, Albert W. Hickman, and Peter F. Crossing, "Christianity in 2017: Five Hundred Years of Protestant Christianity," *International Bulletin of Mission Research* 41.1 (2017), pp. 47–49. The 2010 figures are from Johnson and Ross, *Atlas of Global Christianity*, p.71.

[9] However, a significant double counting is assumed in these two categories.

[10] Mandryk, *Operation World*, p. 177.

congregation.[11] This shows how the Pentecostal church has a saturated presence across the world, reaching out to small villages and urban centres. And the expansion is ongoing.

One critical reason for the difference between the Catholic and Pentecostal presence is the worker-supply issue. The shortage of Catholic clergy has been a widespread problem. As the existing churches struggle to remain open due to clergy shortage, adding new churches is not a priority.[12] On the other hand, Pentecostal business people, for example, can turn to pioneering pastors literally "overnight" due to its "everyone is called" theology. The same democratization of ministry causes the birth of new churches in storefronts and living rooms. This grassroots saturation provides them with an unusual opportunity to deeply penetrate and affect social life. This extensive network of churches and their (both volunteer and paid) workers have a unique potential for witnessing at various fronts of social life.

Mega-Movements

There are two "mega" phenomena in Pentecostal Christianity relevant to evangelism. The first is the megachurch movement. This recent development is primarily a Pentecostal feature. Regardless of denominational links, most megachurches today in large cities of the world exhibit Pentecostal types of worship songs, fervent prayer (for healing, for example), and messages.[13]

At the beginning of the new century, Younggi Hong, a Yoido Church insider, undertook a study among Korean megachurches and concluded that an overwhelming majority are Pentecostal/ Charismatic in their worship, theological orientation, and emphasis on the work of the Holy Spirit. His sample churches include Presbyterian, Methodist, Baptist, and Assemblies of God.[14]

In the Christian-declining West, large churches are of this Pentecostal variety as well. In London, they include the Nigerian-led Kingsway International Christian Centre and a Charismatic Anglican congregation such as Holy Trinity Brompton, known for its Alpha Course.

---

[11] Mandryk, *Operation World*, p. 163.

[12] For example, "Catholic Church Weighs Future in Tuscarawas Country as Priest Shortage Grows," *Times Reporter*, 20 September 2022, https://www.timesreporter.com/story/news/local/2022/09/20/columbus-catholic-diocese-church-grapples-with-shortage-of-priests-immaculate-conception/65648211007/?utm_source=Pew+Research+Center&utm_campaign=37101197f0-EMAIL_CAMPAIGN_2022_09_22_02_00&utm_medium=email&utm_term=0_3e953b9b70-37101197f0-400066549. Accessed 23 September 2022.

[13] Leadership Network, "Global Megachurches," http://leadnet.org/world (accessed 23 March 2023); and Hartford Institute of Religion Research, "Database of Megachurches in the US," http://www.hartfordinstitute.org/megachurch/database.html (accessed 23 March 2023).

[14] Young-gi Hong, "The Backgrounds and Characteristics of the Charismatic Mega-churches in Korea," *Asian Journal of Pentecostal Studies* 3.1 (2000), p. 101.

A large-size gathering or congregation is one characteristic of this Christian family. Does the size matter? Yes, it does, especially in social contexts where Christianity is marginal. When the Hope of Bangkok Church empties thousands of its members into the streets after its worship service, people will look at this size as having the credibility of the Christian faith in this Buddhist nation.[15]

The second "mega" feature is the tradition of mass evangelistic campaigns, often emphasizing healing. For example, Oral Roberts led massive tent meetings in the 1940s and 50s. T. L. Osborne was another popular evangelist known for his international ministries, especially with his en masse healing prayers, setting a new paradigm.[16] Many Pentecostal evangelists formed their own evangelistic associations, raised funds, and expanded their operations. Early Pentecostals, such as William Seymore of the Azusa Street Mission, operated media outlets such as magazines, radio and TV programmes, and a mass mailing system. The stories of healing and salvation travelled far and wide, opening more doors for the gospel. Often such large-scale events are interdenominationally organized and hosted to benefit the local churches in the area from the evangelistic fruits.

Daniel King uses Reinhard Bonnke as a prime example of this unique Pentecostal tradition, mass healing evangelism. Hugely successful in his ministry in Africa for four decades, the magnitude of his gatherings is staggering: 1.6 million people came to hear him on a single day in Logos, Nigeria, in November 2000.[17] King enumerates the following reasons for his success: 1) using miracles as "an attractional method" to the gospel, 2) his popularity, and 3) his ability to carefully plan, organize, and implement massive gatherings.[18] The result of his ministry is over 78 million documented decisions for Christ.[19] Although they differ in scale, Pentecostals have effectively used public "crusades" for mass evangelism.

The Empowerment Cycle

These remarkable dynamics for evangelism and church planting continue the cycle of empowerment. As argued elsewhere,[20] the emphasis on the "empowerment" of the Holy Spirit in Pentecostal missiology responds to the long-standing challenge of Christian mission. Newly evangelized churches in mission fields have not become missionary churches. This has resulted in the

---

[15] "The Hope of Bangkok," (n.d.), https://www.thaimissions.info/gsdl/collect/thaimiss/index/assoc/HASH0296.dir/doc.pdf, (accessed 23 March 2023).

[16] Daniel D. King, "Mass Healing Evangelism: The Unique Contribution of the Spirit-Empowered Movement to the Practice of Evangelism," in Wonsuk Ma, Opoku Onyinah, and Rebekah Bled (eds), *The Remaining Task of the Great Commission and the Spirit-Empowered Movement* (Tulsa, OK: ORU Press, 2022), pp. 303–304.

[17] King, "Mass Healing Evangelism," p. 305.

[18] King, "Mass Healing Evangelism," pp. 305–307.

[19] King, "Mass Healing Evangelism," p. 305.

[20] Ma and Ma, *Mission in the Spirit*, Chapter 4, "Full Circle Mission."

perpetuation of the existing mission pattern: the world is divided between missionary-sending and missionary-receiving places.

However, Pentecostal "empowerment" missiology has motivated and prepared Christians and churches to be active evangelists and church planters. Our experience in the northern Philippines among the tribal groups demonstrated the rise of a new mission paradigm. From the very early stage, congregations actively sent out their members to adjacent villages to evangelize. Some crossed tribal boundaries to establish new churches in the neighbouring tribes. With almost no missionary intervention, within seven years, we saw five-generation churches.

There are four characteristics in this continuing cycle of evangelism and church planting. The first is the intuitive conviction that every believer is called to be an evangelist. Christian children speak to other children, Christian youths engage with other youths, and believing adults speak to their fellow adults. The second is that mission is what any church does from the first day of its existence. The new churches did not wait until a certain point of growth, facility, or maturity. They believed evangelism to be a natural part of being a church. The third is the power of healing and miracles through the Holy Spirit. Many villagers abandon their traditional spirit worship when they witness the manifestation of God's power through healing. Many new churches were established through the healing of a villager.[21] The fourth is the radical severance from the old religious system. We observed other Christian churches that accommodated the indigenous religious beliefs and practices as "cultural". This approach may have reduced any social tension in a community. However, the long-term result is not encouraging: many believers maintain their allegiance to both religious systems.[22] In contrast, Pentecostal preachers demand sole devotion to the Christian God, with a decisive severance from the old religion. This causes social tension, leading to the marginalization and persecution of the new believers. However, it is more likely that such an approach leads to evangelizing the entire village rather than the "compromising" one.

It is also my observation that Korean missionaries put efforts into teaching national churches to be missionary churches. Although it is not certain where this new attitude came from, Mission Naga for the Nagaland churches in Northeast India and Mission Romania are but two examples of structured mobilization of national churches by Korean missionaries. With the rise of the non-Western missionary movement, the "full-circle" mission throughout the globe is a reality. Indeed, the advent of the new missionary movement among the churches once evangelized by the Western churches is a fine testimony to the continuing cycle of mission empowerment!

---

[21] Ma, "More Powerful than Ancestor Spirits," pp. 47–49.

[22] Ma, *When the Spirit Meets the Spirits*, pp. 45–72.

Things That Will Determine This Dream

With a good dose of humility, however, I want to be cautiously optimistic that we are now living with the real possibility that global Christianity can increase over the one-third line, stay on the other side of the line, and even grow further. If this is the case, what would it take from our end to see the movement of the Spirit in this direction?

A Radical Rethinking of Mission

As elaborated elsewhere,[23] the radical southward shift of global Christianity and the rise of new missionary movements in the Global South call for a new understanding of mission and its practice. The current southward gravity is the second occurrence in history, and the first-millennium experience may help forge mission thinking and practice for the third millennium. However, this proposal is not based on a naïve idealization of the early period, including the early church. But a more critical look is required in assessing what is called the "receive" mission thinking and paradigm from the West, because it is that with which the new mission players from the Global South are familiar.

Although this is the product of its own (Western) context, mission thinkers in the South will have to critically evaluate whether this is close to what the Bible is teaching and if this is workable for them. One unmistakable part of the Western mission paradigm is the element of "power", be it political, economic, cultural, or even Christian. The powerful and developed Western nations were the main, or even only, mission players until recently.

This does not mean only the powerful can do mission. The problem is that this perception has become a reality or mission "rule" in the minds of new churches. This is where the early church record becomes highly relevant. Just as with the status of Jesus and Christianity, early believers were marginal: culturally, socially, politically, and religiously. They witnessed Christ through words, lifestyle, and work, but seldom from a position of power. They were ridiculed, marginalized, harassed, and persecuted. For example, Paul's Roman citizenship was never used to give weight to Christian witnesses. His exceptional learning, which resulted in several fine arguments in the New Testament, was not the basis of his preaching. The attitude and approach of early believers were closely related to the life of Jesus they preached: "[T]he Son of Man did not come to be served, but to serve, and to give his life as a ransom for man" (Matt. 20:28, NIV). Even if there is an element of "power", his followers were to deny such, like the Lord, "who … did not consider equality with God … rather, he made himself nothing by taking the very nature of a servant … humbled himself by becoming obedient to death – even death on a cross" (Phil. 2:6-8). This pattern

---

[23] See Chapter 4. Also, Wonsuk Ma, "A 'Fuller' Vision of God's Mission and Theological Education in the New Context of Global Christianity," in Charles van Engen (ed.), *The State of Missiology Today: Global Innovations in Christian Witness* (Downers Grove, IL: IVP, 2016), pp. 84–106.

of witnessing weakness and servitude is the mark of Christian mission. This, however, does not make full use of various "gifts" for effective witnesses, be they political advantage, economic resources, new opportunities, etc. At the same time, this calls us to critically test any "power" in the light of the evidence we have briefly considered. This is a foundational issue that will have endless implications for the understanding and approaches of mission.

Harnessing Simple Evangelistic Fervour

Zeal for and commitment to evangelism is a characteristic of growing churches, regardless of their location. It is especially true for the majority of churches in the South. A simplistic approach may sometimes violate political correctness, especially in religiously pluralistic societies, but this is the core of Christian mission and has been the main engine for growth. Of course, sometimes, "simple" zeal for evangelism can result in an undesirable outcome. Obsession with local church growth can easily betray the very purpose of evangelism: expanding God's kingdom.

With ignorance of Christ's churches' large and diverse reality, zeal for "saving souls" can also target Christians who are different from one tradition, resulting in proselytism among Christians. Nonetheless, evangelism should be upheld as the most crucial element of Christian mission, as evangelism involves ordinary believers and requires little or no training. As a popular saying goes, "Evangelism is a beggar telling another where to find bread." As experienced in one's own personal life, telling the good news of Christ is the main message. This applies to both "home" and "foreign" settings, although cross-cultural settings require additional considerations. This has the strong potential to make mission everyone's calling.

The Transition from Growth to Mission

The growth of new churches in the South is an extremely positive phenomenon which has changed Christianity's global landscape. New mission players are emerging steadily, and cross-cultural mission workers from these churches outnumbered traditional Western workers quite some time ago. Despite this encouraging sign, most churches in the Global South feel inadequate to consider missionary work. Unless these strong Christian nations are helped to become strong missionary nations, the dream of unprecedented growth over the one-third line will not happen.

What is the most significant practical obstacle for these churches? The most common is their struggle over economic resources. Many or even a majority of these nations are still economically developing or under-developed. Some are struggling to feed their growing populations. Some are still in the painful nation-building process. Perhaps for this socio-economic reason, these Christian-rich nations are heavily populated by missionaries. But the nationals, particularly their leaders, have not felt that a missionary call is someone else's.

However, this perception did not come from a reading of the early church's life, but through their experiences of mission as we know it today. Missionaries require substantial monetary resources, and this is not available to them. This requires a serious look at the established notion of mission and at missionary models that are close to the biblical vision of mission. These models will not be based on the availability of economic resources, but on teaching the scriptures, and rich missionary examples often found in the first millennium. For instance, Syriac Christians who spread the gospel to far frontiers such as China and India never enjoyed state sanctions but were constantly persecuted and marginalized.

Many historians argue that it is marginality that fuels missionary movements. Affluence and state protection eventually led the church to complacency and even corruption.[24] How this truth can be relived today in practical terms will be everyone's quest. While various models (old and new) are learned, explored, gathered, and evaluated, as discussed above, evangelism can be inexpensive and every person's mission engagement.

Learning to Live with and Witnessing to Other Faiths

Traditionally, missionary activities have been carried out in religiously crowded places. There are historic and organized religions and animistic ones deeply embedded in everyday life. The Western mission took various approaches to religions: from outright denial to positive accommodation. Today's mission takes religions more seriously, as some have become as "missionary" as Christianity has been. From the former Western mission perspective, one discernible difference is that new mission players are often practitioners of other religions. In earlier days, other religions were "out there", and often, the prevailing mission was to rescue them from the world and into the church. Surrounded by hostile cultural and religious forces, small Christian communities were to persevere until the day of salvation. Now these Christians who live right in the middle of strong religious forces are new mission players. They do not need to cross the sea to experience other religions. They live with them every day. Thus, they will have to construct an existential theology of religion so that Christians can live peacefully with other faiths. This is where mission begins.

Today, often, many cases of tension and violence are religiously motivated. The growing clash between Christians and Muslims in northern Nigeria is only one of many troubling cases. As neighbours, classmates, and workplace fellows, Christians, as followers of a religion of love, will have to make peace-making and reconciliation a mission priority. And this will have a huge implication on overall missionary engagement.

---

[24] For example, see Scott W. Sunquist, *Understanding Christian Mission: Participation in Suffering and Glory* (Grand Rapids, MI: Bakers Academic, 2013), pp. 23–168. Sunquist provides a helpful historical study of mission around the theme of "suffering and glory", suggesting that Christian mission has found hardship as well as power as God's gift for witnessing.

If we turn our eyes to the last frontier, Asia, other religions will be the most important mission consideration. With only one exception (the Philippines), Asia is religiously pluralistic, and this will most likely be the case in the future for good reasons.[25] In fact, in many places, Christianity is the newest organized religion. If this is the case, a realistic and immediate goal of Christian mission will be to learn to understand and live with other religions.

Globally speaking, while the Christians' share of the pie in the world population has shrunk in a century, the advance of Islam in the same period is more than impressive: from 12.6 percent to 22.4 percent, close to double. Why is this so? Numerous studies compare the movements of these two religions, suggesting answers to this question. The very nature of Islam is quite different from Christianity, and closer to Judaism in its social organization and operation. Consequently, according to one suggested theory, it creates a "progressive movement", resulting in a "once Muslim, forever Muslim" pattern. This is compared with the serial movement of Christianity, following a life cycle of birth, growth, maturing, and eventual waning, while it gives birth to new life in another place.[26] With its spread continuing now in the Western world through migration, Islam is expected to grow from 20.4 percent in 2005 to 23.2 percent of the world population by 2025. This is again compared with Christianity, growing from 33.1 percent to 33.6 percent in the same period.[27] The growth rate of Christianity in the same period (1.07 percent of the annual growth rate) is behind that of Islam (1.66 percent) and of Sikhs (1.16 percent).

How can we balance Christian commitment, peaceful living, and peace-building while affirming evangelism as the core of missionary calling? There is no easy answer. However, one important suggestion has been "holistic" evangelism through lifestyle, work, and word. Decades ago, in a survey among former Muslims who turned to Christianity, the experience of love from Christian neighbours was the most critical mode of evangelism. With the increasing number of Muslim immigrants, especially in the West, various evangelistic opportunities are available when promoting peaceful living. The role of Christian immigrants is crucial. This is one important area where mission leaders from the North and the South can combine their experiences for mission cooperations.

There are several other vital areas to consider, including church cooperation in mission. Christian immigrants as God's "plot" for mission, and the role of the Spirit-churches, or Pentecostal-Charismatic Christianity. I am sure other critical areas deserve close attention. As a Korean Pentecostal mission thinker and

---

[25] See Daniel H. Bays, *A New History of Christianity in China* (Malden, MA: Wiley-Blackwell, 2011), pp. 92–95. Bays contests the American idea of Christian China at the turn of the twentieth century.

[26] One recent attempt is Andrew F. Walls, "Christianity Across Twenty Centuries," *Atlas of Global Christianity*, pp. 48–49.

[27] Johnson et al., "Christianity in 2017," p. 7.

practitioner, I like to live with the one-third possibility despite the formidable challenges. One may ask why numbers matter that much: it is the matter of the heart that the gospel must transform. I would put the following, as a rule, in the minds of new mission people: first of all, in this world, there will be no Christianity in visible form without Christians and local churches. The presence of magnificent church buildings empty of worshippers (as we now see in the West) is a scandal to Christian witness. That is where the essential nature of evangelism in Christian mission is convincingly argued. Second, in a social context in which Christianity is a minority and involves being persecuted, a sizeable physical gathering of Christ's followers will serve as a "sign and potent" of the presence of God's kingdom in a particular society. Therefore, God's mission has already been present.

How to bring God's people to be intentionally taught and prepared for active mission is a universal quest, both in the South and the North. Cautiously, but with some assurance, I would like to claim that global Christianity will break the one-third wall in our lifetime, remain on the other side of this barrier, and even grow further. After all, it is God's mission!

11. Blessing

The rise and spread of the prosperity gospel (PG) in the 1960s in North America and worldwide have been controversial. In the minds of many, the PG has become the unfortunate face of Pentecostalism with its sensational promises and claims. Now generally branded as the "Word of Faith" movement, its leaders began to appear in the Charismatic scenes from the 1980s. For example, Kenneth Copleland is listed among the speakers in the 1987 New Orleans Charismatic Congress.[1] It was also called the "name it, claim it" movement.

There has been a plethora of literature by PG preachers, such as Kenneth Hagin, and various critical assessments of the movement. Now, having become a widespread religious phenomenon, the simple understanding of the PG as the combination of Pentecostal Christianity and Western consumerist capitalism no longer holds to diverse socio-economic contexts. More reflections are published, especially from life experiences with various social contexts.[2] Nowadays, such assessments are incredibly nuanced, a stark contrast to the blanket dismissal of many theological analyses.

The purpose of this study is to investigate theological elements of the PG to explore its potential in the shape of a particular social and religious attitude and behaviour. I believe that the Global South's generally positive and immanent religious attitude has much to do with religious dynamism directly and indirectly shaped through PG teachings. If this can be proven, an appropriately revised PG Christianity can continue to fuel the church's growth in the South and provide an essential spiritual key to the rejuvenation of Christianity in the North.

[1] Vinson Synan, *Where He Leads Me: The Vinson Synan Story* (Franklin Springs, GA: LifeSprings Resources, 2019), p. 167.

[2] For example, Katherine Attanasi and Amos Yong (eds), *Pentecostalism and Prosperity: The Socio-Economics of the Global Charismatic Movement* (London: Palgrave Macmillan, 2012).

Sociological studies, for example, have presented a variety of generally positive impacts of the PG in Africa,[3] Latin America,[4] Asia, and even Western Europe.[5]

My own journey with this initially unfamiliar stream of Pentecostalism, in this non-Western social context, will serve as a small window into the PG. From there, I will present several common theological logics among PG preaching. Then the crux of the investigation is the PG's influence on an attitude (both religious and existential) and behavioural change. I conclude the discussion with a reflection on the future development of the PG. Once "redeemed" and appropriately revised, the PG can become a Theology of Blessings (TB). The new expression will have the advantage of moving the issue away from the negatively tainted image of the PG.

Before we move on, several disclaimers are in order. First, it is helpful to remember that there is no such thing as THE PG, but many PGs. Similarities in terminology and even sometimes in behaviours of many PG preachers often conceal racially diverse motivations and theological orientations.[6] This is not to simply condemn the PG's Western original while blindly upholding the PG promoted in the southern continents. Even within the West, significant differences in motivation and context are found between white GP preachers, black ones, and recently emerging congregations among young urban professionals.

Interestingly, most PG preachers are found among Charismatic and independent Pentecostal groups, but less among classical Pentecostal denominations that have been relatively (self-) critical about the PG. Second, due to the motivation of my study, I do not include any historical and theological analysis, particularly of the West. My immediate focus is on the growing South and, eventually, the global scene of Christianity. I published a case study of David Yonggi Cho, and familiarity with this may also be helpful.[7]

---

[3] Paul Gifford's case study on Ghanaian Pentecostal churches provides an excellent window to the PG-type churches in Africa: Paul Gifford, *Ghana's New Christianity: Pentecostalism in a Globalizing African Economy* (Bloomington, IN: Indiana University Press, 2004).

[4] For example, Richard Shaull and Waldo Cesar, *Pentecostalism and the Future of Christian Churches: Promises, Limitations, Challenges* (Grand Rapids: Eerdmans, 2000) on the Brazilian context. Also, Eloy H. Nolivos, "Capitalism and Pentecostalism in Latin America: Trajectories of Prosperity and Development," in *Pentecostalism and Prosperity*, pp. 87–105.

[5] For example, Simon Coleman, *The Globalization of Charismatic Christianity: Spreading the Gospel of Prosperity* (Cambridge: Cambridge University Press, 2000).

[6] See Katherine Attanasi, "The Plurality of Prosperity Theologies and Pentecostalisms," in *Pentecostalism and Prosperity*, pp. 1–12.

[7] Wonsuk Ma, "David Yonggi Cho's Theology of Blessing," pp. 140–59.

A Korean with a Second Pentecostal "Conversion"

I was a post-Korean War lad, growing up out of war rubble and dire poverty. My Christian life was the traditional fatalism with a Western outlook. Growing up under a Christian mother, I became serious about the Christian faith in my early teens when my mother took a sister, stricken by polio, to a healing evangelist in a nearby city. For the first time, I got up early in the morning (yes, 4:30 a.m.), beat the cold, and went to the early morning prayer meeting at the church. The first change I noticed as a boy was a positive expectation of things around me. It was a change in my perspective rather than the circumstances, and this impression has remained with me.

However, a change in my view of God came with much struggle. My family began attending a Pentecostal church in my late teens that was not much different from other churches: God is to be revered or, more accurately, to be feared. The woman pastor of this "weeping church" shared the fatalistic theological outlook, except for more fervent behaviours, such as clapping hands while singing and praying in tongues. Yes, healing was expected, but the fundamental perspective was still other-worldly: there is nothing good about this side of heaven. In fact, through the early 1970s, the imminent return of the Lord was the most popular theme of annual revival meetings throughout Korea. Any hint of material prosperity ran the danger of reducing a high Christian religion to the territory of highly despised shamanism.

When I began my theological education in the early 1970s, my exposure to David Yonggi Cho with his theology and the growing church was a confusing experience. My biggest theological struggle was the difference in the nature of the Christian gospel between my hometown pastor and Cho. The former advocated almost a denial of worldly comforts and prosperity to be more spiritually attuned and committed. But Cho was the exact opposite: God cares not only for our spiritual needs but also our daily needs; thus, our physical and material ones. Another area where nervousness sprang up was the thin line (at least to me at that time) between Christianity and shamanism. Of course, it all boiled down to my understanding of my Christian God. Was he an object of fear or the subject of love?

My faith journey up until this time fostered a relatively passive attitude towards God; that is, we were to accept whatever was laid before us by God. This corresponded with the traditional Korean psyche of fate or lot. But the new Christian stream I encountered brought "I" more prominently into the religious and spiritual equation. My needs, desires, and goals matter as much as what God wanted me to do or become. Initially, my resistance against this kind of gospel was due to the dichotomist view of religions: "higher" religions aim at higher issues, such as holiness, spirituality, and salvation, while "lower" religions cater to mundane matters, such as sickness, prosperity, and good luck. Bringing the "I" factor into a deep dialogue with the "God" factor took a considerable process and time, but my reading of the scriptures, especially the Old Testament, encouraged me to think of human life and the Christian message more holistically. Consequently, I have settled on my own version of the theology of blessing.

This "conversion" process occurred by seriously considering both the scriptures and the social context. Throughout my faith journey, I have concluded that Pentecostal pneumatology has much to do with the "prosperity of life". The role of the Spirit of God in the Old Testament provides a rich resource for this understanding of creation, sustenance, and re-creation of life.[8] This was a significant addition to the traditional Pentecostal emphasis on the empowering role of the Spirit. And the prosperity of life begins with the physical[9] and material dimensions and includes emotional, communal, and spiritual aspects of human and created life.

The early 1970s was a politically turbulent time under a military dictatorship. However, the regime's political oppression and human rights violations were quickly glossed over by the economic agenda: the provision of daily bread and more. A war-torn nation struggled to grow out of the image of naked war orphans, along with shattered and destroyed streets.[10] In this social context, an emphasis on the afterlife looked more like escapism instead of actively engaging with the issues to find a resolution. In this setting, the widespread imminent eschatological expectation was not coincidental. Consequently, Cho's church grew exponentially by focusing on the daily needs, despite harsh allegations against him being "shamanistic".[11] His prayer mountain and the church's (daily) evening prayer meetings (in addition to the early morning ones) drew thousands of believers and non-believers with the expectation of God's intervention. Cho aptly described his half-century ministry as that of "hope".[12] His theology of blessing began with attention to the social context, his own life experience, and the "informed" reading of the scripture. Various influences can be detected throughout his own journey, including North American faith teachers such as Oral Roberts and Robert Schuller. However, the subsequent application of his theology of blessing to the socially marginalized and the care of creation attests

---

[8] A reflection on the Tenth General Assembly of the World Council of Churches deals with human flourishing: Wonsuk Ma, "Life, Justice, and Peace in the Spirit: A Reflection From a Korean Pentecostal Through Isaiah," *Ecumenical Review* 65.2 (July 2013), pp. 225–57.

[9] It is noticeable that classical Pentecostals have grounded their belief in healing not in the work of the Spirit (thus, pneumatologically), but in the atoning work of Christ (thus, Christologically). For example, the "Fundamental Truths" of the (US) Assemblies of God lists one on divine healing based on Christ's atonement. This is one of four cardinal doctrines of the denomination: "Assemblies of God Fundamental Truths (Condensed)," http://ag.org/top/Beliefs/Statement_of_Fundamental_Truths/sft_short.cfm, March 2010. Accessed 4 January 2013.

[10] World Vision and Compassion International began in Korea to care for war orphans.

[11] For more discussion, see below.

[12] Cho, *Dr David Yonggi Cho*, p.162.

to his own unique theological journey and formation.[13] It was just a matter of time before other churches slowly but consistently adopted this theological path, to the point that the main theological focus of Christianity in Korea seems to be on this world rather than the other; thus, another case of lop-sidedness.

Theological Logics Put Forward

From the beginning of the relatively short history, several theological reasonings have been put forward as a foundation for the PG. Several typical types will receive brief attention, with their contributions and weaknesses. It is essential to remember that the issue is neither correct nor wrong. They all have at least one crucial theological element that deserves sufficient attention. Therefore, each has contributed to the development of Pentecostal theology and spirituality and that of the PG. However, we can observe two common weaknesses, making them controversial: 1) theological logic is stressed beyond the limit of biblical evidence, and 2) an overemphasis is made to weaken the balance of theological wholeness.

Sowing Seed

The first is the cause-effect logic. The most typical of this line of theological argument is the sowing-seed preaching. Several biblical passages are frequently referenced. A more traditional one is the admonition of tithing. The first is not to steal what belongs to God. And the second is for God to "throw open the floodgates of heaven and pour out so much blessing that there will not be room enough to store it" (Mal. 3:10). Bringing a financial gift to the church is considered to be an investment for a future return, "thirty, sixty, or hundred-fold" (cf. Mark 4:8). Some preachers take this to the extreme as obligating God to return the gift with multiple blessings. This then becomes a binding "covenant" with God.[14]

In a massive gathering of the El Shaddai Catholic Charismatic movement in the Philippines, the movement's leader, "Mike" Velarde, asked his congregation to pull out their wallets and lift them open so that God could fill them with blessings. Then, people would give this blessing back to God. This giving-returning cycle continues while the volume of transactions grows every time.[15]

---

[13] Lee, *The Holy Spirit Movement in Korea*, pp. 115–29.

[14] Kenneth Copeland, *The Laws of Prosperity* (Fort Worth: Kenneth Copeland Publications, 1974), p. 79, takes a step further by arguing that a tither has a special right to prosperity based on God's covenant, and "Satan has no chance against you [because] God will rebuke the devourer for your sake."

[15] See Katherine L. Wieglele, "The Prosperity Gospel Among Filipino Catholic Charismatics," in *Pentecostalism and Prosperity,* pp. 171–88.

Patrick Ngozi Anwuzia, a Nigerian PG preacher, is quoted as having said, "If you haven't deposited anything, you have no right to ask for anything."[16]

It is not difficult to see the possibility of abuse in several areas. On a theological level, this has the danger of reducing human relationships with God to that of a transaction. The prophets accused Israel of reducing their relationship with God to the level of Baal and its worshippers. This instrumentalization of God is a strong pull in many indigenous religions, such as Korean shamanism and African religions. On the practical level, there are exceptions to this rule of "sowing and reaping". The suffering of the righteous is an age-old quest (as in Habakkuk and Job), and any unqualified claim on the rule can end up with a false promise. The poor of the poorest scrape their barrel to give their last penny to the Lord as the "best" investment. This is a strong possibility of becoming the poor's religious lottery. Several cases have raised an ugly ethical issue when ministries invested in massive property developments and/or their leaders exhibited extravagant and flamboyant lifestyles at the cost of the mass's sacrificial giving based on the presented "secure" promise.

Already in Redemption

This is another relatively simple theological logic that has been widely used. All suffering, including poverty and illness, is a symptom of human sin after the Fall. Through the redemptive work of Christ, our sins have been forgiven, and our status in God has been fully restored. As part of the redemptive parcel, Christians now live with cancelled curses; poverty and illness no longer apply. One often quoted passage is, "with his stripes, we are healed" (Isa. 53:5; 1 Pet. 2:24, KJV). By using the same logic, poverty is also part of a Christian's past and not for today. This is a powerful reorientation of one's self-understanding. The declaration of becoming a "new creation" (2 Cor. 5:17; Col. 3:10) lays a firm foundation for a transformed attitude and lifestyle. At the same time, it is also true that this can lead to a euphoric "realized eschatology": that the full restoration has been completed.

However, biblical evidence is clear that the full consummation is still to come. Indeed, "the whole creation has been groaning as in the pains of childbirth right up to the present time" (Rom. 8:22). Our life is caught between what "already" took place in the redemptive work of Christ and the full consummation that has "not yet" happened. This dilemma provides room for various questions, such as the presence of evil, suffering, and illness. Simple ignorance of this eschatological reality would deprive the Christian life of a legitimate place for hardship. For example, in a PG environment, a persistent illness of a Christian, after a repeated prayer for healing, may be explained as the presence of unrepented sin. Doubting one's Christian authenticity can easily add the excruciating pain of suspicion and marginalization to the existing suffering. The

---

[16] Aeji Isaac Ayegboyn, "A Rethinking of Prosperity Teaching in the New Pentecostal Churches in Nigeria," *Black Theology: An International Journal* 4.1 (2006), p. 74.

other side of the coin is the quick judgement of one's spirituality by health and wealth. This will eventually make the church a place for the rich and the healthy, not the poor and the sick. A more serious concern, however, is the distortion of Christian discipline. If discipleship is to deny oneself and follow Christ bearing one's cross, the PG can present the danger of placing Christians opposite Christ's intent. If Christians pursue what the world does, we fail to be light and salt to the world. God serves only as an extra booster rocket in achieving the same worldly goal. It is a degraded form of Christianity, far from what Christ intends for his own body.

Faith and Power of Word

Frequently observed in many PG preaching is the stress on faith and positive confession to reinforce the power of faith. The Word of Faith movement was born in the United States by Kenneth Hagin, Sr, in the 1960s.[17] However, others held similar views, including E. W. Kenyon and Oral Roberts. Although with a different origin, positive confession became popular in approximately the same period through celebrity preachers such as Robert Schuller. Also, both groups argue about the potent of faith and the spoken or confessed word.[18] This is one line of the PG that many Western, particularly American, preachers propagate through the power of TV.[19] Hagin has popularized the idea of *rhema* vis-à-vis *logos*. He argues that *rhema* is a personalized word of God given in a specific situation.[20] Pentecostal denominations officially condemned such teachings and adopted official responses.[21] Yet, many churches and Pentecostal believers, both in the North and the South, have adopted such teachings. As already seen above, the impact of this strand of the PG has impacted Africa tremendously. According to Vinson Synan, the number of churches in Nigeria exploded after a teaching tour of several faith teachers such as Kenneth Hagin, Jr and Kenneth Copeland

---

[17] E.g. Kenneth E. Hagin, *The Believer's Authority*, 2nd ed. (Tulsa, OK: Kenneth Hagin Ministries, 1985).

[18] Copeland, *The Laws of Prosperity,* pp. 96–97 has a section on "the Power of Confession", in which he teaches that "*You can have what you say!* In fact, what you are saying is exactly what you are getting now" (italics are the author's).

[19] Isaac Phiri and Joe Maxwell, "Gospel Rich," *Christianity Today,* July 2007, p. 24, "The worst brand of African prosperity teaching is, perhaps unsurprisingly, an American export", and "TBN Africa airs wall-to-wall peddlers of plenty" (p. 25).

[20] A heavy emphasis on this is found on the "About Us" page of the Kenneth Hagin Ministries website, repeating "It's all RHEMA" three times. Its central position is clearly stated: "And RHEMA is all about one thing – helping to usher in the last great move of God's Spirit and the second coming of Jesus Christ." http://www.rhema.org/index.php?option=com_content&view=article&id=12&Itemid=2. Accessed 15 February 2013.

[21] See the (US) Assemblies of God's position paper entitled "The Believer and Positive Confession," http://ag.org/top/Beliefs/Position_Papers/pp_downloads/pp_4183_confession.pdf (1980). Accessed 15 February 2013.

in the early 1990s.[22] Although the exact extent of their role is difficult to measure, the contribution of the PG to the growth of African Christianity is generally acknowledged. Also accepted is its role in motivating a better life with hope in the midst of grinding poverty.

Attraction to such preaching is a remarkable contribution to the growth of Christianity. Through millions' transformed attitudes and behaviours, the idea of "positive confession" gained more acceptance.[23] This change, in turn, presents the possibility of community and national transformation. The message of prosperity may be argued as a "starter" towards an introduction to the kingdom, just as Jesus fed the hungry, but ultimately, he preached the Kingdom of God. Nonetheless, like the two models we discussed, the challenge is evident against the authentic message of Christianity. The most difficult problem with this faith-word strand of the PG is the preoccupation with, and priority given to, material prosperity. This misplaced orientation will be problematic for any human being. The distortion of Christian blessing is almost like an unrealistic glitter of stars by night, but in reality, a make-shift town in a desert. An extreme form of this can take Christianity into a territory that is simply foreign to its intended reality. Also, many have criticized the use of certain biblical passages, such as 3 John 2, and the idea of *rhema*.[24] But equally problematic can be the combination of scriptural evidence and positive thinking. There is nothing wrong with faith combined with other elements, e.g. emotion, self-help, etc. However, if the positive-thinking stream becomes a pseudo-biblical truth, then the issue enters risky territory.

"Praying Through"

From the beginning, the modern Pentecostal movement seriously emphasized prayer. Early North American Pentecostals had a concerted, sustained, and dedicated prayer tradition known as "praying through". One does not stop praying until there is assurance from God. Expressed in various ways, such as "breakthrough" [25] or "touching the throne of God", people experience a

---

[22] Phiri & Maxwell, "Gospel Rich," p. 26.

[23] One of the most influential of David Yonggi Cho's books is *The Fourth Dimension: The Key to Putting Your Faith to Work for a Successful Life* (Seoul: Seoul Logos, 1979) which has a chapter titled "The Creative Power of Our Spoken Word" (pp. 75–94). Its sequel, *The Fourth Dimension vol. 2: More Secrets for a Successful Faith Life* (South Plainfield, NJ: Bridge Publishing, 1983), has a similar chapter, "The Creative Ability of Your Words" (pp. 119–145).

[24] See Gordon D. Fee, *The Disease of the Health and Wealth Gospels* (Vancouver: Regent College Publishing, 1985), pp. 10–11, on the 3 John passage.

[25] A strikingly similar experience is reported of the Pyongyang Great Revival of Korea (1907) where Western missionaries, after a seemingly disturbing lack of the Spirit's work for a week, "cried out to God … and refused to let God go till He blessed": Chang Ki Lee, *The Early Revival Movement in Korea (1903–1907)* (Zoetermeer, Netherlands: Utigeverij Boekencentrum, 2003), p. 103.

confirmation often in "tangible" ways. They range from hearing God's voice, a scriptural passage standing out, a message in tongues with interpretation, someone's prophecy, or a word of knowledge.

Various biblical examples are used to admonish one not to give up on hope and prayer. The most frequently heard story is the parable of a widow pleading with an unrighteous judge (Luke 18:2-8). Her persistent and repeated pleas persuaded the unrighteous judge to grant her justice. Equally powerful is Jacob's wrestling with an angel (Gen. 32:23-32), who eventually gave Jacob God's blessing. The efficacy of prayer is best shown in Daniel's prayer (Dan. 10:12-13). This passage is particularly significant as God immediately heard his prayer and sent an angel to him (v. 12). Also, when God's messenger was detained by the prince of Persia, through the prayer, God caused Michael to break the imprisonment of the angel to finally deliver God's message to Daniel (v. 13). Moses' intercessory prayer is also significant as his prayer practically changed God's plan (Exod. 33:12-16). Thus, the power of supplication is stressed as a potent tool to influence God's action, including healing and material prosperity.

In places where existing religions teach devotion, piety, and discipline, many programmes are used to focus on prayer. There are many large Pentecostal gatherings in Africa, sometimes even in millions, to experience God's presence. In Korean Pentecostalism, the prayer mountain movement has been a unique feature, mainly contributing to the Pentecostalism of Korean Christianity. Daily dawn prayer meetings and unison prayer are long-held traditions, tracing their origin back to the 1907 Pyongyang Revival.[26]

There are at least two questions related to this spirituality. The first is the influence of indigenous religious orientations. One renowned scholar criticized Cho as a shaman *par excellence*.[27] East Asian shamanistic religiosities have influenced all other religions, including Christianity. A strong emphasis on prayer is common throughout religions. Korean Buddhism, for example, practices dawn prayer, seven-day, forty-day, or 100-day prayer. Fasting and keeping oneself ritually clean are part of the devotion. Such an influence is not all negative: it has made Korean Christianity far more dynamic than early missionaries might have anticipated. Also, as people move from one religion to another (that is, Christianity), it is natural to look for parallel concepts and spiritual practices. Often the biggest failure in missionary work is when Christianity does not provide a functional substitution for the old religion. Of course, the real danger is when core indigenous religious ideals remain and are repackaged in Christian symbols and language. That is when the shamanization

---

[26] C. Lee, *The Early Revival*, pp. 169–70.

[27] Hollenweger, *Pentecostalism: Origins and Developments Worldwide*, p. 100, n. 2. Also, Harvey Cox, *Fire From Heaven: The Rise of Pentecostal Spirituality and the Reshaping of Religion in the Twenty-First Century* (Reading, MA: Addison-Wesley, 2005), pp. 218–29. Both, however, describe Cho as an excellent model for incorporating indigenous religious functions to Christianity.

of Christianity takes place. The second risk of an overemphasis on prayer is a possible theological imbalance: prayer as merit may stress human agency. Any form of devotion and piety is always positive. However, when it becomes a practice that would warrant what the believer prays for, the answer to a prayer is not graciously gifted by God but rather earned by the believer. Most classical Pentecostal churches have held the "healing in atonement" teaching. This may serve as an example of a theological counterbalance to the PG tendency on prayer as merit.

Summary

Had space allowed, I would have included the somewhat controversial notion of spiritual warfare, introduced by the Third Wave advocates from the early 1980s. Some of its ideas and practices are highly problematic and consequently not taken very seriously in mainline theological circles.

It is also important to realize that there is no "pure" type, and every PG preacher combines two or more, or even all, theological traits. One's preaching often undergoes a developmental process depending on the context and audience and their theological understanding. For instance, Cho's earlier life was characterized by illness, poverty, and external elements such as the nation under colonial rule. As he frequently interpreted for American healing evangelists, it is reasonable to recognize their influence on the formation of his theology. As an Assemblies of God preacher, he subscribed to the standard theological notion of healing in the atonement. Then from the 1970s and on, positive confession was stressed along with faith and prayer, as he developed close relationships with Oral Roberts and Robert Schuller. The inclusion of fasting was more credited to the spirituality of Jashil Choi, his mother-in-law, who was responsible for establishing the renowned Jashil Choi Fasting Prayer Mountain.[28] As Korean society has gained economic prosperity in recent years, he placed an increasing emphasis on philanthropy and missionary work.

Impact to Lifestyle

"Can knowledge change one's behaviour?" is an age-old question among behavioural scientists. The preceding discussion investigated the PG's "knowledge" dimension, which impacts a believer's lifestyle. All of them are potentially controversial. This section explores further Pentecostal resources that have contributed to the formation of the PG and impact the believer's attitude and behaviour. Unlike the previous section, the practices and values presented here are more generally accepted. Being a theologian, I am not claiming any expertise in behavioural science: this is purely a reflection based on a layperson's observation. I have found social science studies, including sociology and economics, extremely helpful. The PG has the potential to turn religious faith

[28] Ma and Ma, *Mission in the Spirit*, pp. 242–59.

into social capital. For example, Heslam's "appreciated enquiry" into the human and social capital towards improving economic life was constructive.[29]

Shaping of Attitude: "Baptism in the Spirit"

It is generally agreed that Pentecostal/Charismatic Christians have developed a unique attitude toward their daily life. First, they tend to possess a more positive outlook on their life and the future. Since early Western Pentecostals came from lower social strata, and today most Pentecostal/Charismatic believers worldwide follow a similar demographic spread, this change in attitude is significant. The cause of the traditionally apprehensive outlook towards life often comes from socio-economic and cultural influence, such as dire poverty, oppressive political systems, and/or a culture that provides few alternative lifestyles. This is the same stock that most Pentecostals come from. As my own story attests, sometimes existing forms of Christianity further reinforce this never-ending cycle of negative attitude. Thus, "poor" is one of the most common adjectives to refer to the socio-economic status of ordinary Pentecostal/Charismatic believers.

Therefore, an important question can be asked: what turns the attitude and behaviour of these "poor" not only to overcome but to become change agents: or, in other words, "to fire up the poor"?[30] One of the most crucial conceptual building blocks is the belief and experience around what is called "baptism in the Spirit". Its primary focus on empowerment has been firmly established among classical Pentecostals based on Acts 1:8.[31] Despite the continuing theological debate on its nature, this belief has a powerful consequence in a change of attitude. When talking about this empowering experience, we already assume the call to be "witnesses to the ends of the earth" (Acts 1:8). In the Old Testament, we notice the process of a divine call as in Gideon (Judg. 6) and Saul (1 Sam. 10) before the Spirit comes upon chosen leaders. For average Pentecostal believers who are "nobody" in the eyes of the secular and even Christian worlds, this is a revolutionary concept that they are really "somebody" in God's eyes. People often testify to tangible experiences as God's affirmation of the call and empowerment. They include speaking in tongues and healing. Some even go through sensual experiences, such as "heat striking from the head through the whole body". They reinforce one's conviction of calling and actual empowerment for God's service.

Even if today's diverse Pentecostal/Charismatic communities do not share exactly the same doctrinal standards throughout the world, no one will object

---

[29] Peter S. Heslam, *Transforming Capitalism: Entrepreneurship and the Renewal of Thrift* (Cambridge: Grove Books, 2010); and "Happiness Through Thrift: The Contribution of Business to Human Well-Being," in John Atherton and Elaine Graham (eds), *Political Economy, Religion and Wellbeing: The Practices of Happiness* (Oxford: Routledge, 2011), pp. 54–65.

[30] See Chapter 6.

[31] For example, Robert P. Menzies, *Empowered for Witness: The Spirit in Luke-Acts* (Edinburgh: T. & T. Clark, 2005).

that Pentecostal Christianity is a radical sort of religion.[32] At the centre of its belief and experience is an encounter with God in somewhat tangible and sometimes striking ways. Pentecostal spirituality does not reduce the divine to a manageable size, as many "worshipper-friendly" religions do, but maintains God's transcendental nature at encounterable proximity. This tendency is particularly prevalent in cultures where such encounters are part of indigenous religiosity. The rise and exponential growth of the African Independent Churches in Sub-Saharan Africa are attributed to the appropriation of this indigenous religiosity into Christian beliefs and practices.

The belief in Spirit baptism further implies the "commissioning" of the Spirit into witnessing. It has a strong behavioural implication. Pentecostals have understood from the beginning that this blessed experience is for every believer, whether for professionally commissioned cross-cultural missionaries or ordinary men and women who live their daily life in the market places and at home. In the process of one's obedience, the believers expect the empowering presence of the Spirit, both in perseverance as well as in signs and wonders.

The effect of this theological orientation is enormous, both in theology and practical living.[33] In simple terms, this translates into new purposefulness in life, a positive outlook on the future, and new confidence in work, forming a positive attitude towards God, life, and the future.[34] However, it is more than hope: it is almost expectancy. The unique religious belief and experience in the Pentecostal/Charismatic circles form a deep sense that the things one hopes for are a real possibility. In many cases, these believers live the future today. The much-criticized emphasis on sowing by offering resources to God is not viewed as a bogus scheme to empty the pockets of the poor but as a sincere investment for a real possibility of blessing. For this reason, it is understandable that David Yonggi Cho of the Yoido Full Gospel Church summarizes the primary character of his half-century ministry that began in war-torn Korea as a ministry of hope. His consistent preaching of God, who is good and able, has resulted in testimonies that typically overcome formidable life challenges.[35] It is, therefore, not difficult for this attitude change to lead to a change in behaviour.

---

[32] Cox, *Fire From Heaven*, pp. 74–76, characterizes Pentecostalism a religious "fundamentalism".

[33] For several areas of its theological effect, see Chapter 6.

[34] This potential is aptly presented in the case study of an urban Christian community: Gerardo Marti, "'I Determine My Harvest': Risky Careers and Spirit Guided Prosperity in Los Angeles," in *Pentecostalism and Prosperity*, pp. 131–50.

[35] Myung-soo Park, "Korean Pentecostal Spirituality as Manifested in the Testimonies of Members of Yoido Full Gospel Church," in *David Yonggi Cho: A Close Look at His Theology and Ministry*, pp. 43–67.

From Attitude to Behaviour: Reinforcing the Values

Max Weber believed Protestantism fosters disciplined, industrious behaviour, and constrains spending, thus building a mindset toward capitalism.[36] If Reformed faith has proven this behavioural possibility, how much would radical Pentecostal belief and experience create a kind of human capital that would produce a radical outcome?[37] Change of behaviour requires more than the correct information. A theological orientation, not just information, provides the right attitude towards a lifestyle or behaviour change. This combination of the energy source and the new direction produces an intentionally directed behaviour. This makes Pentecostalism a dynamic religion, setting it apart from other traditional forms of Christianity today. Repeated and regular reinforcement is necessary to make this orientation and change a permanent lifestyle.

Pentecostal worship is typically loud, full of emotion, body movements, and spontaneous expression, and is at times chaotic. This is a tangible manifestation of the unique Pentecostal belief and experience. At the same time, worship constantly reinforces Pentecostal spirituality and orientation. Preaching is a critical part of worship, where essential theology-making occurs in Pentecostalism. By nature, pastors are to provide pastoral care and encouragement.[38] A typical Pentecostal sermon would challenge worshippers to look beyond the circumstance and have hope in Christ, the miracle worker. Many preachers would adopt some form of the PG theological logic discussed above. Illustrations, mainly drawn from known and contemporary individuals to the congregation, whether in healing or overcoming difficulties, will enhance the sense of hope.

Sufficient time has been allocated in typical Pentecostal worship for testimonies. Any member can share their experience with God with the whole congregation. They become raw material for grassroots theological formation, as the experience is now shared, evaluated, processed, and finally communally owned. Also important is the singing of simple songs, sometimes short lines repeated, to the accompaniment of modern instruments such as drums, guitars, and an electronic organ. They create an ambiance conducive for worshippers to "surrender" to the powerful leading of the Holy Spirit. This highly explosive Pentecostal worship often includes prayer times, sometimes by laying on of hands, or other times in a let-out unison prayer.[39] They all create a powerful atmosphere with a high expectancy of God's intervention. Believers become

---

[36] Max Weber's classic, *The Protestant Ethics and the Spirit of Capitalism*.

[37] For example, Peter L. Berger, "Max Weber is Alive and Well, and Living in Guatemala: The Protestant Ethic Today," *Faith and International Affairs* 8.4 (2010), pp. 3–9.

[38] Ma and Ma, *Mission in the Spirit*, pp. 240–41, argues that a local pastor is the main driver in Pentecostal theological formation.

[39] Today many churches in Korea would begin a season of unison prayer by calling "Lord!" three times, known as *Juyo gido*.

pretty sure that they live with firm promises and that they are with like-minded company.

As a result, zealousness and religious convictions have become a hallmark of Pentecostal/Charismatic life. They are highly motivated and charged with purposefulness and a sense of empowerment. This provides resilience to withstand hardship and creates an immune system to cushion the impact of any adverse circumstances one is facing. This also leads to a persistent pursuit for the better. Often the goals are audacious ones. In many minds, they are not daydreams but reachable realities through hard work, religious devotion, and God's gracious and miraculous intervention. They often live their future today, of course, in hope and faith.

In the early days of my mission work, I made a short visit back to Korea. Once I was asked to accompany a pastor on her visit to a member. One unique Christian pastoral routine in Korea is unannounced visits to homes for prayer. The host family was living in a room-rented house (that means just one room, no separate living room or kitchen) for a family of five (with three school-aged children). The woman, struggling to survive each day, shared with us her audacious prayer of owning a three-story building: two levels with three apartment units for rent and the third level for her family. She ensured that there would be a secluded "prophet's chamber" on the roof of the building for visiting missionaries. She and her pastor had set this prayer item firm in their minds. She was diligent in daily dawn prayers and Friday overnight prayer, and spent a whole week fasting in a prayer mountain. It was not an attitude common among many Christians, including the traditional sort of my growing years. If God answers, that's wonderful. If not, there is nothing to lose. After all, he is the Boss, who knows what's best for us! Years later, we were able to revisit the church and the family. Lo and behold! This time, the family was occupying a three-story building; her husband joined her in the church, although there was not yet a prophet's chamber.

Of course, not everyone who "opens the mouth wide" would have their mouths filled in this drastic way. However, many Pentecostal believers, like this woman and her pastor, attribute any positive outcome to their spiritual capital (or faith) to dream of something big. The effect of the inner reorientation through Pentecostal belief and experience on individual, family, and community life has been well attested.[40] Behaviours change, and a new lifestyle is born with constant community reinforcement, often resulting in betterment in daily life or upward social mobility.

Setting the Course: Eschatology and Context

The net result of this process is a behavioural change based on an attitude change, constantly reinforced and strengthened by Pentecostal worship and religious

[40] For Latin American experiences and beyond, with many case studies, see Martin, *Tongues of Fire*, pp. 205–32.

experiences. The most tangible outcome is a highly positive and aggressive attitude in spiritual and daily life. A goal has been set high, attitude is positive with firm faith, expecting God's supernatural help, and working diligently with a conscientious lifestyle. Spiritual obstacles are countered through prayer, while the Bible provides a stream of God's promises. Social upward mobility is instead a natural outcome. This zealousness can be expressed in various ways, in witnessing, workplaces, family life, and others.

This highly charged theological orientation also interacts actively with a given context. And this interaction produces a wide range of expressions depending on the theological guidance of the time and the context of a given location. One example of the theological guidance system is eschatology.[41] In the early years of the modern Pentecostal movement, eschatological urgency was widespread. The coming of the Spirit was clearly understood as a sign of the last days. Naturally, early Pentecostals had an extreme other-worldly perspective of life and the world. In this context, this dynamic spiritual, emotional, and practical energy was channelled to mission. As a result, within ten years of the modern Pentecostal movement, there were 200 missionaries to Africa, Asia, Europe, and Latin American countries.[42] And they were all voluntary missionaries, as the Azusa Street Mission did not develop any structure to recruit, train, deploy, or support them. *The Apostolic Faith*, the official publication of the Mission, regularly included many missionary reports, and a good amount concerned miraculous works of God. This is a clear example of the Pentecostal PG potential theologically directed to mission. This also shows how mission was understood in that particular circle: crossing a geographical and cultural border to preach the gospel. Other factors, of course, contributed to this move, such as their generally lower socio-economic status.

A discernible shift in the North American scene emerged in the second half of the twentieth century, especially since the emergence of the Charismatic movement in the 1960s. Pentecostal spirituality and experience now found their home in historic churches: socially more middle class and eschatologically less millennial. Also, the second-generation Pentecostals began to exercise pulpit leadership by this time. It is unclear if the mainline churches' more amillennial or post-millennial eschatological tendency also affected this de-eschatological move of Pentecostalism. This time, the Pentecostals were more preoccupied with defending their theological identity. The validity of "speaking in tongues as the initial evidence of the baptism in the Spirit" was at the centre of the debate, criticized from without and within.

Its religious dynamism is expressed in various forms. In the following decades, a host of televangelists rose in the United States, often armed with the

---

[41] See Chapter 9.

[42] G. B. McGee, "Missions, Overseas (N. American Pentecostal)," in Stanley M. Burgess (ed.), *New International Dictionary of Pentecostal and Charismatic Movements*, rev. ed. (Grand Rapids, Zondervan, 2003), p. 888.

PG message of healing and prosperity. In the meantime, the eschatological emphasis slowly disappeared. Such ministries often followed a secular corporate sales model in their funding strategy. Some of them invested in properties in the name of the ministry, a clear sign that the Lord's return was no longer expected any time soon. Some even adopted Hollywood-style celebrity culture. One's eschatological understanding determines the direction of personal and ministerial life. Ethical scandals and legal charges of some "stars" revealed the dark side of this change in eschatology. (Of course, there is nothing wrong with, let's say, post-millennialism or amillennialism. The problem was the lack of an intentional theological process to "revise" Pentecostal eschatology.) A heavy "this-worldly" orientation was also expressed in the rise of large and impressive suburban church buildings. By this time, eschatological urgency remained only in theological memory among Pentecostals. Comparing this observation with Western Europe, the unique American consumerism and entrepreneurial spirit may have contributed to the rise of the PG. If this is the case, it is a substantial theological challenge as Christianity is no longer for worshippers to serve their God but for God to serve his followers.

Pentecostal/Charismatic churches that mushroomed from the 1980s throughout the world generally align with this non-eschatological Charismatic trend more than classical Pentecostal traditions, except for the infilling of the Spirit. Many Pentecostal churches, such as the Yoido Full Gospel Church of the Korean Assemblies of God, adopted several Charismatic elements. The change in eschatological orientation resulted in several tangible expressions. The first is an emphasis on growth. The growth of individual congregations and global Pentecostalism cannot be explained by any organizational ingenuity or training system in its incredibly diverse forms; rather, through the voluntary mobilization of ordinary believers who changed their attitude and behaviour. I was genuinely impressed by everyday housewives who serve as cell group leaders with a minimum theological orientation. At the Yoido Full Gospel Church, many spent several days of the New Year holidays at the prayer mountain for fasting and prayer. Yes, they pray for their own needs, but it is not unusual that they also fast for their cell group members for healing, the salvation of their family members, or the solution to life's problems. What can motivate an ordinary woman, who would enjoy the winter holidays with extended family gatherings for celebration, to devote her time to prayer, especially for someone else? No wonder the church has grown into the largest single congregation in the world! This story repeats itself, in the highly sophisticated urban centres like Hollywood or the deep mountain villages of Latin America.

The second expression is the expanded missionary scope. Unlike the earlier focus on evangelism and church planting, there have been clear signs that Pentecostals have developed, or are developing, a holistic understanding of mission. Although Pentecostals have intuitively exercised the holistic aspect of mission, it was not intentional or theologically articulated. Care for the needy has been motivated by an immediate social context and evangelization.

However, in the last several decades, more Pentecostal denominations and agencies have expressed their commitment to care for the needy and even to justice issues.[43] For example, YWAM has embraced community development, HIV/AIDS care, and even social justice into its mission thinking and operation.[44] The commitment of the Yoido Full Gospel Church to church unity and creation care is another example.[45] These are positive outcomes of the changed eschatology of Pentecostalism, which has brought the potential for attitude and behaviour change.

Towards a Future

If the discussion appears to have blindly endorsed the PG, this is neither my intention nor my belief. But this is to serve as a devil's advocate against "angels" who have been accusing the PG. Most criticisms are very valid and theologically sound, I admit. However, I have assumed that, within the PG package, despite its ugly surface, there may be inherent theological elements that beg to be liberated from abuses and stereotypical dismissal. And some of them may indeed be a unique gift of the Spirit to rejuvenate dying churches while continually fuelling the growth of global Christianity.

My brief study has focused on one of them: the quest for a dynamic and passionate Christianity. With a risk of overgeneralization, today's Christianity may be evaluated by this criterion. The Western church has been losing its strength, numbers, and influence as the average mindset of mainstream Christians has increasingly moved away from an expectation of God's direct and immediate presence and work. The traditional heart-bed of Christianity has been steadily eroded by secularization, pluralism, rationalism, and a high degree of suspicion toward claims of Christianity. Consequently, Christianity's role in the public sphere is decreasing, which is no different even in individual life. Relative affluence and stable social systems have left less room where God is meaningfully needed. The bottom line is clear: not much is expected from God any longer.

On the other hand, in places where Christianity grows, sometimes, despite harsh circumstances, it is almost the exact opposite. God is assumed to be involved in every part of daily life. In many places, this religious expectation may have also been shaped by people's previous religious experiences; thus, Christianity offers a functional substitution. Equally critical is the social context,

---

[43] Understanding of mission as evangelism, care of the needy and the establishment of justice is argued as the full spectrum of Pentecostal mission: Ma and Ma, *Mission in the Spirit*, pp. 7–14.

[44] One example of this expanding mission scope is epitomized in a YWAMer's recent study: Stephanie L. Goins, "The Place of Forgiveness in the Reintegration of Former Child Soldiers in Sierra Leone" (PhD dissertation, University of Wales/Oxford Centre for Mission Studies, 2008).

[45] Lee, *The Holy Spirit Movement in Korea*, pp. 126–29.

where many struggle for daily survival. In such situations, where social systems provide little or no provision for daily sustenance or protection from threats to survival, religions flourish. This can partly explain the expansion of the PG in Africa and Asia and, to a lesser degree, in Latin America. Often in such cases, the PG generally represents Pentecostal/Charismatic Christianity, which takes immediate concerns seriously. The most tangible sign of this vibrancy is the huge size of buildings, crowds, and media presence. Equally oversized is a "big mouth" with audacious claims and promises. Beneath this "size" lies explosive enthusiasm for the Christian message as people receive it. With changes in social and religious attitudes and behaviours, this attitude of involving God in every aspect of human and social life is what is needed to jump-start waning Christianity and continue fuelling Christian expansion. Thus, I have argued that a proper theological "re-visioning" of the PG is an urgent crucial call.[46]

Although not intended to be prescriptive or comprehensive, a healthier version of the PG, or now I may propose to call it a "theology of blessing", may contain the following components while maintaining the religious attitude and behaviour discussed above.[47] The first is repositioning "prosperity" from its place as an end of Christian aspiration to a means of fulfilling a God-given mandate or mission. This may be compared with Jesus' feeding of the five thousand. Seeking physical and material blessing has a rightful place in Christian life, but only as a start or means, not an end in itself. The second is moving one's attention from "what I want" to "what we all need". This has two elements for re-visioning: motivation and community-centred thinking. Physical and material needs for daily living are legitimate Christian things to pray for and expect from God. This is moving the PG from consumerist secular motivation. Moreover, such a quest is for the common good instead of only the selfish desire to serve oneself.[48] The third, I propose, is a holistic understanding of blessing. The current narrow preoccupation with abundance's physical and material aspects is not different from what the secular world is pursuing. They are part of the basic level of Maslow's human needs for survival. A human is distinguished from an animal by our desire for social, emotional, relational, ethical, and spiritual welfare. Vision for God's shalom (for example, in Isa. 32:15ff) reveals this enlarged, holistic view of blessing. The fourth is the recognition of suffering as

---

[46] This call is clearly issued by Frank D. Macchia in "A Call for Careful Discernment: A Theological Response to Prosperity Preaching," in *Pentecostalism and Prosperity*, pp. 225–37.

[47] From an economic perspective, Amos Yong presents several models: Amos Yong, "A Typology of Prosperity Theology: A Religious Economy of Global Renewal or a Renewal Economics?" in *Pentecostalism and Prosperity*, pp. 15–33.

[48] Whether the PG can affect national economy is an ongoing enquiry. At least a South African case is presented with a tentative, inconclusive, yet positive verdict by the Centre for Development and Enterprise, South Africa, "Under the Radar: Pentecostalism in South Africa and Its Potential Social and Economic Role," in *Pentecostalism and Prosperity*, pp. 63–85.

part of human reality. This is where an eschatological balance is essential. The wisdom literature illustrates this reality well. We not only have rules for a successful life in Proverbs, but we also have a clear case of exceptions in the Book of Job. The righteous suffer while the wicked prosper. That is an age-old theological question, as Habakkuk complained to God (e.g. 1:13). A healthy pastoral theology will not criminalize victims as lacking faith, but will build a life with the right existential and religious attitude informed by biblical teaching. Ultimately, this is a matter of Christian discipline: we do not use God but surrender ourselves for God's use. He is indeed our Lord (*kurios*).

Our discussion already suggests problematic areas of the PG. The worst theological combination will be, therefore, combining the wrong extremes together:

1. Making prosperity the goal of the Christian life.
2. Using Christianity to fulfil one's selfish consumerist desire.
3. One's blessing and spirituality are measured only by health and wealth.
4. Denying the complexity of life, condemning poverty and illness as the sign of spiritual bankruptcy.
5. Ultimately God is used and abused for one's own desire.

This worst-case scenario can worsen further if such preachers maintain a lavish and celebrity lifestyle at the cost of the poverty of the mass. It is more than an ethical problem: it's a crime.

The most ideal form of the PG, which we agreed to call a "theology of blessing", provides the key to the dynamic and passionate strength of the church. But the worst-case scenario is so destructive, and we have seen many injured financially and spiritually, sometimes resulting in broken families. In that case, it is a deadly wolf in Christian skin. This is where the role of "theological prophets" can decisively influence the future of Pentecostal mission and the global church. So, God help us!

12. "In Jesus' Name!": Power Encounter Among Pentecostals and Third Wavers

Confronting evil spirits has been a unique spiritual tradition of Pentecostalism. Thus, it has made a significant theological and missiological contribution to demonology, mainly through its healing practices. Its belief in divine healing is partly attributed to its unique holistic worldview. Then the rise of the Third Wave movement significantly added to this discussion.

Introduction

Demonology, long neglected by traditional theologians, has become a hotly debated issue in theological discussions. Pentecostals have inherited the traditional belief and practice of divine healing from the Holiness revivals. Early Pentecostals struggled with the place of medicines in divine healing.[1] When it comes to the source of illness, they assumed the activity of demons as one cause. Then the proponents of the Third Wave movement from the early 1980s brought the role of demons into the spotlight. The subject has inherent elements of controversy, and the recent discussions make many churches uneasy. This uneasiness is especially obvious among Western Christians and mission-initiated churches in the non-Western world. This attitude may have at least two sources: insufficient biblical data and the Western worldview. The latter tends to exclude the world of angels, demons, and miracles in its two-tiered worldview, the supernatural and the natural worlds. Theology, as a product of such a worldview, naturally ignores or "demythologizes" the supernatural. The Asian church, like other "Southern" Christian churches, received this "sanitized" version of Christianity. As a result, it has struggled to live between its traditional worldview (holistic and much closer to the biblical worldview) and the transmitted "Christian" one. This gap is further widened by unconscious attempts to sever emotional ties with the old, so-called "superstitious" and" demonic" religious traditions. Consequently, any discussion of angels, demons, demonization, healing, and miracles has, for the most part, been deliberately avoided in our theological discourse.

The growth and maturity of the Southern church and its theological thinking have challenged the validity of such Western theology in the Southern context.

---

[1] Vinson Synan, "The Pentecostal Roots of Oral Roberts' Healing Ministry," *Spiritus: ORU Journal of Theology* 3.2 (2018), pp. 287–302.

This reassessment of the "received" theology and the earnest desire to construct theologies relevant to the local context are two sides of the same coin. The theological minds in the South did not overlook this fact. Also, locally "initiated" versions of Christianity, be it African Independent Churches, Chinese house church Christians, or even doctrinally questionable groups in Japan, always include the activities of spiritual beings in their theological framework. This may prove that the "primitive" form of Christianity, including that of the early church, inevitably embraces a worldview closer to the non-Western ones.

One outcome of this tension is what is called "split-level" Christianity,[2] as the received theological system provides little or no room for the supernatural world in the followers' Christian beliefs and practices. Their allegiance is divided: the church provides answers for "higher religious" concerns such as sins, salvation, and others, whereas the old and indigenous religion provides answers for "lower religious" matters such as dreams, healing, and others. This dilemma proves that we have lived with a one-sided or handicapped version of Christianity for quite some time. This challenge also presents a new possibility for Southern theological minds to revisit the biblical evidence through a new set of worldview lenses. The active theological explorations by the Global South would certainly pay attention to the study of demonology.

This chapter explores the place of Pentecostalism in the discussion of demonology. I will trace two major groups within the Pentecostal movement and their contribution to the present discussion: classical Pentecostalism and the Third Wave. The concluding section summarizes Pentecostal contributions to theology, missiology, and practical ministry with special reference to principalities and powers. I will also list several areas needing further attention. To avoid the risk of error and to offer a positive contribution to the future of Christian theology and ministry, I will explore this topic from an Asian Pentecostal perspective.

Pentecostals and Demons

Healing Movement

One crucial continuity between the Pentecostal and the nineteenth-century Holiness movements was the belief in and practice of divine healing. Healing ministry was so popular that healing homes were established throughout the United States. Continuing this belief of their Holiness predecessors, Pentecostals confirmed a theological position that healing is rooted in Christ's work of atonement. For example, the Church of God Declaration of Faith (Cleveland,

---

[2] Not to be confused with Jaime Bulatao's concept of "split-level Christianity" that has more to do with the belief-behaviour dissonance among Christians.

TN) has: "Divine healing is provided for all in the atonement."[3] The Assemblies of God, USA, has a more elaborate statement. Still, the belief is identical: "WE BELIEVE … Divine Healing of the Sick is a Privilege for Christians Today and is provided for in Christ's Atonement (His sacrificial death on the Cross for our sins)."[4] This doctrine is elaborated fully in a position paper entitled, "Divine Healing: An Integral Part of the Gospel."[5] This official document, approved by the General Presbytery, further identifies its scriptural base as Isaiah 53:4, 5; Matthew 8:16, 17; and James 5:14-16. Classical Pentecostals throughout the world subscribe to similar doctrinal positions.

An excellent example is David Yonggi Cho's ministry. As he has done for several decades of ministry, he administered a healing ministry during the second Sunday service of his church on 27 January 2007. The title of his sermon was "Through God's Grace", based on the parable of the prodigal son. He stressed the overwhelming grace of the father in receiving his wayward son. Regardless of the subject of his sermon, the healing ministry is a regular part of the worship service. The summary of this healing session may be presented as follows:

> If you come with disease and life's problems, please stand. If you are sick, please lay your hand upon the suffering part of your body. If you come with life's problems, lay your hand on your heart. Let us pray, "God, our father, we come to you with our weakness and disease. Through the work of your Son on the Cross, please heal every disease. Please heal them now, heal them now, heal them now.
>
> All kinds of disease and suffering, I command you in the name of Jesus of Nazareth to lose your grip right now. Leave now, leave now, leave now. Enemy and demon, I command you to leave, leave, leave.
>
> "Lord, through Your work on the Cross, through the stripes, bring healing to us, we plead. Do Your miracle now. As You promised in 3 John 2, prosper every spirit, blessing everything they do, and make everyone strong. In Jesus' name, we pray. Amen.
>
> God is healing now. He is performing miracles now.

The healing ministry did not end there. Toward the conclusion of the worship, Dr Cho pronounced various healings which took place in that service. He did not specify how he obtained this information, but in previous services, he would say,

---

[3] "Church of God Declaration of Faith," available at: http://www.churchofgod.cc/about/declaration_of_faith.cfm. Accessed 19 January 2006.

[4] "16 Fundamental Truths of the Assemblies of God," available at: http://ag.org/top/Beliefs/Statement of Fundamental Truths/sft_short_cfm. Accessed 19 January 2007.

[5] "Divine Healing: An Integral Part of the Gospel," available at: http://ag.org/top/Beliefs/Position_Papers/pp_4184_healing.cfm. Accessed 19 January 2007.

"God spoke to me…" or "I see…" This implies the exercise of a spiritual gift, either a word of knowledge or a simple revelation by God to him. His declaration was as follows:

> God says that a deaf [person] was healed. A brain tumour was healed. Someone with a neck problem has been healed. An intestinal cancer was healed. Muscle pain is healed. Someone with back pain has been healed. Acute skin disease has been cleaned. God wants to heal you. Trust him.

This brief glimpse of Pentecostal healing practices enables us to move our discussion forward. Before we move on, it is essential to clarify that healing is not the most distinct feature of classical Pentecostalism. Pentecostalism's main theological emphasis is on the empowering aspect of baptism in the Holy Spirit. Almost all the classical Pentecostal groups subscribe to speaking in tongues as the initial and physical evidence of Spirit baptism. The movement has been more popularly known for this feature.

Pentecostal Beliefs

I seek here to relate the practice of divine healing and its Pentecostal theological orientation to demonology and the practice of spiritual warfare. I also plan to discuss its implications for pastoral settings.

First, the Pentecostal faith has brought a new Christian worldview and significantly impacted world Christianity. The birth of the Pentecostal movement paralleled the rise of a holistic Christian worldview that takes the supernatural world seriously. Only within a holistic worldview is an expectation for healing and miracles possible. Thus, the presence or absence of the miraculous has much to do with the worldview within when one undertakes Christian theology and ministry. That classical Pentecostalism traces its origin to the West is significant in that the worldview of the New Testament church was holistic. Pentecostalism may be seen as a corrective to Western naturalism and the recovery of biblical holism.

Second, as expressed through Pentecostal healing practices, some illnesses are attributed to the work of evil spirits or demons. Determining the cause of a disease is difficult. Still, basing their beliefs on the New Testament, Pentecostals readily point to the role of demons in causing some diseases and disturbing God's work. Albeit lacking theological sophistication, Pentecostals acknowledge the presence and potency of demons and evil spirits affecting human lives. They assume these demonic spirits are actively causing diseases, misfortunes, and distractions against God's work. More particularly, they readily attribute mental illness to demonic activity and consider power encounter a regular practice. Some Pentecostal-Charismatics suggest that the spirit which causes a disease is afflicted with that same disease (for example, the blind spirit inflicts blindness). As seen in Cho's prayer, Pentecostals often personify diseases and unfavourable circumstances such as poverty. These diseases and events are called and cast out in the name of Jesus, along with demons and evil spirits.

Third, regarding confrontations with demons, Pentecostal theology shows a strong Christ-centred orientation, especially invoking the image of Christus Victor (the Victorious Christ). Except for the mention of the gift of healing, the Holy Spirit has a surprisingly limited role in this practice. In Pentecostal beliefs and practices, healing is anchored in the atoning work of Christ on the Cross. The Assemblies of God (USA) position paper established a doctrine of "healing in the atonement", arguing for the possibility of healing for every case. However, a widespread belief among people in the pews acknowledges the problem of such a tight doctrine. Many have learned to live with the tension between the victory of Christ and the present reality of suffering. Although not always articulated, the present life in an eschatological tension appears to have provided a satisfactory explanation.[6] Christo-centrism is also expressed in the most popular phrase in Pentecostals, "In the name of Jesus…" They take the healing actions of Jesus seriously, e.g. "they will place their hands on sick people, and they will get well" (Mark 16:18).

Fourth, Pentecostals maintain an attitude of having the upper hand, as evidenced in their prayers full of commands and rebukes. Pentecostals seldom "discuss" with the evil spirit during an exorcism event. This practice is due to at least two assumptions: 1) demons are liars, and 2) Christians, as God's children, already have the authority to rebuke and expel evil spirits. However, it is crucial for the exorcist to act with spiritual insight (drawing on the gift of discernment) or to exercise spiritual power through prayer and fasting. For instance, taking Matthew 9:29 seriously, many Pentecostals have taken prayer and fasting as the primary way to confront the devil.[7] By combining a few rites, such as anointing with oil and laying on of hands, spiritual confrontation sometimes becomes a long and challenging battle, even if victory is already assured.

Fifth, how Pentecostals have formulated their demonology is revealed only implicitly in various anecdotes of healing and exorcism. Although much

---

[6] See the recent studies among Pentecostals on "non-healing", e.g. Erlinda Reyes, "A Theological Framework for Non-Healing in the Pentecostal Perspective" (Th.M. thesis, Asia Pacific Theological Seminary, 2007); Wonsuk Ma, "Pentecostal Theological Formation and Education for Tomorrow (Sec 1)," *Pentecostal Education* 7.2 (Fall 2022), pp. 261–73. Also, on the issue of suffering, see Veli-Matti Karkkainen, "Theology of the Cross: A Stumbling Block to Pentecostal/Charismatic Spirituality?" (pp. 150–63) and William W. Menzies, "Reflection on Suffering: A Pentecostal Perspective" (pp. 141–49), in Wonsuk Ma and Robert P. Menzies (eds), *The Spirit and Spirituality: Essays in Honour of Russell P. Spittler* (London: T. & T. Clark, 2004).

[7] For example, Julie C. Ma, "Korean Pentecostal Spirituality: A Case Study of Jashil Choi," *Asian Journal of Pentecostal Studies* 5.2 (2002), pp. 235–54 studies the life and ministry of Jashil Choi, the founder of Jashil Choi International Prayer and Fasting Mountain in Korea. Also, Harold R. Cole, "A Model of Contextualized Deliverance Ministry: A Case Study: The Cordillera Rehabilitation Center," *Journal of Asian Mission* 5.2 (2003), pp. 259–73.

attention is given to demonic activities in individuals, the concept of territorial spirits is embedded in their holistic worldview. Certain places are known for the presence of demonic influence, even though the concept of territorial spirits has not been developed to a level of sophistication. Also, implicitly recognized are different degrees of demonic control over individuals or places. Therefore, "demon possession", in Pentecostal minds, represents only the worst case of demonic control.

Spiritual Warfare of the Third Wave

Third Wave

The rise of the Third Wave (also dubbed Pentecostalism version 3.0), after classical Pentecostalism and the Charismatic movement (Neo-Pentecostalism), traces its genesis to the first part of the 1980s. John Wimber was a catalyst in transforming the worldviews of C. Peter Wagner and Charles Kraft of Fuller Theological Seminary through a controversial course, "Signs and Wonders". Earlier, Kraft and Wagner had been struggling over what they deemed as "powerless" Christianity in their missionary settings and were on a determined quest for an answer to this problem.

The significant contribution of the Third Wave to the discussion of demonology, especially among Evangelical circles, cannot be underestimated.[8] Although the diversity of Third Wave thinking is expanding rather than decreasing, the main focus of this branch of Pentecostalism right from the start has been "power encounter". It is broadly divided into the lower (personal or ground level) and the higher level (strategic or cosmic) power encounter.[9] In the lower level, related concepts include inner healing, deliverance, and inter-generational curses. In comparison, at the higher level, beliefs and practices are associated with territorial spirits, spiritual mapping, and prayer walks. Note that these practices have strong missiological implications. Between Kraft and Wagner, the former seems to have produced more reflections on the lower-level power encounter. The latter focuses on strategic power encounter, especially with his House of Prayer for the Nations in Colorado Springs, Colorado.

Unlike their predecessors (classical Pentecostals), leaders of the Third Wave movement are articulate, popular teachers and writers. Representatives such as C. Peter Wagner, Charles Kraft, and Neil Anderson have written countless books on the theories and practices of the power encounter and, more recently, the

---

[8] The authors, more practitioners than traditional theologians, have engendered intense discussions on demonology even as they construct theories and practices of "power encounters" with evil spirits.

[9] Varying categories have been used among Third Wave thinkers, e.g. Charles H. Kraft, "Contemporary Trends in the Treatment of Spiritual Conflict," in A. Scott Moreau, et al. (eds), *Deliver Us from Evil: An Uneasy Frontier in Christian Mission* (Monrovia: MARC, 2002), pp. 177–202.

restoration of the apostolic and prophetic offices. Now loosely networked among "post-denominational churches" in North America and elsewhere, books and conferences have proven to be the most effective tools in propagating Third Wave beliefs and practices.[10]

Notwithstanding the diversity at hand, my reflection deals mainly with Kraft's insights. I find him a respected scholar with deep pastoral and missional commitment. Also, through his teaching (with his ministry sessions before the class) and helpful publications, I am better acquainted with his manner of effecting power encounters.

Spiritual Warfare

Previously, I analyzed Kraft's theory and practice of deliverance from a classical Pentecostal perspective through a typical ministry session he conducted.[11] Thus, I found his book *Christianity With Power* extremely helpful and valuable. He extensively discusses the Western worldview, the conceptual framework for modern Christian theology and practice. This "defective" worldview, without a proper category for the supernaturals, has deprived the church of the ability to handle demons properly. As a cultural anthropologist, Kraft takes the reader on a journey of discovering Christian life with power and authority. Well-woven with his testimonies, the book shows how one can overcome typical Evangelical limitations by re-reading scripture with a holistic worldview.[12]

This book represents the author's long journey that had "only just begun".[13] His subsequent writings acquire sophistication in theory and practice. My previous analysis represents a developed stage in Kraft's approach. Now he integrates controversial concepts such as the "inner child", increasing the pain level to force demons to reveal information or to induce their obedience, cutting their arms and legs, commanding demons to jump into a box, and others.[14]

---

[10] Kraft, "Contemporary Trends in the Treatment of Spiritual Conflict," pp. 177–202 provides a valuable summary of the development of Third Wave inputs, while pp. 182–87 present details of publications and conferences.

[11] Wonsuk Ma, "A 'First Waver' Looks at the 'Third Wave': A Pentecostal Reflection on Charles Kraft's Power Encounter Terminology," *Pneuma* 19.2 (1997), pp. 189–206.

[12] Charles H. Kraft, *Christianity With Power: Your Worldview and Your Experience of the Supernatural* (Ann Arbor, MI: Servant, 1988). Especially helpful are his later chapters on conducting a "power ministry". His principles are biblically based and theologically sound. Although he leaves several topics for further exploration, I highly recommend this particular book to Christian workers for its strong combination of theory and practical steps for ministry. "Sensitive" topics include the possibility of Christians being demonized, inter-generational curses and also demonic influence attached to objects.

[13] Kraft, *Christianity with Power*, p. 177.

[14] Charles H. Kraft, "Dealing with Demonization," in Charles H. Kraft, Tom White, Ed Murphy et al., *Behind the Enemy Lines: An Advanced Guide to Spiritual Warfare* (Ann Arbor, MI: Vine Books, 1994), p. 114. See also Ma, "A 'First Waver' Look at the 'Third Wave'," pp. 191–92.

With strategic or cosmic-level spiritual warfare, we can readily identify several key practitioners: C. Peter Wagner,[15] Cindy Jacobs, John Dawson, and others. Kraft proposes three categories of spirits involved: 1) "territorial spirits" assigned to various levels of territories including nations, cities, and regions; 2) "religion/institutional spirits", "assigned to religions and organizations"; and 3) "vice spirits", having to do with vices.[16] Using Argentina as the most popular case, Kraft summarizes a common strategy:

> Cosmic-level warfare approaches the breaking of the power of cosmic-level rats through dealing with cosmic-level garbage. This garbage includes sin on the part of human populations (both present and in the past); the breaking of satanic power gained through past dedications and/or sinful use of a place; disunity and competition among spiritual leaders; and neglect of godly use of a place or territory.[17]

The cosmic-level spiritual warfare employs actions such as repentance, spiritual mapping, and intercessory prayer walk. The most apparent confrontation, however, occurs when the "strong man" is identified and "bound". The enemy gains its controlling power through pagan religious devotion or sinful use of the territory. Thus, the key weapon to break its power is warfare prayer. The end result is the liberation of an individual, family, or community from satanic power and the restoration of their relationship with God.

Analysis

Several features have become evident during the development of Third Wave demonology during the last decades. And they all have implications for Pentecostal theology and ministry.

The first is its pragmatic approach. Motivated by pastoral and missionary concerns, Third Wave concepts of demonology have been shaped through biblical evidence and a good dose of experience-based theories. In fairness, this is not the fault of Third Wavers, as scripture does not provide sufficient data to construct a complete biblical demonology. The problem is that most biblical "holes" are sometimes "filled in" by less than biblical concepts. For example, the problematic idea of an "inner child" has no biblical support whatsoever, although psychology has long employed a similar concept. It is important to note that not everything that allegedly works among Christians is biblical, such as the imaginary cage-and-punishment schemes used in spiritual warfare.

This poses a serious theological challenge: what is the limit of theological enquiry, especially when scripture does not provide necessary evidence? This

---

[15] For example, C. Peter Wagner, "Twenty-One Questions," *in Behind Enemy Lines*, pp. 123–47, presents his answers to critical questions raised to the "four-year-old" discipline of strategic power encounter.

[16] Kraft, "Contemporary Trends," p. 189.

[17] Kraft, "Contemporary Trends," p. 193.

problem has been with us throughout Christian history, just as Judaism invented many new interpretations of the law during the exilic and post-exilic eras. Clearly, the church has to live with a certain theological ambiguity, while pastoral concerns demand immediate and unambiguous answers. Often, theologians are pressured to run against biblical limits. I have benefited significantly from Third Wave emphases on, among others, the believer's inherent authority to confront evil power and the believer's responsibility to remove sin ("garbage") rather than the devil ("rat").

The second is the role of experience in theological construction. This is a little different from the case of classical Pentecostals, who were criticized for building their pneumatology based on experience. Against Third Wavers, serious charges are often made that much of the experiential data comes from demons, who are liars by nature. They would argue that these demons were forced to provide valuable information. Another example is the consensus among Third Wave thinkers that believers can be "demonized". Although the new term (being "demonized") points to a broader spectrum of demonic influence than demon possession, there is still much theological homework to do. The doctrinal stance of classical Pentecostal denominations raises pastoral problems. If a believer cannot be demonized (or possessed), a church member experiencing demonic manifestation can only be an "unbeliever". There is no doubt that experience can be a valuable resource for theologizing, yet it should come under the judgement of the scriptures.

The third is the "sensational" tendency of some concepts. For example, the theology of inter-generational curses has raised an unusual interest among Korean Christians, and often sessions are held to "cancel" such curses through inner healing. As a result of insensitive leading, however, family conflicts sometimes arise, posing serious pastoral and ethical questions.

The more fundamental question remains: is the amount of attention given to evil spirits theologically healthy? This is a matter of theological balance. In a theological framework where the devil somehow takes the centre of Christian attention (as we have seen in several places), a distorted theology reduces "God's whole redemptive activity … to destroying the devil."[18] Classical Pentecostals also share this unhealthy view, as they see the Spirit's empowerment (for example, Acts 1:8) in terms of spiritual confrontations. Again, to be fair to Third Wave leaders, it is certain that such disproportionate attention to demons is never by their design. Kraft once said that he was not looking for demons but would cast them out when he found them.

The fourth is the controversy around territorial spirits. This is a hermeneutical issue, dealing with whether or not one can build a theological pattern based on limited scriptural evidence. The concept of territorial spirits has its basis in the

---

[18] Carolyn Denise Baker and Frank D. Macchia, "Created Spirit Beings," in Stanley M. Horton (ed.), *Systematic Theology: A Pentecostal Perspective* (Springfield MO: Logion Press, 1994,) pp. 179–213 (207).

Book of Daniel, where the messenger of God was detained by the "prince of the kingdom of Persia" (Dan. 10:13) until Michael the archangel came to help free him from the twenty-one-day detention. Thus, spiritual warfare in the unseen world caused the delay in God's answer to Daniel's prayer. Here the "prince" is interpreted as the evil spirit assigned to Persia, which tried to hinder God's work. The Third Wavers tend to believe that this pattern applies to every region and political system. In the absence of sufficient biblical support, such a notion appears to me to be overly simplistic and speculative.[19]

Promises and Challenges

The development of demonology in the twentieth century through the emergence of various streams of Pentecostalism has brought both promises and challenges.

Theological

This short survey illustrates how Pentecostal Christianity has dealt with demonology, a long-ignored or unnoticed part of Christian theology. Jesus demonstrated God's power through the Holy Spirit over the evil ones as the typical sign of the presence of God's kingdom (Matt. 12:28). The ignorance of demonology, therefore, has resulted in the general avoidance of the subject. Pentecostalism recovered this topic to the theological and pastoral world, and the Third Wave has further pushed limits through its theological construct and pastoral practices.

Yet the theological challenge remains. The difficulties faced by any theologian addressing the field of demonology come from various directions, some of which we already mentioned. With its explosive nature, I propose to handle demonology "with care". We need also to take into consideration the full context of theology, particularly the biblical teachings on "the last things" (eschatology), of Christ (Christology), and the church (ecclesiology). The dilemma surrounding demonology arises from our present time, caught between the ultimate victory of Christ over Satan through his death and resurrection, and the reality and potency of the principalities and powers in this present age. The New Testament does not deny this eschatological tension. Even a slight bias toward the power of the atonement will lead to the notion of the "kingdom now", engendering a triumphalist attitude. While maintaining Christ as the centre of theology, this imbalance may result inadvertently in ignorance of the complex suffering and struggle which church members experience daily.

On the other hand, any bias towards the reality and potency of evil forces will move the centre of theology away from the atoning work of Christ, thus reducing the Christian life to a struggle with evil spirits. Pastoral sensitivity and commitment cannot justify such a shift in theological attention. The very eschatological nature of our present life should provide the needed balance.

---

[19] Cf. Baker and Macchia, "Created Spirit Beings," p. 200.

Careful attention to demonology is essential. Barth may have meant this when he advised, "Give only a quick, sharp glance to the area of demonology."[20] He warned against granting more attention to demons than they deserve. Early Pentecostals were known for blaming demons for things they never did, and I am afraid Third Wavers have not improved the situation.

Missiological

Classical Pentecostals did not intentionally link healing and exorcism with evangelism and world mission. Considering the unmistakable pattern of Jesus' proclamation of the presence of God's kingdom through healing and exorcism, Pentecostals have generally failed to articulate the missiological implications of such practices. However, Pentecostal missionary work has been known to include "signs and wonders". To the Third Wave's credit, spiritual warfare (particularly the higher, strategic kind) was explicitly motivated by, and applied to, evangelism and mission.

The influence of the Third Wave thinkers and other Pentecostal leaders can be seen in the Lausanne Movement. The 1989 Manila Manifesto included more sharply articulated spiritual warfare language. Particularly noted are two paragraphs under Section 5, "God the Evangelist":

> All evangelism involves spiritual warfare with the principalities and powers of evil, in which only spiritual weapons can prevail, especially the Word and the Spirit, with prayer. We therefore call on all Christian people to be diligent in their prayers both for the renewal of the church and for the evangelization of the world.
>
> Although the miracles of Jesus were special, being signs of his Messiahship and anticipations of his perfect kingdom when all nature will be subject to him, we have no liberty to place limits on the power of the living Creator today. We reject both the skepticism which denies miracles and the presumption which demands them, both the timidity which shrinks from the fullness of the Spirit and the triumphalism which shrinks from the weakness in which Christ's power is made perfect.[21]

As part of this Lausanne process, a study group was formed, resulting in several conferences and producing significant resource material.[22] Particularly valuable is the "Deliver Us from Evil Consultation Statement",[23] which presents the current state of affairs. I find this to be a "balanced" document because it reflects views of varying persuasions: Western and non-Western; advocates (such as Third Wavers) as well as more "reserved" participants. It also takes the

---

[20] Karl Barth, *Church Dogmatics*, 3:3:519.

[21] The Lausanne Committee for World Evangelization, "The Manila Manifesto," available at: http:// www.lausanne.org/Brix?pageID=12894. Accessed 30 December 2006.

[22] A. Scott Moreau et al. (eds), *Deliver Us from Evil: An Uneasy Frontier in Christian Mission* (Monrovia, CA: MARC, 2002).

[23] In *Deliver Us from Evil*, pp. xvii—xxviii.

subject matter positively, while issuing due cautions against excesses. Equally useful is the lead chapter by Asian theologian Bishop Hwa Yung.[24]

A serious challenge arises in non-Western contexts, where some of the newly developed Third Wave ideas take root. It is one thing to herald these ideas within the West, where spiritual beings were totally ignored; it is entirely another when they are introduced to a cultural context already crowded with a myriad of good and evil spirits. For instance, Kraft's contention that demons can be "attached" to an object which could affect the occupants of a building sounds more like an animistic belief rather than a biblical claim.[25] Years ago, a prominent South African Pentecostal church formally adopted a position to denounce the belief in inter-generational curses, even though such practice was enthusiastically adopted by many African indigenous churches. This is to say that, with its many theological "holes," demonology has slippery edges. These edges show themselves in the interaction between churches and local cultures.

Pastoral

Demonology has profound pastoral implications. Pentecostalism has brought a significant additional dimension to Christian ministry. Local pastors now have a greater responsibility to bring balanced demonology to actual-life settings.

I bring two tasks to my fellow Pentecostals. The first is to pay attention to the community dimension of power encounter. Traditionally, healing has been entirely a personal matter. As ministry takes place in a local church, exploring the community dimension of such experiences is essential. Non-Western churches may suggest ways to involve and benefit the faith community through healing ministry. In many small village settings in Asia, the healing experience of an individual is often jointly owned by the community as a whole. Such communal ownership often happens in many church plants.[26]

Another dilemma that any Pentecostal pastor faces is my second point of challenge: the problem of long-term suffering. As much as there is tension between Christ's victory and the devil's continued activity today, any long-term suffering by a faithful believer cannot be explained simply by a theological declaration, such as healing in the atonement. If salvation has been achieved through the atoning work of Christ, yet the full realization of it still awaits the

---

[24] Hwa Yung, "A Systematic Theology that Recognizes the Demonic," in *Deliver Us from Evil*, pp. 3–27.

[25] Edward Rommen (ed.), *Spiritual Power and Missions: Raising the Issues*, Evangelical Missiological Society Series 3 (Pasadena, CA: William Carey Library, 1995) devoted the entire discussion to spiritual warfare. Robert J. Priest, Thomas Campbell, and Bradford A. Mullen, in "Missiological Syncretism: The New Animistic Paradigm," pp. 9–87, lodge a strong criticism against the emerging theories and practices of power encounter. See Charles H. Kraft, "'Christian Animism' or God-Given Authority?" pp. 88–136 for his response.

[26] For example, J. Ma, *When the Spirit Meets the Spirits* reports numerous cases of healing which resulted in church planting in the northern Philippines.

appearance of the Lord, the same can be said of healing. Pentecostals are facing the challenge of preaching the good news of divine healing and ministering to those living with suffering. How to minister to HIV/AIDS-infected individuals is a case in point. Recently the Commission of World Mission and Evangelism of the World Council of Churches proposed two concepts: "cure" and "healing". Healing ministry is much broader than just bringing a cure. Victory over infirmity and disability through the grace of God, even if the actual cure will never be experienced, may be a more theologically desired goal of healing ministry.

One also needs to revisit the controversial argument of the demonization of believers. This subject needs further exploration and rethinking. Within the Pentecostal family, we can learn much from one another.

An open dialogue between different streams of Pentecostalism will be beneficial, as I myself have experienced in the Third Wave movement. With the explosive growth of both indigenous Pentecostal groups and Pentecostals who do not care whether they are indigenous or not, Pentecostal scholars and theologians could offer sympathetic, insider articulations of their beliefs and practices. Here I have Chinese house church networks especially in mind. In such an exchange, however, it is critical that the "helping hands" do not impose their theological discourses and categories on these indigenous groups. Rather, their job is to help these churches rediscover their God-given spiritual and theological gifts.

And so, our task continues. With Pentecostal-Charismatic beliefs and practices becoming widespread in the Global South, how can we formulate a demonology that is theologically balanced yet contextually and pastorally sensitive?

13. Spirit-Motivated Leadership and Service to the Poor: Hawaii's (Korean) Cedar Church

Introduction

Pentecostal mission has expanded over the decades from evangelism to community service and justice issues.[1] This chapter is a case study investigating an immigrant church's service to its community and the role of church leadership.

This study began in 2018 with our first visit to a relatively small Korean-immigrant Pentecostal church on the outskirts of Honolulu, Hawaii. Two distinct features of the church immediately caught our attention. The first was its outstanding worship, marked by the immediacy of the Holy Spirit's presence and work. The second was its aggressive and equally striking outreach to its neighbours, which included weekly food distribution and care for the homeless and the elderly. In light of the church members' own struggles as ageing first-generation immigrants, we would describe our initial encounter with this community as truly mind-blowing. We made another visit in 2020 and again observed the church's worship and food distribution. We interviewed senior pastor Rev. Duk-hwan Kim, and two lay leaders in charge of one food distribution programme, as well as two senior centres. I (Wonsuk) also interviewed the state representative of the district in which the church is located, as well as several staff members of the church who were coordinating various programmes. What impressed us most was their enthusiasm and commitment, despite their limited resources of personnel and finances. Our main enquiry here involves the correlation between the Pentecostal faith of an immigrant community and its aggressive social engagement. What aspects of Pentecostal faith have given this congregation the confidence, even audacity, to tackle so aggressively the social needs they have seen around them? Thus, the focus is limited to theological enquiry.[2] There are two relevant areas to the study.

---

[1] See Ma and Ma, "Missiology: Evangelization, Holistic Ministry, and Social Justice."

[2] Therefore, the study precludes any assessment of its operational, financial, and legal details. Hence, this study does not imply an endorsement of the ministry.

"Progressive Pentecostals"

Early Pentecostals showed a keen interest in the well-being of daily life.[3] Primarily drawn from the lower social strata, they had a deep belief in God's supernatural healing and miraculous work, which motivated them to hope for a better future.[4] Various studies have identified the biblical and theological foundations for Pentecostal social engagement.[5] The publication of *Global Pentecostalism* (2007) by Donald Miller and Tetsunao Yamamori marked the first systematic field study attesting to Pentecostal efficacy in social change.[6] The authors, who are not Pentecostals themselves, looked for growing and vibrant local churches in the Global South tackling social issues without relying on outside assistance. When they compiled the initial list according to these criteria, they saw that, to their surprise, most of the churches were Pentecostal, which led to the term "progressive Pentecostal". This study went one step beyond the Pentecostal experience of upward social mobility, as observed by David Martin in Latin America.[7] *Global Pentecostalism* identified needy social contexts, the zeal of the Pentecostals, and the role of leadership as the main components shaping this "progressive" ethos.

Migration Studies

Ever-increasing migration has been one of the top areas of interest in international studies.[8] Accordingly, the role and impact of immigrant Christian communities, especially in Western host nations, is a topic of ongoing discussion, which ranges in tone from extremely positive to reserved. The former may be found in Jehu Hanciles' study of African immigrant churches in North America. Hanciles discusses four missionary roles that immigrant churches can play. One is the Samuel-Eli type, found mostly among mainline churches. The immigrant members bring new dynamism and zeal, which attract young members to declining congregations, ultimately replacing the "old" leadership of the Western church.[9] Paul Freston, also discussing immigrant churches,

---

[3] See, for example, Julie C. Ma, "Touching Lives of People Through the Holistic Mission Work of the Buntains in Calcutta, India," *International Bulletin of Mission Research* 40.1 (January 2016), p. 72.

[4] For example, Daniel Isgrigg, "'I Tried Poverty': Exploring the Psychological Impact of Poverty and Prosperity in the Life of Oral Roberts," *Spiritus: ORU Journal of Theology* 5.1 (Spring 2020), pp. 5–24.

[5] The groundbreaking work is Dempster, Klaus, and Petersen (eds), *Called and Empowered.*

[6] Donald E. Miller and Tetsunao Yamamori, *Global Pentecostalism: The New Face of Christian Social Engagement* (Berkeley: University of California Press, 2007).

[7] Martin, *Tongues of Fire.*

[8] For more statistics, see the International Organization for Migration, *World Migration Report 2020* (Geneva: International Organization for Migration, 2020), www.iom.int/wmr (accessed 22 March 2023).

[9] Jehu Hanciles, *Beyond Christendom: Globalization, African Migration, and the Transformation of the West* (Maryknoll, NY: Orbis Books, 2008), p. 327.

questions the legitimacy of this claim of "reverse mission" among Christian immigrants to Europe. Considering the relative isolation of immigrant churches from the mainstream church, he sees little possibility of them having a major mission impact.[10] As a first-generation immigrant congregation, Cedar Church and its experience are of interest to students of migration.

Hawaii, the Context

Korean Christians in Hawaii

Korean immigrants arrived in the tropical paradise of Hawaii during two distinct periods. The first was between 1903 and 1905, when several thousand Koreans came as labourers on Hawaiian sugar plantations. With Korea gradually falling into the colonial grip of the Japanese, the opportunity for a new life in the American territory attracted many Koreans. Initially drawn from Methodist circles in the Inchon area, a high proportion of Korean laborers in Hawaii were Christian. By 1910 their number had reached 7,000, including 1,100 "picture brides" who had immigrated since 1905.[11] By 1908 there were 2,800 Korean Christians and thirty-nine churches in the Hawaiian Islands.[12] These churches served as social and community centres for the labourers, in addition to being their spiritual haven, and they actively supported the independence movement against Japanese colonial rule. They provided financial assistance to the independence government and its armed activities against the Japanese imperial army. The churches also nurtured several key leaders of the independence initiatives. Syngman Rhee, the first president of independent Korea, was a Methodist leader who spent several years in Hawaii from 1913.

The second wave of Korean immigration to Hawaii occurred in the mid-1960s, swelling the Korean American population to 30,000. The new arrivals also added a sizeable number of Korean churches, which reached 100 in Honolulu in the 1980s. Currently, sixty-four Korean churches are formally registered in the entire state, with perhaps eighty in all, including house churches.[13] According to the list of major Korean churches, Cedar Church was the second of the churches established in the 1970s. After the surge of Korean

---

[10] Paul Freston, "Reverse Mission: A Discourse in Search of Reality?" *PentecoStudies: An Interdisciplinary Journal for Research on the Pentecostal and Charismatic Movements* 9.2 (2010), pp. 153–74.

[11] K. Kale Yu, *Understanding Korean Christianity: Grassroots Perspectives on Causes, Culture, and Responses* (Eugene, OR: Pickwick, 2019), p. 246.

[12] Hyung-chan Kim, "The History and Role of the Church in the Korean American Community," in Hyung-chan Kim (ed.), *The Korean Diaspora: Historical and Sociological Studies of Korean Immigration and Assimilation in North America* (Santa Barbara, CA: ABC-Clio, 1977), p. 50.

[13] Sabin Kim, "Korean Churches in Hawaii," in *Thirty-Year History of Hawaii Cedar Church: 1975–2004* (in Korean) (Honolulu: History Publication Committee of Hawaii Cedar Church, 2004), p. 190.

immigrants and churches in the 1970s, people began to leave the churches, as they no longer needed their immediate help. Also, many Koreans (and others) left the islands for better opportunities elsewhere.

Hawaiian Social Context

Between 1778 and 1890, the native Hawaiian population in the islands plummeted from approximately 300,000 to 37,656.[14] In addition, there has long been a steady exodus to the mainland, where it can be much easier for people to make ends meet.[15]

An online list of reasons why *not* to move to Hawaii is revealing; five of the top twelve reasons are economic:[16]

- There's a good chance you'll be living in what feels like poverty.
- It's one of the worst places to start a business.
- Pay is below national averages, despite a much higher cost of living.
- First-time home ownership is nearly impossible.
- Everything is really expensive.

The cost of housing, for example, is 202 percent of the national average, followed by utilities (89 percent higher), groceries (62 percent higher), and transportation (35 percent higher). Overall, the cost of living in Honolulu is 88 percent higher than the national average.[17] Compounded by the weak educational system and various social challenges, these paradise islands are a paradise lost. The recent COVID-19 pandemic has hit tourism, the state's primary industry, hard. Currently, the state's highest priority is dealing with homelessness. The lieutenant governor's office has declared it "one of the worst homeless epidemics in the country, with the highest rate of homelessness per capita in the nation". Around 15,000 people are homeless, representing about 1 percent of the state's population. Some 13,000 are enrolled in Medicaid, and this number accounts for $1.2 billion of a $2 billion annual Medicaid budget. The governor's office

[14] R. Kuykendall, *The Hawaiian Kingdom – Vol. 1: Foundation and Transformation, 1778–1854* (Honolulu: University of Hawaii Press, 1938), p. 387, quoted in Paul Miller, "The Holy Spirit and the Nineteenth-Century Mission to Hawaii," *Spiritus: ORU Journal of Theology* 5.1 (Spring 2020), p. 79.

[15] United States Census Bureau, "2019 US Population Estimates Continue to Show the Nation's Growth Is Slowing," 20 December 2019, https://www.census.gov/newsroom/press-releases/2019/popest-nation.html (accessed 22 March 2023).

[16] LivingInHawaii.com, "12 Reasons You Should NOT Move to Hawaii!" https://www.livinginhawaii.com/12-reasons-you-should-not-move-to-hawaii/ (accessed 22 March 2023).

[17] PayScale, "Cost of Living in Honolulu, Hawaii," https://www.payscale.com/cost-of-living-calculator/Hawaii-Honolulu (accessed 22 March 2023).

confirms there is "almost total overlap with these high utilizers and the chronically homeless population".[18]

The ageing population is another social challenge. In 2020 the proportion of people sixty years of age and older in Hawaii was 25.3 percent of the state's population. By 2030, this group will reach 27.9 percent.[19] This large and still increasing aged population has strained the state's healthcare resources. Furthermore, alcohol and drug abuse have become widespread.

Cedar Church

In this section, after reviewing the nearly fifty-year history of Cedar Church, we focus on its present pastor and the scope and "tone" of its many ministries.

History

In 1975 Yoido Full Gospel Church, Seoul, Korea, commissioned Rev. Hee-chul Ahn and his wife to be missionaries to the Korean immigrants in Hawaii. Riding the second wave of immigration, the Hawaii Full Gospel Church was born with four families.[20] In the well-established Korean Christian circle, dominated by Methodist and Presbyterian churches, this first Pentecostal church introduced several other firsts to the Korean Christian community: daily dawn prayer meetings, gospel songs, Friday overnight prayer, and a fellowship meal after Sunday worship.[21] The church lived up to its name, for it seemed full of the Holy Spirit, faith, and love, serving as an epicentre of revivals. However, this super-active church attracted both admiration and harsh criticism. Eventually, several other churches adopted the "full gospel" prayer programmes.[22] By 1981, when the Ahns moved on to another pastoral position, the church had grown to 150 registered members.

There were several leadership changes between the founding pastor and Duk-hwan Kim, the current senior pastor, who began in 2002. The church reached its height during the tenure of the third pastor, Keun Oh (1987–98). He invested in daily dawn prayer, Bible studies, preaching of repentance, and the fullness of the Holy Spirit.[23]

---

[18] Lieutenant Governor of the State of Hawaii, Josh Green, "Homeless in Hawaii: Facts and Resources," https://ltgov.hawaii.gov/homeless-in-hawaii-facts-and-resources/ (accessed 22 March 2023).

[19] Department of Health, "2017–2019 Hawaii State Plan on Aging" (Executive Office on Aging, c. 2019), p. 10, http://www.advancingstates.org/sites/default/files/Hawaii_draft_20192023%20Hawaii%20State%20Plan%20on%20Aging%20rev%2005-17-19.pdf (accessed 22 March 2023).

[20] *Thirty Year History of Hawaii Cedar Church*, p. 46.

[21] *Thirty Year History of Hawaii Cedar Church*, pp. 48-49.

[22] *Thirty Year History of Hawaii Cedar Church*, p. 49.

[23] *Thirty Year History of Hawaii Cedar Church*, p. 69.

As the spiritual foundation was solidified, the church began to pray for a property on which to build. The surprising – and no doubt miraculous – purchase of the Kahili lot in 1988 and the groundbreaking the following year for the church building became the turning point. Situated in a residential area, the church committed itself to serving its immediate community by providing childcare, parking spaces, and areas for community events. When the church dedicated the worship centre in 1989, the Full Gospel Church (Cedar Church's original name) became the seventh Korean church with its own building.[24]

By 1990 the church had 300 registered members, with 200 adults and 60 children regularly attending services. In that year, the growing church broke ground for its education wing and ordained the first elder. Various initiatives followed, such as the launch of Trinity Bible College and a Korean-language school, both short-lived. In 1997 the church began various mission programmes: the organization of Paul Mission, mission seminars, and the first short-term mission trip.[25] During 1993–95, the House of Love was established as a residential facility, with the church providing over $4,000 in monthly support. At least eleven individuals stayed in this facility under the pastoral care of a residential clergy and his family.[26] The nature of the residential rehabilitation programme is not specified, but we suspect it related to drug addiction, as there was a special revival meeting in the same year on drug issues.

When Pastor Oh resigned from the church in 1998, the membership had dwindled to only eighty registered members, with just ten children. History attributes this sudden decline and Oh's resignation to his frequent travel for revival meetings and "the attraction of many women to his handsomeness and eloquence".[27] The church had two different pastors in the next four years before Kim took the leadership in 2002. During this interval, the sharp decline in membership continued.

Pastor Duk-hwan Kim

We have known Pastor Kim from his college days in the 1970s, observing his theological studies and accomplishments. And we knew he had been a missionary to Las Palmas in Spain's Canary Islands. But we had not had contact with him until we reconnected during our visit to Hawaii in 2018. At that time, we encountered a radically changed minister who had become a social activist. Our previous knowledge of Cedar Church had been almost nil, although Rev. Hee-chul Ahn, its founder, was a college classmate of mine (Wonsuk).

Duk-hwan Kim began his pastoral responsibility with only eight members – and an $800,000 debt! He immediately announced several changes. First, the

[24] *Thirty Year History of Hawaii Cedar Church*, p. 71.
[25] *Thirty Year History of Hawaii Cedar Church*, pp. 82-85.
[26] *Thirty Year History of Hawaii Cedar Church*, pp. 96-99.
[27] *Thirty Year History of Hawaii Cedar Church*, p. 103.

church changed its name to Cedar Church.[28] Second, he made a long-term commitment to remain as the church's pastor, identifying frequent leadership changes as the leading cause of the church's instability and decline. Third, he would not draw any salary from the church for the first year. His message was, "Let's forget the past, forgive and reconcile with one another so that we can rebuild the church in unity and love".[29] For the next two years (2002–3), the main topic of his sermons was "Receive the Holy Spirit." Amazingly, the church soon recovered to 280 registered members, with an average of 150 worshippers attending weekly services by October 2003.[30]

What the Church Is and Does

After its peak in the 1970s, the Korean immigrant population has steadily aged, with only a trickling of new arrivals. At the same time, churches are losing their younger generation, and Cedar Church is no exception. In our two visits, we observed that most of the members were in their sixties or older.

Cedar Church is located in the area known as Kalihi Valley. A realty group provided the following statistics for 2018 for the area: 39.6 percent of the 53,886 residents were born outside the United States; the median household income was $80,546, which is $6,023 below the poverty level; and more people live in rented properties (6,391) than own their own home (5,675).[31] We saw a massive public housing compound for low-income families in the vicinity. John Mizuno, the state representative of this area, describes his constituency as "mostly Filipino, hard-working-class, with two or three blue-collar jobs, often two or three families in a lot"; also, "most kids are qualified for free meals".[32]

During our first visit, we were immediately struck by the accommodation facility behind the main church building for homeless families. Kim told me that he opened the church lot and pitched tents for homeless people.

The 9:00 a.m. service was sparsely attended, with about thirty mostly grey-haired women. However, worship was electric during the three Sunday services, characteristic of true Pentecostal worship. But the prayer time after the sermon caught us off guard. More than a dozen worshippers moved to the front seats to be prayed for by the pastor. Kim spent about thirty minutes laying his hands on the troubling part of the body of each member. He knelt to his knees to hold the feet of several members, and what surprised us most was the extended time he spent praying for healing and the passion he poured into his prayer. I (Wonsuk)

---

[28] This was the name of the churches that Pastor Kim had previously established in Spain and in the UK.

[29] *Thirty Year History of Hawaii Cedar Church*, pp. 138-39.

[30] *Thirty Year History of Hawaii Cedar Church*, pp. 152, 177.

[31] Point2, "Kalihi Valley Demographics," https://www.point2homes.com/US/Neighborhood/HI/Honolulu/Kalihi-Valley-Demographics.html (accessed 22 March 2023).

[32] Interview with John Mizuno, Honolulu, 3 February 2020.

preached at the 11:00 a.m. service, which had about sixty worshippers, and he asked me to do as he did after the service. His singular emphasis on the supernatural work of the Holy Spirit was evident. Among the Korean Pentecostal churches, he has been a popular speaker on the Holy Spirit, especially with the clergy.

Among many social programmes of the church, the food bank is tops in its frequency, participants, and impact. We participated in one of the two weekly food distributions on Tuesday of the same week. Administered under the auspices of the Good Samaritan Foundation (est. 2010), the church's social service arm, the church lot was filled with trucks, tables, volunteers, and people with bags and carts. While a score of volunteers, from both within and outside the church, prepared the food distribution routine and cooked a hot meal to serve the attendees, about eighty sat in the church for worship. By the time the food distribution began, about 150 filled the church lot. On our second visit, the two weekly food distributions continued, now the largest in the city. The signed distribution list in Kahili on 22 January 2020 indicates that 244 people attended church, and 469 adults and 193 children were served dinner. Only two employees were on the list for the day.[33] Considering that about 6,000 persons live below the poverty line in the Kalihi Valley, the church has been serving a significant portion of the struggling families.

The "marshal" of the day's food distribution was Mrs Yong-im Kim, a seventy-seven-year-old senior deaconess of the church, also in charge of a senior centre. Although frail in appearance, she exercised complete control over the challenging food distribution. She also recruited, trained, and organized volunteers. When the church first began the programme in 2014, she and the pastor visited many food distribution centres and programmes to learn how to operate such a charity. She was extremely proud of the programme, as many area churches have followed its example, although no other Korean churches in the city have.[34] Coming to the church every day and serving has become the centre of her life and transformation.[35]

This transformative effect is also found among other volunteers. Muhammad Ashram, a retired Pakistani professor, saw an announcement for volunteers on Mrs Kim's social media. Although Muslim in faith, he came to the church two or three times each week "to do things that nobody else likes to do", such as cleaning. After suffering two strokes, he said, "Serving the programme makes my day". Now, after volunteering for a year, he calls Mrs Kim "Mama" and the church "different from other churches" in its community orientation.[36] Mrs Kim

---

[33] Hawaii Cedar Church, "Regular Food Distribution Log, Jan 22, 2020." Various reports were graciously provided by Ilbo Park and Miyeo Yoo.

[34] This fact is confirmed by the list "Hawaii Food Bank Member Agencies" (n.d.), which includes over 210 churches, ministries, and civic groups.

[35] Interview with Yong-im Kim, Honolulu, 5 February 2020.

[36] Interview with Muhamad Ashram, Honolulu, 5 February 2020.

told us that many volunteers are disabled: two are deaf, two are active cancer patients, and many others are ill. It is the poor serving other poor, well representing the early Pentecostal culture.

The senior centres are another active programme of the church. Mrs Kim oversees one in Wahiawa, where the original Korean immigrants settled as sugarcane labourers. Running for two years now, this daycare programme serves between thirty and forty elderly individuals. Daniel Ham manages the centre in Kaliki (at the time, he was seventy-eight years old). He was a founding member of the church and served as an elder. The senior centre, now in its eighth year of operation, has between fifty and sixty in regular weekly attendance. In addition to the usual programmes such as singing, dancing, aerobics, English lessons, and games, a cooked meal and food packets are provided. The January 2020 Agency Activity Report shows that 154 adults (or 176 households) were served food, as well as food packets, in the Kaliki senior centre, and 96 individuals (or 147 households) in the Wahiawa centre. Ham said that no other Korean churches have a similar programme.

Ham previously had a successful business career, including a Christian broadcasting company, exercising his influence in Korean American and Christian circles. After recovering from two bouts of late-stage cancer, liver surgeries, and the dismissal and reinstatement of his eldership, he found a new life under Pastor Kim's pastoral leadership and has often accompanied Kim on his preaching tours to share his testimony. Kim led a full-week relay prayer of the whole church for him, during Ham's illness. He attributes miraculous healings to the power of the Holy Spirit mediated through Pastor Kim's preaching and prayer.[37] His life again exemplifies God's transformation of life through the power of the Holy Spirit channelled through human agency.

The third area of the church's service is for homeless people. Pastor Kim took homelessness seriously from the beginning of his ministry and opened the church grounds for tents for the homeless. Later he built a fifteen-room extension at the back of the main sanctuary to house homeless people. In 2012, thirty-five people lived on the church premises. Some of them serve as volunteer staff for the church and social programmes. The third Sunday English worship was instituted in the afternoon so that they could join the worship. As Ham mentioned, the homeless members join the meal during the Sunday lunch hour between the second and third worship services. This radical decision of Pastor Kim caused a sizeable loss of (Korean) membership.

Several other social service programmes are listed in a booklet of the Good Samaritan Foundation (c. 2010):

- House of Love (drug rehabilitation)
- Korean Cultural School
- Scholarship Programme

[37] Interview with Daniel Ham, Honolulu, 5 February 2020.

- Evangel Theological Seminary
- NGO Projects in Europe and Africa
- Nursing Home Project.[38]

Conclusion

As previously stated, our objective was to discover the motivation of this ageing immigrant church in its unrelenting passion for social issues. A full assessment of the efficacy of the programmes would require a more in-depth analysis of the management and financial documents. In this concluding section, I highlight some lessons this church provides to fellow immigrant Christian communities and to the host (American) church. We then revisit the possible correlation between Pentecostal faith and social service.

Lessons We Gleaned

The first lesson is the challenge the church offers to first-generation immigrant churches. The church has defied many obstacles that typically keep first-generation, non-English-speaking Christian immigrants from engaging with society. Pastor Kim has to use an interpreter in dealing with the city and the state legislature, which he does not feel is a hindrance. The lack of human, relational, or financial resources did not stop the church from reaching out to the needy in the community.[39] The church has demonstrated that each local congregation can contribute to its local life with its unique social and spiritual gifts. Pastor Kim has a unique sense of indebtedness to American society, which had received the immigrants and offered them a better life – and it was time to return the favour.[40]

The second lesson is the role of leadership. Throughout the church's half-century history, the current level of social engagement has been new with Kim's pastoral leadership. Both the Pentecostal identity of the church and the pressing social needs around the church remain unchanged. From where, then, did this difference come? The lay leaders attribute it to the vision and direction of the church leader.[41] Until 1986, Pastor Kim was a "decent" preacher, stressing an ethical life. After a week of fasting and prayer, he experienced the presence and work of the Holy Spirit in his ministry. His theology of the church is simple: infilling of the Holy Spirit (internally) and serving the community (externally).[42]

The third lesson is the church's cooperation with various civic and government agencies. Mizuno praised Kim for taking the initiative to reach out to his office and the local government. The massive food distribution

---

[38] "Good Samaritan Foundation" (c. 2010), an information booklet.

[39] In the interview Ham stated that the lack of young people in the church has empowered the elderly to serve.

[40] Interview with Rev. Duk-hwan Kim, Honolulu, 2 February 2020.

[41] Ham interview; Y. Kim interview.

[42] D. Kim interview.

programmes require close cooperation with various agencies to provide food.[43] Mizuno commented that such a spirit of collaboration is rare among first-generation immigrant churches.[44]

Pentecostal Faith and Social Engagement

What is the correlation between Pentecostal faith and social engagement? Although not every Pentecostal church maintains the same set of beliefs or exercises what it claims to believe, several tenets are common, including in Cedar Church.

The first is the immediate and supernatural work of the Holy Spirit experienced by the believers. The "fullness in the Spirit" and healing are two main emphases of Pastor Kim and the church. This pastor pays particular attention to praying by laying on his hands, as the external evidence that a minister believes and anticipates the supernatural work of the Holy Spirit.[45]

The second is the empowering effect of vibrant spiritual life. Ham confessed that, at his age, serving the church and managing the senior centre is hard, but he believes, as does Mrs Kim, that as he serves, the Lord has drastically improved his health. In this way, the Holy Spirit is the motivation and the sustaining power for God's work. Indeed, the passionate involvement of the members, mostly elderly and even handicapped, in the church's social services and the enthusiastic leadership of their pastor (who has persevered despite his inability to speak fluent English) attest to this theology of empowerment.

The third is the realignment of ecclesiology because of the experiential pneumatology. The radical action of the church to welcome the homeless was the theological turning point for the church. According to Ham, serving the community became the church's priority, and he witnessed God's miraculous supply of resources when the church initiated social programmes.

The fourth is the belief that the true mark of the Spirit-empowered believer is serving others and that the fullness of the Holy Spirit is the fullness of Jesus' heart, which would direct one's heart toward the poor and the sick. Pastor Kim was motivated to organize the Holy Spirit Camp to prepare church leaders, primarily clergy, to experience baptism in the Holy Spirit and train them to carry out their ministry in the fullness of the Spirit. He has stated that anyone who claims to be filled with the Holy Spirit but is not giving priority to serving the needy is selfish or mistaken about serving in the fullness of the Spirit.[46]

---

[43] Ron Mizutani, president of Hawaii Foodbank, praised the church's working closely with his agency: his message is published in the fundraising brochure by the Foundation and Hawaii Cedar Church (2018).

[44] Mizuno interview.

[45] D. Kim interview.

[46] D. Kim interview.

This model of "the poor serving the fellow poor" is the heart of Pentecostal ethos.[47] Even so, the accomplishments of this unlikely, aged immigrant church are admirable and exceptional. Its theology and experience of the Holy Spirit seem to account for the motivation and the energy to carry out its many ambitious programmes. Representative Mizuno's belief that "being an immigrant church is an advantage"[48] may be fully realized only when the community embraces the empowerment theology of the Holy Spirit.

This study may have identified one source of the "fuel" that fires a church's social service. However, the question remains: why do not all Spirit-empowered individuals and churches exhibit the same passion? I do not expect a reflective answer from Pastor Kim or similar activists, who "do not just talk but do".[49] And we have to recognize that the future of many immigrant churches is uncertain, including that of Cedar Church. With the primary workforce now in their seventies, sustainability is not their priority question. Kim does not expect his church to continue indefinitely with business as usual. He is now talking with the city to explore donating his property so that a high-rise community facility can be constructed, with the church continuing to manage part of the social and spiritual programmes.

Although most of his fellow Korean American ministers do not see their churches following the same path, this study has reminded us that "we are all sojourners". Therefore, let us live our lives as full as possible of the Spirit's empowerment and purposefulness! This is the final lesson we learned from our old friend.

Postscript: The COVID Pandemic

The data point for this study was February 2020. Since then, the unprecedented COVID pandemic has deeply touched every part of social life. At the close of 2020, the church graciously provided the latest data, allowing us to update this study. First, there are contextual changes. The state's population decline continues for the fourth straight year, with a net loss of 8,607 people in the fiscal year 2020 (compared with 7,487 in 2019).[50] In the 2020 election, John Mizuno was re-elected as a state representative, a position he has held since 2006.

As expected, the pandemic has seriously impacted the church's social outreach. First, it has expanded the number of beneficiaries. For example, according to the report of 9 December 2020, the church distributed food to 325

---

[47] See Chapter 6.
[48] Mizuno interview.
[49] Mizuno interview.
[50] United Census Bureau, https://www2.census.gov/programs-surveys/popest/tables/2010-2020/state/totals/ (accessed 22 March 2023).

households, representing 1,204 people.[51] This represents almost a 100 percent increase from the January data referenced above, reflecting the economic challenges in the COVID environment. All other distribution points were closed, except the Kalihi site, because of various pandemic restrictions.

Second, according to Rev. Yoo, who oversees all the social outreach programmes, the church has faced formidable challenges in securing food since the pandemic broke out. The recent monthly reports reveal that the agencies are only able to provide produce, pantry items, and snacks, having had to discontinue cooked food. Accordingly, the amount of food has been significantly reduced, while the number of recipients has nearly doubled. Additionally, the church has now assumed the responsibility of food delivery, as the agencies are no longer providing this logistics service. These new data further affirm that the challenges from COVID have not diminished but have strengthened the church's resolve and commitment to its social outreach.

---

[51] Hawaii Cedar Church, "Report to Office of Community Services of the State of Hawaii," 9 December 2020.

14. Pentecostal Gift to Christian Unity

On a beautiful September day in Oxford, a modest celebration took place to mark the close of the Edinburgh 2010 programme.[1] In a redundant English church building, which once housed a vibrant mission community, mission thinkers, leaders, and practitioners met from many parts of the world. They came together to celebrate the publishing of the Regnum Edinburgh Centenary Series. Its unprecedented thirty-five-volume series was hailed for its diversity in themes and geographical and ecclesial representations. The highlight of this auspicious occasion was a presentation by a world-renowned mission historian on church unity and mission.[2] Various rejoinders, reflections, and conversations ensued that afternoon.[3] The day's theme, "One Christ, Many Witnesses", was fitting in the sense that church unity was the dominant theme in the 1910 Edinburgh Missionary Conference, and the modern ecumenical movement was birthed as a concrete expression of the Edinburgh discussion. Hence mission and unity were part of the central framework for the concluding volume of the Edinburgh Centenary Series.[4]

Dana Robert, a mission historian with a broad global perspective and strong African connections, was one of the presenters. In her presentation, she assessed the current state of ecumenical affairs and pleaded for new directions toward church unity. She helpfully characterized the conceptual and practical development of unity within three eras: "Cooperation for World Evangelization and the Kingdom of God (1910)", "Ecclesiocentric Ecumenism: One World, One Church, One Mission (1948–63)", and "Worldwide Networking: Many

[1] An earlier and shorter version of this study was presented under the title of "A Pentecostal Reflection on Christian Unity in the New Christian Millennium" at the Global Forum for the Future of World Christianity confer- ence, Jeju Island, Korea, in May 2015.

[2] She was also the keynote speaker for the Edinburgh 2010 conference in June 2010, Edinburgh, Scotland. See Dana L. Robert, "Mission in Long Perspective: Keynote Address," in Kirsteen Kim and Andrew Anderson (eds), *Edinburgh 2010: Mission Today and Tomorrow*, Regnum Edinburgh Centenary Series 35 (Oxford: Regnum Books, 2011), pp. 55–68, followed by rejoinders.

[3] All the presentations of this occasion were later published in *Transformation* 33.4 (October 2016).

[4] Kenneth R. Ross et al., *Ecumenical Missiology*.

Witnesses, One Christ (2010)".[5] According to her, the 1963 mission conference marked the era of diversity in world Christianity and its mission. Affirming the central message of one Christ, she pointed out a clear need for reconceptualizing Christian unity. The basis for her proposition is two-fold. Firstly, according to Robert, there is a clear limitation to the approaches toward church unity by the organized ecumenical instruments, such as the World Council of Churches (WCC). This "big tent" ideal, the creation of the Western church, has been undermined by the steady weakening of the Western church through the rise of secularism. Secondly, the radical shift of world Christianity has posed a serious question as to how the growing churches in the Global South could meaningfully participate in or even lead this "Edinburgh project" of church unity. The proliferation of contextual and local theologies, particularly from the Global South, has been growing to replace the "one church, one mission" ethos. Considering that almost two-thirds of world Christians live today in Africa, Asia, and Latin America, the viability of the traditional methods of ecumenism is scrutinized by both the North and the South.[6] Robert then concluded with four "frameworks" for the conceptual and practical development of Christian unity and mission for this and the next generation.

Dana Robert's presentation inspires the following reflection. This study aims to bring the role and contribution of Pentecostal Christianity to the quest for church unity. Robert's proposed "frameworks" are: "Common Witness Through Global Networking", "The Power of Testimony", "Centrality of the Holy Spirit", and "The Ecumenism of Blood".[7] All four are relevant to the life and witness of Pentecostals. However, for this reflection, I will explore potential Pentecostal contributions to Christian unity and mission through three essential aspects of Christian life: presence, worship, and service. Each topic will be developed by asking the following questions: (1) How have Pentecostals fared so far? (2) What has caused Pentecostals to be or to do? (3) How can they contribute to or hurt Christian unity? In the process, I will engage with the latter three of Robert's frameworks, namely testimonies, the Holy Spirit, and marginality. In doing so, I will incorporate real-life stories (that is, "testimonies") into this discussion. These narratives are to illustrate the point and be faithful to the concrete thinking of Pentecostals.

Numerical Growth

A potential gift of Pentecostal Christianity to unity comes from its expansion, which provides an increasing Christian presence. The presence of a vibrant Christian community in society is a "sign and portent" of God's kingdom in their

[5] Dana L. Robert, "One Christ, Many Witnesses: Visions of Mission and Unity, Edinburgh and Beyond," *Transformation* 33.4 (October 2016), pp. 271–74.
[6] Robert, "One Christ, Many Witnesses," pp. 273–74.
[7] Robert, "One Christ, Many Witnesses," pp. 274–78.

midst. It is especially true when Christianity is present as a minority religion among other dominant religion(s). This unique gift of Pentecostalism is expressed in several areas. To put it bluntly, there is no church without warm bodies (or believers). Without churches, there is nothing to unite. The church is the gathering of God's people with Christ as the head. People are essential in the church, as much so as Christ.

There are several distinct contributions of Pentecostal Christianity to the growth and expansion of global Christianity.[8] The first is its exponential growth throughout its history. It is generally agreed that Pentecostalism's birth, rise, and expansion were among the most significant twentieth-century developments in Christianity. In many parts of the world, Christian growth was led by Pentecostal churches. The second is the megachurch movement. This recent development is primarily a Pentecostal phenomenon. Regardless of denominational links, most megachurches today in large cities of the world exhibit a Pentecostal type of worship songs, fervent prayer (for healing, for example), and messages.[9] The third are mass evangelistic campaigns, often emphasizing healing. Large-scale events are interdenominationally organized and hosted to benefit the local churches with evangelistic fruit. The fourth is the saturated presence of Pentecostal congregations. In reality, most of them are small community churches in urban and rural settings. The gift of Pentecostal "presence" is felt through the saturated presence of its congregations.

What has caused this incredible growth and enabled Pentecostalism to penetrate almost all church traditions and socio-cultural contexts? This is where Robert's "frameworks" play a helpful role. The centrality of the Holy Spirit is the foundation of Pentecostal life. It is the "Holy Spirit [that] links the work of Christ to the world [as the] focus on the Spirit opens witness of healing (both personal and communal)".[10] The foundation of Pentecostal life is an encounter with God through the Holy Spirit. Recovering the "apostolic" dimension of Christian spirituality, Pentecostalism is known for its emphasis on and experience of healing and miracles. This experiential characteristic affects one's religious life, including lively and expressive worship[11] and witnessing through testimony. The power of testimony is essential in the participatory dimension of

[8] For more discussion, see Chapter 10.

[9] Leadership Network, "Global Megachurches," http://leadnet.org/world (accessed 22 March 2023).; and Hartford Institute of Religion Research, "Database of Megachurches in the US," http://www.hartfordinstitute.org/megachurch/database.html (accessed 22 March 2023).

[10] Robert, "One Christ, Many Witnesses," p. 277.

[11] For example, see Ma and Ma, *Mission in the Spirit*, Chapter 15, "Local Church, Worship, and Theological Formation," which characterizes Pentecostal worship by intensity and liveliness, participation, spontaneity, and experience of the transcendental.

Pentecostal worship.[12] Filled with the Holy Spirit and personal testimonies, every Pentecostal believer is a potential evangelist. They are now motivated and empowered through the Pentecostal teaching of the baptism of the Holy Spirit. More often than not, this draws hostile attention, especially from the dominant religion in a given context. For example, it is well documented that the highest number of churches attacked and burned by Islamic mobs in Indonesia were Pentecostal churches.[13]

How does this ever-expanding presence of Pentecostal Christianity contribute to, or hurt, Christian unity? To be frank, the growth of Pentecostal churches has resulted in countless divisions of existing churches. In the movement's early years, Pentecostal believers were forced out of their churches due to their Pentecostal experience. However, aggressive evangelism and an emphasis on local church growth often damage Christian unity.[14] Large churches have also brought the so-called Walmart effect to smaller churches in the area. At the same time, as seen below, the size and spread help initiate interchurch projects and active ecumenical involvement. On a macro level, sharing testimonies has become a prominent feature of the new ecumenical method. The Global Christian Forum (GCF) has created a "neutral space" for all the churches to come to share their journey with Christ and with one another. Other gatherings have adopted this methodology. Its theological document states:

> The most important practice in the development of the GCF and its meetings is the telling of faith stories. It was discovered that this approach enabled the full participation of those Christian communities in which sharing testimonies occur regularly, including notably Pentecostal, Evangelical, and African Instituted churches ... In these communities, the stories are a means to spread the Gospel, seeking through one's own story of conversion and God's continuing faithfulness to encourage and strengthen the faith of others in their praise and service of God. All members are recognized to have a story; testimonies are not reserved for those with special positions. In the GCF setting, faith stories brought together ... experience with the practice has brought a new recognition that sharing such stories has long been part of many traditions.[15]

The bottom-line question is this: with their increasing and powerful presence in local and global settings, how can Pentecostals be conscious stewards of the

[12] For a Korean Pentecostal case, see Myung Soo Park, "Korean Pentecostal Spirituality as Manifested in the Testimonies of Members of Yoido Full Gospel Church," in Wonsuk Ma, William W. Menzies, and Hyeon-sung Bae (eds), *David Yonggi Cho: A Close Look at His Theology and Ministry* (Baguio, Philippines: APTS Press, 2004), pp. 43–67.

[13] Gani Wiyono, "Pentecostalism in Indonesia," in Anderson and Tang, *Asian and Pentecostal*, p. 262.

[14] The 1987 allegations of the Evangelical Fellowship of Thailand against the Hope of Bangkok Church is a case: see "Hope of Bangkok," pp. 9–11.

[15] Global Christian Forum, "Our Unfolding Journey," 2.2.

influence they have? "From everyone who has been given much, much will be demanded; and from the one who has been entrusted with much, much more will be asked" (Luke 12:48b, NIV).

Worship in the Spirit

The renewal possibility of Charismatic Christianity has been well attested. It applies to both individuals and communities. A spiritual revival causes the renewal of the church through experiences of an encounter with God and an eager commitment to share this good news with others. When a community is formed by such people, primarily drawn from lower social strata (thus, the "poor"),[16] an alternative world is created, and this draws others who long for such a community. When people of desperation come together to seek an encounter with God, their solidarity forms a strong bond. We see this in the Choi Jashil International Mountain of Prayer and Fasting, outside of Seoul. This large facility draws people needing physical healing and financial breakthrough for profound spiritual experiences from all walks of life and various church traditions. While they are all in one accord in seeking a personal encounter with God – be it healing, baptism in the Spirit, or simple renewal of one's faith life – a shared quest for spiritual experience and exchanged testimonies instantly generates a social and spiritual bond. Regardless of denominational affiliations, their shared needs and desires result in a new spiritual community for the needy. This can be termed spontaneous ecumenism.

This critical term was coined by a Pentecostal sociologist, Koichi Kitano. While serving in the Philippines as a missionary, he observed in the early 1980s the emergence of the Charismatic movement, especially among Catholic believers. In this Catholic-majority nation, Protestants and Catholics lived with much suspicion toward one another and in virtual isolation on an ecclesiastical level. At the outbreak of the renewal movement, he noticed a lively exchange on various levels between Catholic Charismatics and Spirit-filled Protestants. But the most important finding of his year-long participant-observation enquiry was the consistent narrowing of the social distance between the two groups through their shared experience of the Holy Spirit. That is, Protestant Pentecostals felt closer to Catholic Charismatics than to non-Pentecostal Protestants. The same could be said among Catholic Charismatics: they felt closer to Protestant

[16] The common Pentecostal demography is made of people from the lower socio-economic strata of society. Thus, they are referred to in different terms: the "poor", "marginal", "disinherited", "deprived," etc. See, for example, Martin, *Tongues of Fire*, and Cox, *Fire From Heaven*. For a critical assessment, see Stephen J. Hunt, "Deprivation and Western Pentecostalism Revisited: The Case of 'Classical' Pentecostalism," *PentecoStudies* 1.1 (2002), pp. 1–32. In Korea, *han* has been a subject of discussion, as it represents a suppressed grudge.

Pentecostals than Catholic non-Charismatics. The main crux was their shared belief and experience in the Holy Spirit.[17]

Another case is the multi-denominational celebration of Charismatic Christianity in North America. Vinson Synan, a Pentecostal historian, played a crucial role in organizing large Charismatic conferences in the 1970s. The 1977 Kansas conference presents a glimpse of Christian unity brought about by the common spiritual experience found in worship. This massive gathering of 50,000 was attended by Catholics, the "shepherding group", non-denominationals, Lutherans, Episcopalians, Presbyterians, Baptists, Mennonites, Pentecostals, Messianic Jews, and United Methodists.[18] A speaker espoused that three streams (Pentecostals, Protestant Charismatics, and Catholic Charismatics) were now coming together to form a mighty river to be one in the Spirit, "so that the world will believe that You have sent me".[19] On the third day, three special seats were prepared on the platform for "Cardinal Suenens (Roman Catholic Primate of Malines, Belgium), Bishop J. O. Patterson (Presiding Bishop of the Church of God in Christ and an African American), and Thomas Zimmermann (General Superintendent of the Assemblies of God)". Synan said, "Seeing these three churchmen from such widely differing backgrounds sitting together in this stadium setting was a special sight",[20] and "the crowd erupted in a roar of approval and praise." A prophecy delivered by Larry Christensen is noteworthy. He revealed that a serious struggle would take place in South Africa due to its apartheid policy. In his vision, he said, he saw "a white leader and a black leader reach across the political confusion, shake hands and bring peace through the power of the Gospel".[21] His prophecy shows that Christian unity can reconcile divided communities. On a mass scale, these gatherings fostered a powerful Christian unity through the Spirit.

This observation leads me to suggest that God did intend the modern Pentecostal outbreak around the close of the nineteenth century and the early twentieth century to be a movement to renew the whole church. He did not intend it to be reduced to a denominational movement. However, various social and historical developments and contexts reduced this renewal, ecumenical, and interracial movement into Pentecostal denominations. To further regret, most of these were divided along racial lines. This move practically limited its powerful renewal potential to a handful of church families. After half a century of denominational existence, this movement was rebirthed among historic churches to fulfil its renewal mandate. This is now called the Charismatic movement, as

[17] Kitano, "Socio-Religious Distance Between Charismatics and Other Religious Groups," pp. 231–42.

[18] Vinson Synan, *An Eyewitness Remembers the Century of the Holy Spirit* (Grand Rapids, Mich.: Chosen, 2010), p. 89.

[19] Synan, *An Eyewitness Remembers*, p. 91.

[20] Synan, *An Eyewitness Remembers*, p. 92.

[21] Synan, *An Eyewitness Remembers*, p. 93.

illustrated above. It is time for all the global Pentecostal families – denominational Pentecostal, Charismatic in different churches, and the ever-growing independent or indigenous Pentecostal churches (or "neo-Charismatics") – to make their primary focus spiritual renewal. Through this, the Holy Spirit brings diverse Christian churches into one place in worship and spiritual experience. It can be a Hillsong music conference, a weekend Alpha Course, or a week-long Easter celebration with millions gathered in Southern Africa. Deep worship, intense corporate prayer (like the famous Korean "juyo" prayer), or prayer for healing can make denominational differences slowly disappear. The differences shrink because everyone draws close to each other and the Lord as his people. A witness of the Azusa Street Revival aptly described this unifying work of the Holy Spirit: "The color line was washed away in the Blood."[22]

The Holy Spirit is the Spirit that makes us one, thus bringing spontaneous (at least to us humans) ecumenism. In a recent study, Cecil Robeck provides a list of Pentecostal entities participating in the national and regional ecumenical bodies. There are thirty-one in Africa, six in Asia, sixteen in the Caribbean, thirty-three in Europe, twenty-nine in Latin America, seven in North America, and nine in the Pacific.[23] The numbers may mislead our conclusion, as Pentecostal denominations in the Global South are more open to their participation in church unity. While spiritual solidarity is to be celebrated among Spirit-experienced believers, as evidenced in the case of spontaneous ecumenicity, two important questions should be raised. First, does this particular ecumenical possibility emerge at the cost of other divisions? Are Catholic Charismatics consciously working to maintain the existing unity with non-Charismatic Catholics? The same applies to Pentecostal/Charismatic Protestants in their relationship with non-Pentecostal/Charismatic Protestant believers. Second, if we endorse "spontaneous" potential, what are we doing to preserve and enhance this potential? Where are the concerted efforts, both on the practical and theological levels, to organize systematic programmes to nurture the spontaneous impetus and develop theological foundations? Yes, there have been several ecumenical dialogues with Catholic, Reformed, Lutheran, and Orthodox churches. Did Pentecostals initiate any one of them? How are Pentecostals actively engaging in the new ecumenical spaces such as the GCF? There seem to be more questions than clear answers. Nonetheless, togetherness in worship is a powerful testimony to Christ and is a unique Pentecostal contribution to Christian unity.

[22] Frank Bartleman, *Azusa Street: The Roots of Modern-Day Pentecost* (S. Plainfield, NJ: Bridge Publishing, 1980), p. 54.

[23] Cecil M. Robeck, Jr, "Christian Unity and Pentecostal Mission: A Contradiction?" in *Pentecostal Mission and Global Christianity*, pp. 201–206.

Serving the Fellow Poor

Pentecostalism has been a "religion *of* the poor". As the Pentecostal poor have become empowered, the movement has also become a "religion *for* the poor". This fits a popular definition of mission and evangelism by D. T. Niles: one beggar telling another beggar where he found bread. Examples are mounting as Pentecostal believers and communities are more actively engaging with social issues.

Two (non-Pentecostal) Evangelical scholars undertook a systematic field study of what they call "progressive Pentecostals". They sampled churches in the Global South that were 1) growing, 2) engaging with social issues, and 3) not depending on external resources. To their surprise, nearly 85 percent of them were Pentecostal.[24] This study used a social science approach. It was groundbreaking because it challenged the common perception that Pentecostals were not engaging beyond evangelism and church planting. How such mission activities promote church unity was outside the book's purview. Now I will present two "testimonies".

Philippe Ouedraogo is a Pentecostal minister of Burkina Faso. The nation is ranked among the poorest in the world, and it cannot seem to find any prospect of breaking this chain of generational poverty. A high national debt ratio (39 percent of GDP) and low educational levels, especially among girls, make things grimmer. Considering that more than half (55 percent) of the total population is under fifteen years old, the national enrolment rate for elementary education for girls is only 24 percent.[25] The rate would be even lower for those from Muslim families (which make up about 52.2 percent of the total population). The government and private sectors have singled out education as the most crucial problem in the nation. Seeing education as God's gift to the entire country, Philippe decided to focus the mission of the church (which makes up only 20.7 percent) on education.

Various churches, mission organizations, and Christian NGOs came together in 1992 under the Association Évangélique d'Appui au Développement (AEAD). In 2006, they set up an intense and accelerated nine-month educational programme in the nation's northern region, where about 80 percent of its population is Islamic. By 2012, a total of 2,255 boys and girls between nine and twelve years of age, who missed their opportunity for elementary education, had completed this programme. After the nine-month fast-track programme, 90 percent achieved the three-year equivalent of formal elementary education when placed in public schools.[26] Also, local churches run formal schools under AEAD,

---

[24] Miller and Yamamori, *Global Pentecostalism*, pp. 5–6.

[25] Philippe Oedraogo, "Transforming Communities through Education," in *Good News from Africa*, p. 81.

[26] Oedraogo, "Transforming Communities," p. 87.

and an overwhelming majority of the 5,035 students in 2008–9 (or 62.5 percent) were girls.[27]

This ecumenical mission initiative has shown strong potential to alter the nation's future. Indeed, the prime minister of Burkina Faso hails this programme as an "innovative way to improve female education". The programme has influenced the government's policies, contributed to gender balance, and promoted the national language in education, while the schools "continually dominate in the national examination league tables". [28] The power of transformation offered by churches working together has motivated a broader partnership, including Catholics and Muslims. The government has adopted the effectiveness of AEAD's education strategy and now runs a similar nationwide programme. Also, Mali and Niger, two neighbouring countries, invited Philippe and his team to organize churches and train Christian leaders to implement similar programmes.

Another Pentecostal "Philippe" is Joshua Banda of Zambia, the pastor of a large congregation in Lusaka. His church is known for its comprehensive and holistic HIV/AIDS programme for patients and their families. The programme is based on the principles of a Christian lifestyle, coupled with medical, educational, social, and spiritual care. The Expanded Church's response to HIV/AIDS, along with hundreds of its member congregations and organizations, has provided treatment and care for close to 30,000 people. The Health Care Association of Zambia, to which Banda's Northmead Assembly's programme belongs, accounts for over 50 percent of health care in the nation.[29] Christian intervention into AIDS by local congregations has substantially impacted society, and Banda was invited to lead the National AIDS Council.[30] Also, as chairperson of the National Constitutional Conference committee, he wrestled with national and international policy issues. His research on the church's response to HIV/AIDS has enabled him to engage robustly with civic and financial institutions as he defends the Christian lifestyle as part of a viable response to the AIDS pandemic.

The common Pentecostal belief in the baptism of the Holy Spirit is for the empowerment of every believer for witnessing. The experience of the Holy Spirit provides an empowering dynamic to the believer's life. This is more than spiritual enlightenment. Instead, it affects every aspect of human attitude, habit, and lifestyle. A powerful Pentecostal social ministry among street gangs is called

---

[27] Oedraogo, "Transforming Communities," p. 86.

[28] Tertius Zongo, "Foreword," in Philippe Ouedraogo, *Female Education and Mission: A Burkina Faso Experience* (Oxford: Regnum Books, 2014), p. xiii.

[29] Joshua Banda, "Engaging With the Community: The Fight Against AIDS," in *Good News from Africa*, p. 42. The churches also provide the bulk of social services; for example, caring for orphans, who are estimated to be 71,000 throughout the country. Mandryk, *Operation World*, p. 894.

[30] Wonsuk Ma, "Circles of Hope for Tackling AIDS," *Sojourners: Faith in Action for Social Justice* (January 2017), p. 33.

Teen Challenge. Its primary approach to counter habitual drug use and a destructive lifestyle is a spiritual tactic through conversation and experience with the Holy Spirit. The Pentecostal believes that, when the inner core of a human being is transformed, it will have a comprehensive and long-lasting impact on individuals and affect all others they may encounter. Therefore, it has the potential to affect all corporate human existence. In this way, those in the Teen Challenge programme overcome their own challenges – be they poverty, chemical intoxication, sexual promiscuity, suicidal tendencies, or broken marital and family life – and are empowered to bring God's good news to many others. Thus, the "poor" are "fired up" by the Holy Spirit to become witnesses. This is the genius of Pentecostal theology.[31]

How does this contribute to church unity? Today, an average global Christian may be a young African woman in poverty, facing social challenges, and often surrounded by a strong religious presence. This is radically different from a hundred years ago. The fledgling Pentecostal congregations are where people struggle to survive daily. Again, the research by Miller and Yamamori tells where these "progressive Pentecostals" are and how they courageously responded to their challenges. Pentecostal churches are, therefore, primarily a grassroots phenomenon. When humans share their suffering and challenges with little help from the government and international institutions, one of two things can happen. Due to the survival instinct, more fragmentation and violence can occur, especially if there is an obvious fault line, often in racial and religious differences. This can include denominational differences. On the other hand, a solidarity spirit can emerge to affirm the common challenges and God's call to action. In the process, humans overcome differences.

It often takes a leader who can help different (denominational, religious, ethnic) communities to come together. They are "Philippes", as observed above. They are a part of the sons and daughters of the "poor" fellowshipping in suffering. They have a strong sense of calling and empowerment; often, they have worked out creative initiatives in their own communities/congregations. Because of their Pentecostal worldview and orientation, spiritual renewal is often part of the process. As seen in the Azusa Street Revival, African Americans and whites worshipped together while sharing their common spiritual quest. This interracial gathering angered and disgusted the public. One newspaper described the scene in a derogatory tone: "Colored people and a sprinkling of whites compose the congregation [of the Azusa Street Mission]."[32] This potential can further expand to bring warring religious communities together for peaceful coexistence and a shared future. Although often failing, Pentecostals are to probe whether they are living up to this high calling.

Are these "Phillippes" typical Pentecostals? What is so Pentecostal about their otherwise brilliant work? Did Joshua lay on his hands for the cure of AIDS, and

---

[31] See Chapter 6.

[32] *Los Angeles Times*, 18 April 1906, as quoted in Bartleman, *Azusa Street*, p. 175.

did Philippe cast out the demon of illiteracy? I am sure they prayed for the destitute, but their *Pentecostalness* or *Charismaticity* is not what we see or hear. Instead, we see how their hearts were moved after seeing the people's hurts, hearing the cry of God's Spirit, experiencing the empowering presence of the Holy Spirit, and taking action by faith and research. As they carefully read the Bible within their social context, they understood the holistic nature of life, the gospel, and the mission of Christ's church. This results in ministries that care for physical, material, emotional, social, and spiritual needs. Their mission engagement also includes policy issues, both national and international. They know that God's missional call is to be "keepers of our brothers (and sisters)" regardless of religious affiliation. Christ calls us one by bringing various church families into a united voice and action.

"Self-Critically Speaking": A Way of Closing

Like in any other church tradition, socio-historical context, spiritual experiences, ways of understanding the scripture, and divine revelation have uniquely shaped Pentecostalism. Using Robert's "frameworks", the Pentecostals are specifically prepared to bring the gift of their testimonies, the central position of the Holy Spirit in their life and work, and solidarity in suffering as the "poor". Thus, like any member of the body of Christ, Pentecostal Christianity is God's gift to the church and the world. Their committed zealousness in witnessing has been, as mentioned above, an essential contribution to global Christianity. In fact, without a believing community, a quest for unity is meaningless, especially unity in witness.

Indeed, the growing awareness among Pentecostal churches toward church unity is encouraging. Through the courageous pioneering work of leaders such as David du Plessis and Donald Gee, Pentecostals are now engaging more in the ecumenical platforms. Cecil M. Robeck, considered to be the "guru" of Pentecostal ecumenism, recently produced a helpful overview.[33] There are two significant ecumenical "spaces" in which Pentecostals have actively participated. The first is the bilateral theological dialogues. The International Roman Catholic–Pentecostal Dialogue began in 1972 and completed six rounds.[34] This was followed by the Reformed–Pentecostal Dialogue from 1996,

[33] Cecil M. Robeck, Jr., "Growing Opportunities for Pentecostal Ecumenical Engagement," *Pentecostal Education* 7.2 (Fall 2022), pp. 173–90.
[34] Robeck, "Growing Opportunities," pp. 178–80.

and its latest joint document was adopted.[35] The third is the dialogue with Lutherans from 2005. A joint report is expected in 2022.[36]

Just as in any individual or faith community, giftedness means "un-gifts". That is, the areas where Pentecostals critically need the hospitality of others to share their gifts. Like many other church groups, Pentecostals once lived with the Spirit's incredible gifts and glorious potential. However, we (including me as a Korean Pentecostal) quickly brought in our human agenda and shortsightedness. Consequently, in its short history, we have lived with our share of big disappointments and failures. The creation of Pentecostal denominations soon usurped racial unity, clearly divided along the racial lines of North America and elsewhere. We have divided more churches as we opened our Pentecostal congregations and treated others as less than "spiritual". We insisted on a particular way that the Holy Spirit manifests himself. We try hard to convert other Christians to our way of believing. This is a good case of ignorance and arrogance. We invented deeply selfish versions of the gospel in the name of miracles; more Spirit-filled leaders fell through greed and failure. Only the gracious and powerful intervention of the Holy Spirit has kept this movement flourishing as it is today.

We Pentecostals must humble ourselves. Despite the giftedness and opportunities of the Spirit God gave us, we must critically reflect on our shortcomings and repent before the Lord and other churches. We must earnestly seek the restoration of the community-forming gift of the Holy Spirit. At the same time, I, along with my fellow Pentecostals worldwide, plead to other Christian families to pray with us and help us be faithful in our stewardship of the gifts so that we are successful on this journey. I propose to seek together a theological humility and a learning spirit from our shared past.

For the same reason, this proposal of "organic" or "missional" ecumenism should not be viewed as replacing the traditional efforts through theological discoveries, for which perhaps the Western church is well gifted. Nor is this proposal intended to minimize the importance of work toward visible and structural unity. Although it appears less intentional, the proposed approach to Christian unity is from-the-ground-up, spiritual, on-the-work, and pragmatic. This may strongly appeal to many worldviews of the Global South and complement the traditional and institutional format. We can begin with a theological affirmation of oneness in Christ. Then, through life, worship, service,

---

[35] "Called to God's Mission: Report of the Third Round of the International Dialogue between Representatives of the World Communion of Reformed Churches and Representatives of the Pentecostal World Fellowship, 2014–2020," *Pentecostal Education* 6.1 (Spring 2021), pp. 55–86. For the elaborate history, see Jean-Daniel Plüss, "The Reformed-Pentecostal Dialogue: A Journey in Discipleship," *Pentecostal Education* 7.2 (Fall 2022), pp. 191–205, and a rejoinder by Karla Ann Koll, "The Gifts of Dialogue: A Reformed Response to Jean-Daniel Plüss," *Pentecostal Education* 7.2 (Fall 2022), pp. 207–10.

[36] Robeck, "Growing Opportunities," pp. 182–84.

and studying together, we recognize and experience unity. After all, we have been baptized in one Spirit!

Selected Bibliography

Aikman, David. *Jesus in Beijing: How Christianity is Transforming China and Changing the Global Balance of Power*. Washington, DC: Salem Books, 2006.

Anderson, Allan. *To the Ends of the Earth: Pentecostalism and the Transformation of World Christianity*. Oxford Studies in World Christianity. Oxford: Oxford University Press, 2013.

_____. "Towards a Pentecostal Missiology for the Majority World." *Asian Journal of Pentecostal Studies* 8:1 (2005), 29–47.

Anderson, Robert M. *Vision of the Disinherited: The Making of American Pentecostalism*. Peabody, MA: Hendrickson, 1979.

Archer, Kenneth J. *A Pentecostal Hermeneutics for the Twenty-First Century: Spirit, Scripture and Community*. London: T. & T. Clark, 2004.

Attanasi, Katherine, and Amos Yong, Eds. *Pentecostalism and Prosperity: The Socio-Economics of the Global Charismatic Movement*. London: Palgrave Macmillan, 2012.

Banda, Irene Mutalima. "Listening to the Poor in Microfinance." In *Good News From Africa: Community Transformation Through the Church*. Ed. Brian Woolnough. Oxford: Regnum Books, 2013, 25–39.

_____. *Microfinance in Sub-Saharan Africa: Responding to the Voices of Poor People*. Oxford: Regnum Books, 2023.

Banda, Joshua. "Engaging with the Community: The Fight Against AIDS." In *Good News From Africa: Community Transformation Through the Church*. Ed. Brian Woolnough. Oxford: Regnum Books, 2013, 41–54.

Bartleman, Frank. *Azusa Street: An Eyewitness Account to the Birth of the Pentecostal Revival*. Plainfield, NJ: Logos International, 1980.

_____. *Azusa Street: The Roots of Modern-Day Pentecost*. S. Plainfield, NJ: Bridge Publishing, 1980.

Bays, Daniel H. *A New History of Christianity in China*. Malden, MA: Wiley-Blackwell, 2011.

Cho, David Yonggi. *Dr David Yonggi Cho: Ministering Hope for 50 Years*. Alachua, FL: Bridge-Logos, 2008.

_____. *The Fourth Dimension: The Key to Putting Your Faith to Work for a Successful Life*. Seoul: Seoul Logos, 1979.

Coleman, Simon. *The Globalization of Charismatic Christianity: Spreading the Gospel of Prosperity*. Cambridge: Cambridge University Press, 2000.

Cox, Harvey. *Fire From Heaven: The Rise of Pentecostal Spirituality and the Reshaping of Religion in the Twenty-First Century*. Reading, MA: Addison-Wesley, 1995.

Dahle, M., S. Dahle, and K. Jorgensen, Eds. *The Lausanne Movement: A Range of Perspectives*. Oxford: Regnum Books, 2014.

Dempster, Murray W., Byron D. Klaus, and Douglas Petersen, Eds. *Called and Empowered: Global Mission in Pentecostal Perspective*. Peabody, MA: Hendrickson, 1991.

Esterline, D. "From Western Church to World Christianity: Developments in Theological Education in the Ecumenical Movement." In *Handbook of Theological Education in World Christianity: Theological Perspectives, Ecumenical Trends, Regional Surveys*. Eds D. Werner, D. Esterline, N. Kang, and J. Raja. Oxford: Regnum Books, 2010, 16–19.

Fee, Gordon D. *The Disease of the Health and Wealth Gospels*. Vancouver: Regent College Publishing, 1985.

Freston, Paul. "Reverse Mission: A Discourse in Search of Reality?" *PentecoStudies: An Interdisciplinary Journal for Research on the Pentecostal and Charismatic Movements* 9:2 (2010), 153–74.

Gee, Donald. *Spiritual Gifts in the Work of Ministry Today*. Springfield, MO: Gospel Publishing House, 1963.

Gibaut, J., and K. Jorgensen, Eds. *Called to Unity: For the Sake of Mission*. Regnum Edinburgh Centenary Series 25. Oxford: Regnum Books, 2014.

Gifford, Paul. *Ghana's New Christianity: Pentecostalism in a Globalizing African Economy*. Bloomington, IN: Indiana University Press, 2004.

Global Christian Forum. "Our Unfolding Journey with Jesus Christ: Reflections on the Global Christian Forum Experience" (2013). https://globalchristianforum.org/wp-content/uploads/2018/07/GFC-Our-Unfolding-Journey-ENG.pdf (accessed 22 March 2023).

Goff, James R. *Fields White Unto Harvest: Charles F. Parham and the Missionary Origins of Pentecostalism*. Fayetteville, AR: University of Arkansas Press, 1988.

Gruchy, S. de. "Theological Education and Missional Practice: A Vital Dialogue." In *Handbook of Theological Education in World Christianity: Theological Perspectives, Ecumenical Trends, Regional Surveys*. Eds D. Werner, D. Esterline, N. Kang, and J. Raja. Oxford: Regnum Books, 2010, 42–50.

Guder, D. L. "Theological Formation for Missional Faithfulness After Christendom: A Response to Steven de Gruchy." In *Handbook of Theological Education in World Christianity: Theological Perspectives, Ecumenical Trends, Regional Surveys*. Eds D. Werner, D. Esterline, N. Kang, and J. Raja. Oxford: Regnum Books, 2010, 51–55.

Hanciles, Jehu. *Beyond Christendom: Globalization, African Migration, and the Transformation of the West*. Maryknoll, NY: Orbis Books, 2008.

Harrell, David Edwin. *Oral Roberts: An American Life*. San Francisco, CA: Harper & Row, 1987.

Hattaway, Paul. *Back to Jerusalem: Three Chinese House Church Leaders Share Their Vision to Complete the Great Commission*. Waynesboro, GA: Authentic Media, 2003.

Heslam, Peter S. "Happiness Through Thrift: The Contribution of Business to Human Well-Being." In *Political Economy, Religion and Wellbeing: The Practices of Happiness*. Eds John Atherton and Elaine Graham. Oxford: Routledge, 2011, 54–65.

_____. *Transforming Capitalism: Entrepreneurship and the Renewal of Thrift*. Cambridge: Grove Books, 2010.

Hodges, Melvin L. *The Indigenous Church*. Springfield, MO: Gospel Publishing House, 1963.

Hollenweger, Walter J. *Pentecostalism: Origins and Developments Worldwide*. Peabody, MA: Hendrickson, 1997.

Hong, Young-gi. "The Backgrounds and Characteristics of the Charismatic Mega-Churches in Korea." *Asian Journal of Pentecostal Studies* 3:1 (2000), 99–118.

Hwa, Yung. "Endued with Power: The Pentecostal-Charismatic Renewal and the Asian Church in the Twenty-First Century." *Asian Journal of Pentecostal Studies* (2003), 63–82.

_____. "The Missiological Challenge of David Yonggi Cho's Theology." In *David Yonggi Cho: A Close Look at His Theology and Ministry*. Eds Wonsuk Ma et. al. Baguio, Philippines: APTS Press, 2004, 85–90.

_____. "A Systematic Theology that Recognizes the Demonic." In *Deliver Us from Evil: An Uneasy Frontier in Christian Mission*. Eds A. Scott Moreau et. al. Monrovia, CA: MARC, 2002, 3–27.

Isgrigg, Daniel D. *Imagining the Future: The Origin, Development, and Future of Assemblies of God Eschatology*. Tulsa, OK: ORU Press, 2021.

_____. "'I Tried Poverty': Exploring the Psychological Impact of Poverty and Prosperity in the Life of Oral Roberts." *Spiritus: ORU Journal of Theology* 5:1 (Spring 2020), 5–24.

Jacobsen, Douglas. "Pentecostalism Today: A Review of Brill's *Encyclopedia of Global Pentecostalism*." *Pneuma* 44:2 (July 2022), 251–60.

Jenkins, Philip. *The New Faces of Christianity: Believing the Bible in the Global South*. Oxford: Oxford University Press, 2006.

_____. *The Next Christendom: The Coming of Global Christianity*. Oxford: Oxford University Press, 2002.

Jin, Mingri. *Back to Jerusalem With All Nations: A Biblical Foundation*. Oxford: Regnum Books, 2016.

Johnson, Todd M. and Gina A. Zurlo, Eds. *World Christian Encyclopedia*. 3rd ed. Edinburgh: Edinburgh University Press, 2019.

Johnson, Todd M. and Kenneth R. Ross, Eds. *Atlas of Global Christianity*. Edinburgh: Edinburgh University Press, 2009.

Karkkainen, Veli-Matti. "Theology of the Cross: A Stumbling Block to Pentecostal/Charismatic Spirituality?" In *The Spirit and Spirituality: Essays in Honour of Russell P. Spittler*. Eds Wonsuk Ma and Robert P. Menzies. London: T. & T. Clark, 2004, 150–63.

Kim, Sebastian C. H. "The Problem of Poverty in Post-War Korean Christianity: *Kibock Sinang* or Minjung Theology?" *Transformation* 24:1 (2007), 43–50.

King, Daniel D. "Mass Healing Evangelism: The Unique Contribution of the Spirit-Empowered Movement to the Practice of Evangelism." In *The Remaining Task of the Great Commission and the Spirit-Empowered Movement*. Eds Wonsuk Ma, Opoku Onyinah, and Rebekah Bled. Tulsa, OK: ORU Press, forthcoming 2022: 303–304.

Kitano, Koichi. "Socio-Religious Distance between Charismatics and Other Religious Group Members: A Case Study of the Philippines in the 1980s." *Journal of Asian Mission* 5:2 (2003), 231–42.

Kraft, Charles H. "Contemporary Trends in the Treatment of Spiritual Conflict." In *Deliver Us From Evil: An Uneasy Frontier in Christian Mission*. Eds A. Scott Moreau, et al. Monrovia: MARC, 2002, 177–202.

_____. "Dealing with Demonization." In *Behind the Enemy Lines: An Advanced Guide to Spiritual Warfare*. Eds Charles H. Kraft, Tom White, Ed Murphy, et al. Ann Arbor, MI: Vine Books, 1994.

_____. *Christianity With Power: Your Worldview and Your Experience of the Supernatural*. Ann Arbor, MI: Servant, 1988.

Lee, Younghoon. "Life and Ministry of David Yonggi Cho." In *David Yonggi Cho: A Close Look at His Theology and Ministry*. Eds Wonsuk Ma, Hyeon-sung Bae and William W. Menzies. Baguio, Philippines: APTS Press; Goonpo, Korea: Hansei University Press, 2005, 3–23.

_____. *The Holy Spirit Movement in Korea: Its Historical and Theological Development*. Oxford: Regnum Books, 2009.

Ma, Julie C. *Mission Possible: The Biblical Strategy for Reaching the Lost*. 2nd ed. Oxford: Regnum Books, 2016.

_____. *When the Spirit Meets the Spirits: Pentecostal Mission to an Animistic Tribe of the Northern Philippines*. Frankfurt: Peter Lang, 2000.

_____ and Wonsuk Ma. *Mission in the Spirit: Towards a Pentecostal/Charismatic Missiology*. Oxford: Regnum Books, 2010.

Ma, Wonsuk. "A 'First Waver' Looks at the 'Third Wave': A Pentecostal Reflection on Charles Kraft's Power Encounter Terminology." *Pneuma* 19:2 (1997), 189–206.

_____. "David Yonggi Cho's Theology of Blessing: Basis, Legitimacy and Limitations." *Evangelical Review of Theology* 35:2 (April 2011), 140–59.

_____. "Global Christianity: Where Are We and How Did We Get Here?" *Pentecostal Education* 6:1 (Spring 2021), 35–59.

_____. "Lord and Giver of Life: The Holy Spirit Among the Spirits in Asia." In *Christian Theology in Asia: Evangelical Perspectives*. Eds Timoteo D. Gener and Stephen T. Pardue. Carlisle, UK: Langham Global Library, 2019, 119–38.

_____. "More Powerful than Ancestral Spirits: Prayer, Material Blessing, and Healing." *Christian History* 142 (February 2022), 47–49.

_____. "Pentecostalism: A New But Big Kid on the Global Christian Block." *Pentecostal Education* 7:1 (Spring 2022), 73–91.

_____. "The Spirit of God in Creation: Lessons for Christian Mission." *Transformation* 24:3/4 (2007), 222–30.

Ma, Wonsuk and Julie C. Ma. "The Making of Korean Pentecostal Missionaries: Our Personal Journey." In *Together in One Mission: Pentecostal Cooperation in World Evangelization*. Eds. Arto Hämäläinen and Grant McClung. Cleveland, TN: Pathway, 2012, 159–76.

_____. "Missiology: Evangelization, Holistic Ministry, and Social Justice." In *Routledge Handbook of Pentecostal Theology*. Ed. Wolfgang Vondey London: Routledge, 2020, 279–89.

Macchia, Frank D. "A Call for Careful Discernment: A Theological Response to Prosperity Preaching." In *Pentecostalism and Prosperity: The Socio-Economics of the Global Charismatic Movement*. Eds Katherine Attanasi and Amos Young. London: Palgrave MacMillan, 2012, 225–37.

Ma, Wonsuk, Veli-Matti Kärkkäinen, and J. Kwabena Asamoa-Gyadu, Eds. *Pentecostal Mission and Global Christianity*. Oxford: Regnum Books, 2014.

Macchia, Frank D. *Baptized in the Spirit: A Global Pentecostal Theology*. Grand Rapids: Zondervan, 2006.

_____. "The Struggle for Global Witness: Shifting Paradigms in Pentecostal Theology." In *The Globalization of Pentecostalism: A Religion Made to Travel*. Eds Murray Dempster, Byron Klaus and Doug Petersen. Oxford: Regnum Books, 1999, 8–29.

Mandryk, Jason. *Operation World: The Definitive Prayer Guide to Every Nation*. 7th ed. Gerrards Cross, UK: WEC International, 2011.

Martin, David. *Pentecostalism: The World Their Parish*. Oxford: Blackwell, 2002.

_____. *Tongues of Fire: The Explosion of Protestantism in Latin America*. Oxford: Blackwell, 1990.

Menzies, Robert P. *Empowered for Witness: The Spirit in Luke-Acts*. London: T. & T. Clark, 2004.

Menzies, William W. "Reflection on Suffering: A Pentecostal Perspective." In *The Spirit and Spirituality: Essays in Honour of Russell P. Spittler*. Eds Wonsuk Ma and Robert P. Menzies. London: T. & T. Clark, 2004, 141–49.

Menzies, William W. and Robert P. Menzies. *Spirit and Power: Foundation of Pentecostal Experience: A Call to Evangelical Dialogue*. Grand Rapids, MI: Zondervan, 2000.

Miller, Donald E. and Tetsunao Yamamori. *Global Pentecostalism: The New Face of Christian Social Engagement*. Berkley: University of California Press, 2007.

Moreau, A. Scott et al., Eds. *Deliver Us from Evil: An Uneasy Frontier in Christian Mission*. Monrovia, CA: MARC, 2002.

Murray, S. *Post-Christendom: Church and Mission in a Strange New World*. Milton Keynes: Paternoster, 2004.

Ott, B. "Mission Oriented Theological Education: Moving Beyond Traditional Models of Theological Education." *Transformation* 18:2 (2001), 74–86.

Ouedraogo, Philippe. *Female Education and Mission: A Burkina Faso Experience*. Oxford: Regnum Books, 2014.

_____. "Transforming Communities Through Education." In *Good News From Africa: Community Transformation Through the Church*. Ed. Brian Woolnough. Oxford: Regnum Books, 2013, 81–90.

Pachuau, Lalsangkima. *World Christianity: A Historical and Theological Introduction*. Nashville, TN: Abingdon, 2018.

Park, Myung Soo. "Korean Pentecostal Spirituality as Manifested in the Testimonies of Members of Yoido Full Gospel Church." In *David Yonggi Cho: A Close Look at His Theology and Ministry*. Eds W. Ma, W. Menzies and H.S. Bae. Baguio, Philippines: APTS Press, 2004: 43–67.

Petersen, Doug. *Not by Might, Nor by Power: A Pentecostal Theology of Social Concern in Latin America*. Oxford: Regnum Books, 1996.

Plüss, Jean-Daniel. "The Reformed–Pentecostal Dialogue: A Journey in Discipleship." *Pentecostal Education* 7:2 (Fall 2022), 191–205.

Robeck, Cecil M. *The Azusa Street Mission and Revival: The Birth of the Global Pentecostal Movement*. Nashville, TN: Thomas Nelson, 2006.

_____. "Christian Unity and Pentecostal Mission: A Contradiction?" In *Pentecostal Mission and Global Christianity*. Eds Wonsuk Ma, Veli-Matti Kärkkainen, and J. Kwabena Asamoah-Gyadu. Regnum Edinburgh Centenary Series 20. Oxford: Regnum Books, 2014, 201–206.

_____. "Growing Opportunities for Pentecostal Ecumenical Engagement." *Pentecostal Education* 7:2 (Fall 2022), 173–90.

Robert, Dana L. "Mission in Long Perspective: Keynote Address." In *Edinburgh 2010: Mission Today and Tomorrow*. Eds Kirsteen Kim and Andrew Anderson. Regnum Edinburgh Centenary Series 35. Oxford: Regnum Books, 2011, 55–68.

_____. "One Christ, Many Witnesses: Visions of Mission and Unity, Edinburgh and Beyond." *Transformation* 33:4 (October 2016), 271–74.

Rommen, Edward, Ed. *Spiritual Power and Missions: Raising the Issues*. Evangelical Missiological Society Series 3. Pasadena, CA: William Carey Library, 1995.

Ross, Kenneth R., Jooseop Keum, Kyriaki Avtzi, and Roderick R. Hewitt, Eds. *Ecumenical Missiology: Changing Landscapes and New Conceptions of Mission*. Oxford: Regnum Books, 2016.

Seleky, Trinidad E. "The Organization of the Philippines Assemblies of God and the Role of Early Missionaries." *Asian Journal of Pentecostal Studies* 8:2 (2005), 271–82.

Shaull, Richard and Waldo Cesar. *Pentecostalism and the Future of Christian Churches: Promises, Limitations, Challenges*. Grand Rapids: Eerdmans, 2000.

Stronstad, Roger. *The Charismatic Theology of St Luke*. Peabody, MA: Hendrickson, 1984.

_____. *The Prophethood of All Believers: A Study in Luke's Charismatic Theology*. Sheffield: Sheffield Academic Press, 1999.

Sunquist, Scott W. *Understanding Christian Mission: Participation in Suffering and Glory*. Grand Rapids, MI: Bakers Academic, 2013.

Synan, Vinson. *An Eyewitness Remembers the Century of the Holy Spirit*. Grand Rapids, MI: Chosen, 2010.

_____. "The Pentecostal Roots of Oral Roberts' Healing Ministry." *Spiritus: ORU Journal of Theology* 3:2 (2018), 287–302.

_____. *The Spirit Said "Grow": The Astounding Worldwide Expansion of Pentecostal and Charismatic Churches*. Monrovia, CA: MARC, 1992.

_____. *Where He Leads Me: The Vinson Synan Story*. Franklin Springs, GA: LifeSprings Resources, 2019.

Tizon. Al. *Transformation After Lausanne: Radical Evangelical Mission in Global–Local Perspective*. Oxford: Regnum Books, 2008.

Warrington, Keith. *Pentecostal Theology: A Theology of Encounter*. London: T. & T. Clark, 2008.

Woolnough, Brian and Wonsuk Ma, Eds. *Holistic Mission: God's Plan for God's People*. Regnum Edinburgh Centenary Series. Oxford: Regnum Books, 2010.

World Council of Churches. *Together Towards Life: Mission and Evangelism in Changing Landscapes*. Geneva: WCC Publications, 2013.

Yong, Amos. "A Typology of Prosperity Theology: A Religious Economy of Global Renewal or a Renewal Economics?" In *Pentecostalism and Prosperity: The Socio-Economics of the Global Charismatic Movement*. Eds Katherine Attanasi and Amos Young. London: Palgrave MacMillan, 2012: 15–33.

Yu, K. Kale. *Understanding Korean Christianity: Grassroots Perspectives on Causes, Culture, and Responses*. Eugene, OR: Pickwick, 2019.

Index